The Name on the Envelope

by Michael M. Dowd

DORRANCE
PUBLISHING CO
EST. 1920
PITTSBURGH, PENNSYLVANIA 15238

Dorrance Publishing Co
585 Alpha Drive
Suite 103
Pittsburgh, PA 15238
Visit our website at *www.dorrancebookstore.com*

ISBN: 978-1-4809-8675-6
eISBN: 978-1-4809-9977-0

DEDICATION

I wish to thank all of my family and friends who have inspired me to write this book. I include co-workers, close friends, my brothers and sisters, and my parents who have suggested I share my story.

This book is the result of the inspiration I got when I told family and friends about how this journey started and how I figured it all out. Those people who were aware of my story knew it was a big mystery to me, so it was only fitting they were the first to be told when I finally resolved this forty-seven-year-old riddle.

I finally found the right people who led me down the correct path. The funny thing is, it was kind of like an ending to a television show. It really took about only ten days to solve, once I had all the correct information.

I also wish to thank mylife.com, who has not only been supportive but has written a short story on my journey and were kind to enough to publish it on their website. My thanks to Monica, Kashia, and Joe from mylife.com for all their help. If it was not for the fact we now have this great thing called social media like mylife.com, as well as Facebook, I think that this journey would still be unfinished.

I want to dedicate this book to all of the people I met on this journey, and all the kind things they did for me to help me find the person I was looking for the most. I thank you for your honesty and your help with my journey. I also want to thank my family, who raised me as one of their own. I owe them everything in my life and I always will. If it was not for them, as well as my other close family members, I would be lost in this world. I also wish to thank my grandparents, my parents, my sisters and brothers, my great aunts and uncles, aunts and uncles, as well as my many cousins from all families that I am related to. I have many close friends who have been with me for many years of my life, and I wish to thank them, as well. I wish to thank my close friends' families for their support and for treating me like one of their own family members. You all know who you are.

Finally, I wish to dedicate this book to all of the family and friends who passed away before this book was published. This includes grandparents from all families, great aunts and uncles, aunts and uncles, cousins from all families, close friends, and former co-workers. May God bless them all.

I would also like to state that everything that has been written in this book is the truth. Some people may disagree with events, or perhaps the part they might play in the story, but that is their opinion and I have mine. I have also left out the names of family members and friends' names for security and legal reasons. I have no wish to upset any family or friends.

I hope you enjoy reading this book, and I also hope that not only will you find it interesting but that it inspires you to find your family members if you are looking for them. The memories I acquired along the way are for a lifetime. I quote a former stepfather who once said, "Everyone has the right to know who you are and where you come from."

I have to agree; he is so right.

Michael M. Dowd

CHAPTER 1: IN THE BEGINNING

Everyone has his own story. Everyone knows, or should know, what city and what hospital he was born in. Everyone should know who his parents are, who his brothers and sisters are, and where he grew up; what city or town and what high school and college from which he graduated. Everyone should know who his grandparents are, his aunts, uncles, cousins, and family ancestors. People should know this information. But sometimes they do not. I was among one of those people.

My life is and has been complicated from the beginning. My life was even complicated before I was born and, fifty-five years later, nothing has changed. You may laugh, but it is true. Complicated, confusing, and stressful. In my life, I have had health issues, too, and will discuss those later. My life has had happiness, sadness, pain, and suffering, as have we all. But I have had some great things happen to me, as well. I am not asking for you to feel sorry for me, as I don't feel sorry for myself. This is the story of what happened to me.

My life story is about me and the people who made it happen kept me alive; those who took responsibility for me when others did not or could not. My story is also about circumstances and decisions that were made, and why these decisions might have been made. I want to say right now, that I do not blame anyone for actions they took that affected my life. As I learned a long time ago, you can't change the past. It is what it is, and for the most part, all our friends and families do the best they can at any one time and simply do the best they can with what they have.

Some of the people that were in my early life are no longer with me now, as they died before this book was even conceived, including my paternal grandmother, Granny Fran, and my grandfather, who both played significant roles in my early life. This also includes my father, Tom. Granny Fran died in May 1965 when I was about a year and a half. Grandpa remarried several years later, and he lost his life due to cancer when I was fifteen years old in March 1979. I'll never forget that event as long as I live. I was a sophomore in high school at the time.

I may not remember my Granny Fran, but I am certain she has always been my guardian angel. As most grandmothers go, she was loving and adored her family. She wanted and expected to raise me as one of her own when my father Tom could not take care of me. As I have been told, my grandfather was not in favor of their raising me, but she insisted. There were many reasons, and I will try my best to explain them as I move through my story.

My paternal grandparents came from working class families. Grandpa's roots go back to the late 1800s and early 1900s, as do my grandmother's. Granny Fran was one of eleven children: five sisters and five brothers. Again, like my grandpa, she was a child during World War I, the roaring twenties, and grew into adulthood during the Great Depression and World War II. Most of her brothers served in the military during this war. Grandpa told me that he was drafted and sent to Indianapolis. However, as World War II ended, he was not needed and released.

Grandpa and Granny Fran had three children. Their first two children were Chuck and Tom, and their third child was a girl, Bonnie. Tom was the second child—the middle child. He always had to listen to his older brother, Chuck, and take orders from him because when his parents were not home, the oldest son was always in charge. Grandpa was an ironworker, and Granny Fran worked in an ammunition factory.

My father, Tom, was born in 1936 and died in 1996. I would like to say he had a great life, but I know I would not be telling the truth. He was my father, and I always knew that and respected that. But it was the whereabouts of my mysterious birth mother that I did not know. This mystery began for me when I was in my early teens and continued on until I was forty-seven years old. That is thirty-four years…a lifetime for some people. But for now, let me continue to explain my beginning.

I guess you could say my life started back in November 1958 when Tom married his first bride. Their daughter, my sister, Katy, is the daughter from my father's first marriage, so she is my half-sister. I was visiting her house some time ago when she showed me photos from that wedding in the album from her mom after she died. Even more surprising to me was discovering that this wedding was the event that started it all for both of us. That is how my sister was brought into this world and how a few, short years later I came to be. I'll talk about that visit later on in this book, as well.

Katy, my first sister, was born in Hammond, Indiana. While living in Hammond, my father, Tom, had a job as a bartender just across the border in Lansing, Illinois. It is at this bar, Tom told me in later years, where he met my birth mother. Now, I don't know if she worked at this bar, too, or was a patron in this place, but this is where the two of them met.

As it turns out, my birth mother probably was already married with two daughters of her own at the time. Her husband was from Chicago, which is not far from Lansing. One of the many unanswered questions I have is whether my birth mother was already separated from her first husband, or if she met Tom at this bar in Lansing while visiting relatives and was in a relationship with him while still married. At any rate, my father was cheating on his first wife, Katy's mother, with the woman who would become my birth mother.

Tom's early background was fairly simple. He was born and grew up in Valparaiso, Indiana, the middle child of three. His older brother, Chuck, was best man at his first wedding. The youngest child in the family was my father's only sister, Bonnie. They were my aunt and uncle from that side of the family, and these two people, Uncle Chuck and Aunt Bonnie, would become decision-makers in my life at a later time.

While Tom was attending Valparaiso High School in the early 1950s, he decided to quit school for some unknown reason and joined the Marines. He was underage when he joined, but I guess he lied about his age, and they accepted him. While he was in the Marines, Tom received a high school diploma and then did his tour of duty.

He never really told me what he did in the Marines, but I found out later from a cousin that he was in the Intelligence Division. Tom was good in math and accounting, and he always had a really good memory. My father told me he had a number of jobs when he was younger. He did jobs like washing dishes at a restaurant in Valpo, and he was an ironworker and tended bar. Tending bar seemed to be his favorite job, and he said that it was one of the hardest jobs to have.

After Tom completed his tour of duty in the Marines, he came back to Valparaiso for a short time, got married, like I mentioned, and got accepted to Indiana University in Bloomington, Indiana. This is where he studied accounting. He and his first wife lived in Bloomington, but for some reason, he never got his degree. He attended all four years of college, and when it came time to take his finals in the last semester, he just never showed up and took them. Because of this, he did not receive his bachelor's degree in accounting. After that my father and his first wife left Bloomington and came back to Valparaiso and then moved to Hammond. It was then that Grandpa told me he got Tom a job as an ironworker in Gary, but he was also still working as a bartender in Lansing.

I am guessing that it was in late 1962 or so when Tom and his first wife divorced. It was an ugly divorce, from what I have been told. I heard that when my father was getting ready to leave, his soon-to-be ex-wife packed his clothes into a suitcase and poured pancake maple syrup on his nicely packed clothes.

I am not sure who did his laundry after that escapade. With that marriage over, and my birth mother's first marriage now over, the two of them got together in early 1963. The way I understand it, my father moved in with my birth mother, again in Lansing, Illinois. Tom's ex-wife got custody of their daughter, Katy, and they moved to Valparaiso. She then went on to work in the post office in Valpo, and that is where she met her second husband. The two of them were married and had two sons. I met them and Katy's stepfather some years later. I also met my sister Katy's mother, who was also my father's ex-wife a number of years later, as well.

This whole family left their northwest Indiana roots and wound up in Naples, Florida. Now, compared to Valpo, Naples was paradise! Years later I went to Naples and found it to be such a very nice, tropical part of warm, sunny Florida. I'll talk about that trip later on in this book, too.

So, now you know who my grandparents were, who my father was, as well as his older brother and younger sister. Very few of my family met my birth mother. I was told that Granny Fran did meet my future birth mother at some point when she and Tom were getting ready to leave for Las Vegas, Nevada. I think at this same time, my Aunt Bonnie was still living at home and might have met my birth mother, as well. Grandpa told me years later that he never met her.

Again, I am not sure of the circumstances, but my father and his girlfriend, my future birth mother, decided to go west to the booming city of Las Vegas, Nevada. I don't know what would inspire Tom and his girlfriend to just pick up and leave the Chicagoland/Northwest Indiana area and go to Sin City. It might have been that back in the early 1960s, Las Vegas was such a boomtown. New hotels and casinos were being built everywhere. The Las Vegas Strip was being developed. Fremont Street was *the* place to be. Who knows what my father and his girlfriend were thinking? Maybe it was the job possibilities due to all of this development.

What I do know is that sometime early in 1963, the two of them went to Las Vegas and either before they left or after they got to Vegas, I was created. That is the bottom line. I was a life created by the two of them. That seems so simple, but yet the complications just continue. It is my understanding that back in the 1960s, if you had a child out of wedlock, it was a huge, moral issue. Unmarried mother. A single, pregnant woman in the early 1960s was treated like an outcast in the family at that time. My, oh, my, have times changed.

As I said before in this chapter, there are still many unanswered questions I have about my origins. To the best of my knowledge, something happened to the relationship between Tom and my birth mother, and for some unknown reason, the two of them split up. I don't know if my birth mother just one day moved out or what might have been the reason, but according to Tom, one day he came home from work to the apartment in Las Vegas that the two of them shared and my birth mother had left. He had no idea where she went, and I do not even think Tom knew that my birth mother was pregnant.

At least that was his version of the story. I found out later that she was incredibly good at hiding her pregnancies, and she was very good at not always telling the truth. Later I also found out she had a job at the phone company in Las Vegas. I will discuss later in this book some possible reasons why she and Tom might have split up.

I have not previously told you about the relationship Tom had with his close family members. It was my understanding that my father was very close to his mother, my Granny Fran. He got along with his father, but they were not close like Tom was to his mother. I am told she ALWAYS bailed him out of trouble. Whether it was money or any other kind of trouble, she bailed him out. I don't know all the circumstances but, clearly, my father was his mother's favorite son. Tom's brother was my grandfather's favorite son. Of course, my Aunt Bonnie, my father's sister and the youngest of the family, was favored by both parents, my grandparents. This relationship between Tom and his mother had a huge effect on me. It was this relationship between them that would determine my fate for a number of years after my birth. It was the decisions made right at this time that set up the circumstances for the rest of my life story. So amazing. This is why, as I said in the early part of this chapter, I will always think of Granny Fran as my guardian angel.

It was during my grandmother's visit to Las Vegas in November 1963 when my life all started. While she was there, the phone rang. The day was Tuesday, November 19, 1963. Tom answered the phone. It was somebody from Southern Nevada Memorial Hospital in Las Vegas, and they were looking for Thomas Dowd. He said, "Yes, that is me. I am that person."

My grandmother was there and heard Tom talking to someone from the hospital. She heard him say, "Okay, my mother and I will be down in a few minutes to pick him up." Probably Granny Fran asked my father, Tom, what the phone call was all about since she heard her name mentioned. Maybe she thought Tom had to pick someone up at the airport.

But he explained, "Mother, we have to go to Southern Nevada Memorial Hospital here in Las Vegas over on Lewis Boulevard." He went on to say,

"You may not believe this, Mom, but I have a son to pick up at the hospital, your grandson."

I would have loved to have seen the look on my grandmother's face when Tom told her that. I can only imagine what was being discussed in the car on the ride to the hospital. I mean, think about it. Is it not ironic that Granny Fran just happens to be on vacation in Las Vegas seeing her favorite son, and there they are, the two of them, in Tom's apartment talking about who knows what, and all of a sudden, the phone rings and someone tells them that they have a son/grandson to pick up at the hospital? I find that amazing.

So, Tom and Granny Fran picked me up at Southern Nevada Memorial Hospital in Las Vegas. It was near Fremont Street, not far from where Las Vegas Boulevard intersected. That was the place to be back in the early days of Las Vegas before the Strip was developed. I am sure that they had to sign paperwork for my release.

I suppose it was then they found out that I was considered and diagnosed a "blue baby." The doctors and nurses may have explained that I might not live very long because of a heart condition. What doctors may or may not have known back then was that I had a condition called Tetralogy of Fallot. This is, by definition, a heart defect that is understood to involve four abnormalities of the heart. It is the main cause of Blue Baby Syndrome.

A blue baby basically has holes in the heart that cause the heart to work improperly. And this causes the baby to turn blue. This issue did not seem to worry Granny Fran or Tom. They took me home. I guess that was the first big decision that was made for me. The second big decision must have been Tom giving me my name. He named me Michael McKinley Dowd. My middle name was Grandpa's middle name, as well.

So, now I have a name, a birthdate, and a family. My mother had given birth to me and left me there, but now I had a family and a home. I grew up always knowing who my father was. Even though Tom did not raise me, he did try to take care of me during my first few months of life.

However, my heart problems meant I needed surgery, and with no health insurance, Tom was unable to help financially. This left him in a dilemma. So, Granny Fran came back to Las Vegas to the rescue. She decided when I was about seven or eight months old that she would come and pick me up and bring me to my new home in Valparaiso.

With my birth mother gone and nowhere to be found and my father Tom having no insurance to cover my medical expenses, he felt that sending me to Valpo with his parents was the best option. It could have been Tom's only option. My grandfather most likely did not want me to come live with them, but I am guessing he was told by Granny Fran that there were really no other options. With that said, I was to be raised by my grandparents and grow up in Valparaiso, Indiana. That was another decision made for me. My dear Granny Fran was my guardian angel right from the beginning.

I have been told that she thought the world of me and did so much for me. Among other things, she was a very talented seamstress. She could sew clothes and made some really neat outfits for me. She not only made these outfits for me but also had me professionally photographed in these outfits. She made me a baby blanket, which I still have to this day. One of the outfits is the pinstripe suit that I am wearing on the cover of this book. She was very loving and caring. She loved having me around, and she loved showing me off to her brothers and sisters, my great-aunts and uncles. I know that I was loved and well cared for.

Then, in May 1965, it all changed. A couple of weeks before Mother's Day of that year, Granny Fran was sent to the hospital by her doctor because she was having some really serious headaches. Those headaches were much worse than migraines, so when she had to go to the hospital, she asked her youngest sister, Corky, and her husband, Harold, to take care of me while she was in the hospital.

There were many reasons for this decision. Mainly, Grandpa, who was an ironworker at the time, had to work and therefore could not take care of me. Tom, I think, was still in Las Vegas, so he was not available. It only made sense that my grandmother's family was to care for me. Little did we all know that this was going to be a life-changing decision for me, as well as my Great Aunt Corky and Uncle Harold and their two daughters, my cousins, Sharon and Susan.

I was only a year and a half old when, on Mother's Day 1965, Granny Fran suddenly passed away. I remember Grandpa talking about it some years later when I was older. She went very quickly and did not suffer, for which I am grateful. Grandpa told me she died in his arms at the hospital in Valparaiso, Indiana. Tom never really spoke about it when I was older. When I was able to spend time with him later, that was the one thing he almost always refused to discuss—his mother's death. I found out some time ago that my grandmother died from a blockage in the back of her neck. I think it might have been a ruptured aneurism. Granny Fran was gone. I don't remember her, but thanks to photographs, home movies, and family stories, I will always have her in my memory heart.

CHAPTER 2: A NEW BEGINNING...
HEART SURGERY AND SCHOOL

As you can imagine, after Granny Fran passed away, a lot of things changed. My dad, Tom, was still single and living on his own. I was less than two years old, and Grandpa had to make some serious decisions again; more decisions about my future. He was in a bind, having to take over where Granny Fran left off. Originally, as I mentioned, Grandpa was not particularly happy when he first found out I was coming to live with them. However, years later, he told me that he grew to love me. In fact, I think I became his favorite.

All the time Granny spent with me and things she did for me gave him the opportunity to draw closer to me. His house was his castle, and all of his kids had moved out and either gotten married or were on their own. My dad's older brother, Uncle Chuck, was married and had two kids already, a son and a daughter. My dad's sister, Aunt Bonnie, was married and had three kids, a girl and two boys. Tom was gone to computer school when the computer revolution was just beginning. Grandpa decided he would take care of me somehow.

Right after Granny's funeral, Aunt Bonnie suggested that she and her husband could take care of me. They lived in South Bend, Indiana, with their three kids. This worked for a while, but because of my heart-related health issues, she had to spend more time with me than with her own family. I was told this put a strain on their marriage, so I was taken back to Grandpa's in Valpo. He was again in a bind. Again, he faced a dilemma. He wanted to make a deal with someone in the family and he had to do it quickly. Grandpa was working full-time in the steel mills of Gary, Indiana, as an ironworker by trade. But he was also single with a young grandson to raise, who had serious health issues. This was not going to be easy for him.

The story from this point on was told to me by the couple I call my parents: my Great Aunt Eileen (Corky) Eileen, known as Corky, and Great Uncle Harold, who raised me as their own. They raised me, took care of me—despite my heart issues—along with their two daughters, who became my sisters. At this time in my life, I was about one and a half years old, and my birth mother was not a part of my life at all. Granny Fran, who brought me to Valpo to be raised as one of her own, was now gone also. Tom, my father, was living downtown at the Hotel Lembke. I don't remember what kind of a job he had back then.

Great Aunt Corky and Uncle Harold, plus their daughters, Sharon and Susan, had just a few months prior to these events, moved into a bigger house on Oak Street. It was a large older home with big rooms and lots of space inside. The funny thing is, after I became a permanent resident, this big house was going to become even more crowded.

According to Aunt Corky and Uncle Harold, my grandpa showed up at the doorstep of their home on Oak Street in tears. He stated that Aunt Bonnie and her husband could not take care of me anymore and that he was REALLY in tough situation. He needed someone to take care of me and needed someone right away. He thought that Granny Fran would have wanted it this way. My grandpa said I was being brought back from South Bend later on in the day, and that he needed to know if my great aunt and great uncle could take care of me for a while. He did not know how long this would be, but he needed to know right there and then if they could do it. Well, Aunt Corky and Uncle Harold said yes, and the rest is history. It was a life-altering decision for me and for them. My grandpa now had some peace knowing that I was going to be in good hands. But he was not done making decisions about my future, and he knew that he was going to have to make things happen on a permanent basis—a decision for me that would give me a permanent, stable home.

Because of my ongoing heart and health issues, Grandpa knew that I was going to need medical care, including heart surgery. As I understand it, he would to have to get custody of me and then put me on his health insurance through work. He had to hire an attorney to accomplish this to get a birth certificate from Las Vegas, Nevada, with my name, my father's name, as well as my birth mother's name on it. After my birth certificate was complete, Grandpa's attorney had to get a court date, so he could get legal custody of me. At this court date, my grandfather became my legal guardian and my great aunt and uncle were to take care of me. Now they had a young child in their home again, and my cousins had a "little brother."

By this time, I was almost two years old, and my heart issues had to be addressed. After Grandpa became my legal guardian, he made a deal with my great aunt and uncle. Aunt Corky and Uncle Harold would raise me, and I would spend every other weekend at Grandpa's house. He also paid them for my basic living expenses: clothes, medicine, doctor visits, and so forth. With this arrangement, my grandfather now had peace of mind knowing that he could go to work on a daily basis, leaving me in good hands. Very good hands! Probably the BEST hands I could have been in. This was the beginning of my family experience. I grew up with parents and sisters. People who took great care of me. Grandpa had not only made a good decision, but a GREAT decision for me.

It was sometime after I had turned two years old that I had my first of two operations. This first surgery was going to help me breathe better and get more oxygen into my blood. It was performed by a team of heart specialists in Chicago at Children's Memorial Hospital. This surgery would help me get ready for the big surgery when I turned four years old in 1967. The surgeons took an artery out of my right arm and replaced the pulmonary artery that runs between the heart and lungs.

After this first successful surgery when I was four years old, I was then ready to have my big heart surgery. Back in the 1960s, this was new, and these techniques used were really in the experimental stages. I found out, years later, that many kids who had this kind of surgery did not survive. I was lucky. God and my guardian angel were watching over everything. I will ALWAYS believe that. I had that surgery in December 1967. I have photos of me in a "caged bed" for kids at the hospital and with Santa Claus. I still have one of the gifts I received at that time: a plastic Vroom truck that made a lot of noise. There were visits from a lot of people and even an article in the local paper, the *Vidette-Messenger*. The story told about the surgery and how the disease, Tetralogy of Fallot, had been defeated by this great team of surgeons. I would survive this thing and grow up as a normal kid. I could not wait.

At this time, I want to acknowledge the doctors and staff of Children's Memorial Hospital in Chicago, as well as the nurses and technicians, for helping me survive this heart ailment. Without this surgery, I would not be here today. With that said, I thank you all. I especially want to thank my lead surgeon, the late Dr. Idris, as well as Dr. Roger Cole and Dr. John Poncher. If it were not for these and many other brilliant people, I would not be here today. I personally thank you all very, very, much!

So, with my surgeries done and successful, it was now time to grow as a kid. I got to start school at the age of four. The principal allowed it, and off to kindergarten I went. I guess it was the September after my heart surgery that I began. As a four-year-old, I was going to kindergarten at Banta Elementary School in Valparaiso, Indiana. Yeah! And I knew who was taking care of me. I knew who my father and grandfather were. I knew I did not have a grandmother. I had a great aunt and uncle that I now could call my parents, Mom and Dad. My two cousins were my sisters. I did not know who my mother was back then, but at the time, I did not care. I also did not know I had a half-sister, either. I was told this many years later.

I was making friends at school. I really enjoyed being in the classroom at Banta with my teacher, Mrs. Gertzmeyer, and my friends. I even remember a Halloween party we had that frightened one girl so much that it made her run out of the room and all the way to her house. That story I will explain later. Some of the people I started school with in the fall of 1968 would continue on and graduate from high school with me many years later. To this day, these people are dearly valued friends. I guess when you look back on your life, like

I am doing now, you never forget these childhood friends. You never forget those friends who become good friends, and you never forget those who become very special friends. Some of those people were with me from the very beginning of my school years.

From the age of four when I started school at Banta in 1968, until the time I was seventeen years old and graduating from Valparaiso High School on Wednesday, June 3, 1981, I began the process of growing up. I was at Banta Elementary School until I was in third grade. Then the school district decided to shut down Banta and transferred us to a school just a few blocks away. As it turned out, a new high school opened in Valpo in 1972, and my sister was in the first graduating class from the "new" high school. The former high school now became Ben Franklin Junior High School. And the building that had been Ben Franklin Junior High School now reverted back to Central Elementary School. This is where I attended grades four and five.

Although I was supposed to go to sixth grade at Central Elementary, my mother made the decision to transfer me to Parkview Elementary. I guess that was for some very good reasons. Again, like the last two schools I attended, I was going to make new friends with kids that would go on to be fellow graduates in the Class of 1981. And some of these kids, including one, would become very close personal friends to this day. After sixth grade, I went on to Ben Franklin Junior High School. I was there about twelve weeks when my parents decided to move from Oak Street to Hastings Terrace in Valpo. This was 1975. So, from this point on, I attended the crosstown rival school, Thomas Jefferson Junior High. I was not happy with this decision. But it was a decision that had to be made, and my future changed because of it. After I finished ninth grade as a freshman, I was then sent to Valparaiso High School for the rest of my high school education. I liked high school much better than junior high. I'll talk more about this later. As it turned out, I got bad grades, got into fights with fellow students, and overall just did not like the attitude of some of my teachers at that time. Not all of them were assholes, but let me just say, some of them were. Some of those teachers, and especially a vice-principal, I would not be able to speak to today. I think it is clear that I was not happy at that school.

However, I will say that there were some things that I did enjoy at Thomas Jefferson. When I was in the ninth grade, one of my classmates and I became managers for our ninth grade football team. That was fun, getting to travel to different local cities with the team, getting to wear a game jersey on game days, flirt with the cheerleaders, and again make new friends. We had a pretty good team that year with a record of six wins and two losses. We lost to Merrillville and Chesterton. They were our conference rivals. The other cool thing about going to TJ was playing basketball on the Jefferson freshman team. There were two teams: the "A" team and the "B" team. I was really on the "C" team because there were so many players like me who wanted the chance to play, but rarely got it. I was not a very good player. I did not know how to run an offense until I learned later, and I did not know what a zone defense was either until later. We had to learn "out of bounds" plays, as well. We did drills in practice and shot a lot of free throws. I did get some playing time, although it was fairly limited. It took a while after the season started for me to be able to join the team because my local doctor did not want me to play. I remember going into his office with a physical form already filled out, and he simply refused to sign it. My doctor said, "You know, your body is like a car, and your heart is like an engine. And what happens to engines in cars when they go too fast? They blow up, and those cars become junk cars." He went on to say, "I have known you since you were one and a half years old. I first saw you when you were a blue baby. I saw what that disease did to you. You could not walk, talk, or anything else. Then these doctors at Children's Memorial were like car mechanics. They fixed your engine and made it function again. I do not want to see your engine (heart) blow up. If it does, it could be deadly, and I do not want to be the one responsible for that decision."

I was not pleased with his answer. With my mom in the room, I said, "What can I do to change your mind?"

He said, "Nothing!"

I could not believe that this doctor, who had been like a best friend my whole life, would tell me that I could not play basketball. I played basketball in fifth and sixth grades at Central and Parkview. I could see why he did not want me to play football when I wanted to. At that time, I was really thin, and he said, "You would get creamed on the first hit."

And this was why I was a manager. But the sport of basketball was my favorite. I did not run track or cross country; I was not a swimmer, and I did not wrestle. I did not play football, even though I would have loved to. But being denied basketball, and in Valparaiso, Indiana, at Thomas Jefferson Jr. High School...well, that just plain stunk. I wanted to wear the proud green and white jersey. I wanted to be on that team. I wanted to be out on that court, grabbing rebounds. I wanted to play, period.

So, then, my doctor said, "I'll tell you what. I will send a message to your doctors at Children's Memorial in Chicago, and if they say it is okay for you to play, then I will sign your physical."

It was about two weeks later that Mom got a call from my doctor's office. So, after school at the doctor's office, I got the good news. I asked, "Did you hear from the doctors at Children's Memorial Hospital?"

He responded, "Yes, I did. They have given me permission to sign your physical."

After my physical was signed, I was given an eye test. He said that I was nearsighted, and I might need glasses. I eventually did get glasses and had to wear them while I was in the classroom. But I did not have to wear them while playing basketball. I was not so nearsighted that I couldn't see what was happening on the court. If there is anything I got from being on that freshman basketball team at Thomas Jefferson Jr. High that year, it was the fact that I was ON the team. I loved it! I loved playing, and I loved it when it was time to go to the locker room and get dressed for the game. I loved warming up. And I loved it when I would get put into the game. I was good friends with my teammates. Some of those teammates would go on to star at Valparaiso High School. We had some really good teams back then. I was never good enough to do that. Even though I was over six feet tall, I just was not a good player.

I really liked the coach I had in ninth grade. He was an English teacher and also my homeroom teacher in eighth grade. Coach John Knauff was the one person who taught me how to play. I have stayed in touch with him all these years via Facebook. I will never forget him as a teacher, coach, and friend.

He was always supportive of me and others who played for him. My number was fifty-four. To this day, it is my all-time favorite number. It is not uncommon for me to go into a restaurant where the servers and staff know me and know that I want Booth 54.

During the many years I played softball in the park league in Valpo, I always had that number on my jersey. The one thing that I never expected to get was the chance to own my former jersey. I bought it for $1 from the athletic director at Thomas Jefferson many years after playing and wearing that number. It was only fitting that I had the chance to keep it forever. This jersey is still a prized item.

A few years ago, I was fortunate to have dinner with Coach Knauff and his wife. I brought the jersey to show him. He was nice enough to sign it for me, along with a book he had written about the history of Valparaiso High School boys' basketball. To this day, these two items are very important to me. As I mentioned previously about my basketball days at Thomas Jefferson Jr. High School when as a freshman, I was not talented, and I was not a smart player. But not only did I have fun being on the team and learning the sport and making new friends, I got revenge! I proved to a lot of people, including myself, that I could play this sport. My revenge was one of those things in life that kind of comes full circle.

I mentioned previously that I spent about twelve weeks at Ben Franklin Junior High School when I was in seventh grade. What I failed to mention was that I tried out for the seventh grade team after playing in fifth and sixth grades for Central and Parkview Elementary. While I was trying out for seventh grade basketball, I got cut and failed to make the team. I look back on it now, and I know there were a lot of better players than me, which is why I got cut. But this was awful for me. I cried that night. I could not fathom that I was not good enough to make the team. However, when I got to ninth grade at Thomas Jefferson, this was not the case. Because our coach did not believe in cutting team members, we were invited to play. So, after I got my physical approved, I was now on the team.

Revenge is sweet. It was one of the things that had gone my way for a change, and it was one of those decisions that had actually worked out in my favor. It was a month later in the season when I was put on the team, and because of the physical issue, I started on the team late. I was not able to practice with the team. I would go to practice and watch. Then I would practice those skills on my own. Then, on game nights, when we did not have a team manager, I would dress up to travel with the team on road games, or dress up for home games, too, and help out Coach Knauff with equipment and so forth. I guess I missed about three or three or four games. Maybe more, but as I said, I finally got to dress with the team and be on the team.

How did I get revenge, you ask? Well, we went through the whole season playing out our schedule. Then, because of a forfeit from another team, Ben Franklin Junior High School was going to be our last game of the season. I had practiced with the team all year, except for that early part, and now I was ready for the revenge game. We were playing BF on their home court—the same court I got cut on just about two years before. And they were being coached by one of the coaches who cut me. I was on the "B" team, and our coach always played as many players as he could. If we were winning by a large margin, the more playing time we benchers would get. If I got to play in the last minute of a game, I was lucky. Sometimes, it would be the last ten seconds of a game. But that was fine with me. If I played, my name got into the paper the next day, along with a write-up about my other teammates who did the scoring and made the great plays.

So the game started. The first quarter ended, and we had the lead. I had never previously been nervous before a game, but for this game I was nervous. I was back in a familiar place. It was Boucher Gym in Valpo. This gym now is Ben Franklin Junior High School and was the old Valpo High School until 1972, when the new high school opened. This is the gym where the famous coach Virgil Sweet coached. When I was a young kid in elementary school, my dad would take me to see games there. This was the gym floor that my older sister and her future husband graduated from in 1969.

I used to get the chance to meet players from VHS when I was younger and would be getting my hair cut at the place called Joe's Barber Shop. Players from those basketball teams often got their haircuts there. I would get autographs and be able to talk to them. These were players like Tom O'Neil,

Joel Vickers, and others. It was the friendly influence of these players and others, along with the famous Coach Sweet, which is what made me want to wear the green and white uniform and be a Valparaiso Viking. I looked up to those players and Coach Sweet.

And when you add the fact that I had been cut from the Ben Franklin Junior High School team a couple of years before, it was only fitting that I was here to get even. The second quarter ended, and we still had a lead. Then the third quarter started and ended, and I was wondering if I was going to get into the game. My parents were there watching. I had invited friends on my bus ride home from school that day to come and watch us play, and those friends were watching. It was the second biggest gym I had played in, next to the gym I had played in at Michigan City that season.

When we had a decent lead late in the fourth quarter, I got the call from Coach Knauff. I had taken off my warm-up top before I entered the game, as I had to check in. Then, for at least the last minute or so, I was in the game. We were the road team, so we were wearing our road green uniforms. Those road green uniforms were my favorite anyway, and I was wearing my Number 54. God, was I nervous! My legs shook. I started to sweat the second I got into the game. The last minute of the game seemed like it took more than twenty minutes to finish. Ben Franklin Junior High School never really gave up until the game was over. It occurred to me that I was now out on the court with a few opposing players who I had known since day one of the first day of school.

That went back all the way to 1968 when I started school at Banta. I had to concentrate on the game, but how dramatic was this? I mean, my basketball career had come full circle. Not only was I on the court with my teammates, against our cross-town rival Ben Franklin Junior High School, but here I was, playing against some of these guys I had known my whole life. Well, since I was four, anyway. And then to think I was playing against the school I used to attend and one of the coaches who had cut me back in seventh grade. Revenge? Is it sweet? You bet. I played in the last minute of that game at Boucher Gym in Valpo and my team won! The Jefferson "B" team in freshman boys' basketball had beaten Ben Franklin Junior High School on a cold, snowy night in January 1978. I, along with my teammates, walked off of that court at Boucher Gym as winners! Was it a rivalry game? You bet! Beating your cross-town rival? Sweet as pie!

I never thought of it then, but this was like the Chicago Cubs vs. the White Sox. This game was like the famous rivalry between the Chicago Bears and the Green Bay Packers. This game was like the Boston Celtics vs. the Los Angeles Lakers and Purdue vs. Indiana. You get the picture.

Like I said, we walked off that court as winners, and I could not have been happier. That game I played in Boucher Gymnasium in Valparaiso, Indiana, at Ben Franklin Junior High School School was now over, and so was my basketball career. I did not know that it was going to be over until we went to practice the next day. To this day, REVENGE was sweet! I got back what I was looking for and that was to be on a basketball team!

Coach Knauff was the one person who taught me how to play and helped me personally grow and mature as a player. I was able to get permission from my doctors at Children's Memorial Hospital and from my local doctor to play this sport, and I proved that I could play. I wish my career in basketball could have lasted longer.

I loved playing the game, and I loved the sport. I still do! I miss the friendships you make with your teammates and coaches. I did not realize this until I went to my thirtieth class reunion of 1981 in July 2011. Some of those teammates were there at the reunion, and some who I had not seen since graduation. I had dinner with Coach Knauff a few years ago (2010). I had acquired a game jersey from the athletic director and an old friend from what is now called Thomas Jefferson Middle School. I bought Number 54 game jersey for $1. And Coach Knauff signed it for me. My Number 54. It was just like a retirement party for me. I love this jersey, and I will treasure it forever! If I had thought to take my jersey with me to the reunion, I could have had a number of former teammates sign it, too. I wish now that I had.

CHAPTER 3: END OF AN IMPORTANT PERSON'S LIFE AND YET ANOTHER NEW BEGINNING

My short-lived basketball career ended that night after we beat Ben Franklin Junior High School on their home court. When I reported to practice the next day, Coach Knauff told us that our last opponents had forfeited both the "A" and "B" team games. As I recall, the forfeit happened because most of the team members had failed in school and therefore had to forfeit the remainder of their season. What a shame because I thought we had at least one more game to play.

I wish we could have scheduled one more game and that game against our next scheduled opponent could have happened. But the season was officially over. We were done, and I was done as a player, too. We had one of the worst winter seasons that year. Snow was on the ground from Thanksgiving through spring. Games had to be rescheduled. School was missed for snow days. Practices were cancelled. It was during the 1977-78 school year, and the weather really took its toll. Later, when the snow was almost gone, each team member was able to have a one-on-one talk about our season with Coach Knauff. I thanked him for letting me be on the team and having the opportunity to play. I thanked him for coaching me and his patience with me as a player. Not too many people would have done this for me, but he did.

Although it was not the conversation I wanted to hear, it was the one I needed to hear. Coach Knauff pointed out that of those who would be trying out for the sophomore team, junior varsity, and the varsity basketball teams at Valpo High, I would probably not make any of the teams; that is, unless I dramatically improved my game or grew really tall. I knew my game was over. I knew that I would not be able to play anymore. I knew I was going to have to concentrate on other things. So, after meeting with Coach Knauff for the final time, I turned in my green and white uniform, warm-up sweater, and game shorts. I asked him then if I could buy one of those uniform jerseys, but he stated said that they were not getting new ones anytime soon and they would need them all back.

However, when you wish for something, you just never know when that wish might be granted. As I said previously, I did get one of those game jerseys a number of years later. So, once again, my life in the game of basketball and wearing the green and white Viking uniform came full circle. So many things in my life would come full circle. Again, I have to be careful of what I wish.

Now I had to concentrate on other things, which included getting ready for the move from Thomas Jefferson Junior High School to Valparaiso High School. This was not really a huge transition as far as academics, but it signaled a major change in my family and it was really a big deal for my grandfather. It was on my birthday, November 17, 1977, just before I started playing basketball in ninth grade, that I got the news that my grandpa was in the hospital because he needed to have some fluid drained from his lungs. His test results indicated that he had lung cancer and it was terminal.

My grandfather was an ironworker in the steel mills of Gary, and it turned out that a group of them, including my grandfather, worked in a section of the mill that was loaded with poisonous, airborne chemicals. Because U.S. Steel did not supply any breathing protection equipment, Grandpa had inhaled these fumes for years. He now had lung cancer. It was inoperable. The doctors administered chemotherapy, but it did not help. I'm sorry to say my grandpa had a slow, painful death.

Have I told you how close my grandfather and I had become? Like Forrest Gump said, "We were just like peas and carrots." If you remember, my grandpa got custody of me at an early age after Granny Fran passed away. He did remarry a few years later. But before that, he made a deal with my great aunt and uncle to take care of me, and every other weekend I would go to stay at his house. We would do so many things together. We would take Sunday rides down to see one of his brothers. His oldest brother had a big farm near Culver, Indiana.

We also had a good friend who lived outside of Knox in a tiny town called Ober. Her name was Iva Hacker. Her nickname was "Old Lady Hacker." Mrs. Hacker was known for a lot of things, but especially for her tremendous, home-cooked meals. She actually outlived my grandparents to the ripe old age of ninety-five, if I am not mistaken. Mrs. Hacker was a very dear friend to me, my grandparents, as well as others who knew her. I can remember going to her house when I was staying at Grandpa's house on weekends. We would go down there for Sunday afternoon dinner. I swear to this day, I have never known anyone who could cook like she did. If mean, if you went to her house for dinner or lunch, or even a snack, if the table were not covered edge-to-edge with food, she thought there was not enough food on the table. This is just how generous she was.

Mrs. Hacker lived on a farm that she ran after her husband passed. Her house was old and small, but it was big enough for her. I can remember going there before she had an indoor bathroom. This is where I became used to using an outhouse. She also had a three-acre yard with a garden that my grandpa helped her maintain. It was such fun to run around there when I was a young kid. I'll talk more about Mrs. Hacker again.

Uncle Everett was my grandfather's oldest brother, who had a farm in the Culver, Indiana, area. It was always fun to go to his house, particularly during farming season. My great uncle Everett had been a farmer his whole life. He had several kids who were second cousins to me. It was all part of the Dowd family. I remember, as a kid, he used to let me drive his John Deere tractor. I used to mow his yard. He taught me how to drive a tractor and plow and disk a field. I used to ride with him when the corn was being picked and harvested. I remember being on the trailer when hay was being baled. I guess you never forget things like that. My great uncle Everett was a rather large influence on me when I was a young kid, and he knew it.

My grandpa had five brothers. As I mentioned, Uncle Everett was the oldest. After Uncle Everett, there was Uncle Glenn, the second oldest, Uncle Kenny, Uncle Joe, and my grandfather, Charles McKinley, followed by his younger brother, William. I grew up knowing my grandfather and his three remaining brothers: Uncle Everett, Uncle Glenn, and Uncle Bill. Uncle Kenny died before I was born, and Uncle Joe passed about 1965.

As you know, my grandpa and I were about as close as you could get. My grandfather had other grandchildren—eight others, to be exact, but because I was the only one who lived in Valparaiso, I guess that made me closest to him by default. My grandfather's daughter, Aunt Bonnie, and her husband had four kids. My Grandpa's son, Uncle Chuck, and his wife had two children. So, there were eight grandchildren.

Here was a man who raised me as one of his own and made a promise to my dying grandmother that he would take care of me after she passed. As I said, my grandpa was an ironworker. This had to be one of the dirtiest jobs. I can remember waiting for Grandpa to come home from work with really dirty work clothes and a nearly blackened face. The only way I knew it was him was when he took off his glasses. He would say hello and then hit the bathroom for a much-needed scrub-down.

He was like a new man when he cleaned up from taking a bath and putting on clean clothes. I did not know this at the time, but here was a man who was working in a dirty, smelly, steel mill and paving the way for my future. He had nothing more than an eighth-grade education. Back in those days, you worked first, and school was second. My grandfather's father passed away when he was young, so it was up to him and his brothers to work and run the farm. They worked full-time on the farm to get things done, so that the family had food on the table.

By the end of eighth grade, there was no time for school. He told me he had other jobs, as well. He used to drive a dump truck for his brother, Glenn. The dump truck business was well-known for many years in the Dowd family as Dowd Trucking. My cousin, Glenn Dowd II, took over that business from his father, Glenn Senior. Sometimes I wish that I had taken it over when my cousin decided to retire from it. Many people in Valpo knew this business, and I must admit that it was always kind of cool knowing that my last name was on the truck every time I would see it. There were even times when I got to ride in that dump truck with my cousin, Glenn. That was family. That was a really cool thing to do back then. That old International red-colored Load-Star was really a family icon, and it had my last name on it. It was sometime later my grandfather gave up the trucking business and got a job as an apprentice in the steel mill as an ironworker. I guess he was either in his late twenties or early thirties when he went to the mill for work. It was a union job that paid him a good wage, as well as benefits and a pension. It was a job that he had for nearly forty years. But it was also the job that caused the cancer that led to his death.

It was his job with good insurance benefits that paid for my first open heart surgery in 1967. It was a tough job that he was proud to have and proud to say that he did it for a living, but it was the job that killed him in the end. I still say to this day, if I could take a time machine (whether it was a DeLorean or a phone booth) back to about 1973 or so, I would convince my grandfather to retire and take another job doing something else. Or maybe I would do like they did in the *Back to the Future* movies and pick up a certain sports almanac and give it to him and tell him to go to Las Vegas and use it to win money on sports betting. He could have made millions. I know I could have convinced him to do it because in the long run, it would have saved his life.

It was only four years later after my grandfather's death that Grandpa's second wife died in 1983. She died from injuries suffered in a bad car accident. I remember I was going to college at Vincennes University then, and she died the day after Christmas of that year. She sent me a Christmas card while I was at Vincennes with a check for $5. She was in the car accident about two days later after she mailed that card. I remember that Dad and I were pallbearers for her funeral. I could have stopped their deaths all in one visit. I guess if time travel were for real, I could still do it today.

As I mentioned, Grandpa remarried in the early 1970s. He met his second wife while he was a member of the local Moose Lodge in Valparaiso. His wife's maiden name was Johnson. She had been married before, and her name now was Mary Ralston. She was divorced, and she was also a cousin to my dad from the Johnson side of the family. The things I remember about my second grandmother was that she kept an extremely clean house and she was a very good cook, too. She always took care of the things in the kitchen like the cooking and the dishes, as well as the laundry and the house cleaning. I must say, that now as a single man, I would really appreciate that! Everything in my grandparent's house was clean. I mean, it was spotless. No dirt anywhere—no dust, no grime, no mess. I know there are women who believe in the spotless house, and she might have written the book on it. She also knew how to sew, as well as dance. I used to see my grandparents dance at family weddings, and I can remember dancing with her, as well at the wedding reception of my older sister, Sharon, and Bob in 1974. Mary really knew how to take care of a house. My second grandmother never owned or drove a car and always wore a dress, even if she was doing housework. You never saw her in jeans or any kind of pants. She never believed that a lady should wear pants. And for that matter, neither did Mrs. Hacker. I guess that is old school, or maybe it was just what the two of them believed in doing.

The best thing about going to my grandparents' house every other weekend was being able to spend time with them both. I never knew it as a kid, but now as an adult, you remember those things as significant. You never realize that one day you will never have those good times again.

We often went out to eat at places in Valpo, like The Big Wheel, Lucky Steer, and the old lunch diner at the dime store called Harvey's. My weekends with my grandparents were about going to Mrs. Hacker's house for Sunday dinner. It was about going to see my Uncle Everett and Aunt Mable. Sometimes we would go to Grand Rapids, Michigan, to see my Aunt Bonnie and Uncle Roger and my four cousins, April, Mark, Shawn, and Francie.

We often went up there in the summertime to the Forrest Hills area of Grand Rapids. It was a great vacation. My cousins lived in a large, two-story house in a newer subdivision that had an Olympic-sized pool. These experiences with my aunt and uncle, as well as my cousins, have left me with a lifetime of memories, too.

It was about playing baseball in their front yard with Mark and Shawn and neighborhood kids. It was about swimming and playing tennis with my cousins, April and Francie. I remember the tennis store my aunt and uncle owned. Grandpa would buy me a Fred Perry tennis polo shirt when we would go there to visit. As my cousins Mark and Shawn grew older, they started buying cars and fixing them up and then re-selling them. Then there was movie night. I can remember as a young kid the bunch of us going to the movie theatre and seeing the film *Patton*. I remember that monologue at the beginning with the extreme language and people busting up laughing because of it. I remember the film being so long that there was an intermission about half-way through it. As I said, it was always fun in Grand Rapids. I have never forgotten those memories. I just never knew when I was a young kid that Aunt Bonnie and Cousin Shawn would become such important people in my life later as a young adult. That is a story to be told later. Much later.

It was these and other memories from time I spent with my grandparents that I remember fondly. We also spent different holidays together. I always got to see them my grandparents on Christmas morning, usually right after we opened our presents. I have never forgotten those events, and to sit here and write about my life back then, I realize how fortunate I was. I realize that my grandparents loved me. I stuck around my grandfather for those intimate talks, like fathers have with their sons. I never forgot some of those conversations. I remember one time, I missed giving a Father's Day card to Grandpa. I never saw him more upset. He never yelled at me, but he had a right to be disappointed. I had let him down, when he NEVER let me down. Here was a guy who bought just about everything for me: toys, clothes, and other things, and all he wanted in return was some respect. He was still an ironworker who paid for everything he owned with his hard-earned money. That time I showed him no respect. This hurt him. I never forgot another Father's Day for the rest of his life after that incident. I still remember that conversation like it was yesterday. I learned a valuable life lesson from it, and I have never forgotten it.

One big disappointment in my life was that Grandpa was not able to attend any of my basketball games when I was in ninth grade. He was battling lung cancer then, and he just did not feel well enough to go. He would have enjoyed seeing me play. My father, Tom, lived in New Orleans then, so he also never got to see me play.

Of course, at that time, I had no idea where my birth mother was, either. This was the second time in my life that I wondered who she was. The first time I remember seeing her name was on a medical record that I read when I had a heart catheterization at Children's Memorial Hospital in the summer of 1977. I used to go to there to visit my heart doctors and to make sure that everything was working correctly. After that heart surgery I had when I was four years old, I got to see my doctors in Chicago about every other year. This time I would stay in the hospital for a few days while they did the stress test and heart procedure.

It was a rather stressful time that week leading up to going to the hospital in Chicago for two procedures could get pretty stressful. A few days prior to this, my dad's mother passed away (my great uncle's mother), and the funeral was during the day. I then remember our family had the post-funeral dinner, so we had lots of family at our house for this gathering. I remember my grandparents came over later that afternoon, and we all went in my parents' new Pontiac Grand Prix. All I can say about that day and night was that it was one, LONG day. The funeral in the morning, the interment about midday, and then the family dinner at our house in the afternoon made for a long day.

We left the family gathering about 5:00 P.M., and my dad drove us to Chicago for my checkup. My grandpa was no fan of two-door cars. But Dad drove us to Chicago with Grandpa and me in the front seat. Mom and my grandmother sat in the backseat. We got up to the hospital and proceeded to get me checked in. It took a while, as it usually does, to get a bed in a ward. This ward had at least four other beds. I remember waiting for the doctor to sign me in, and it took some time for the doctor to return. Grandpa had to get back to Valpo, so he could get to bed and then wake up around 5:30 A.M., so he could go to work. In a few minutes, my grandfather came back with the doctor, who then signed off on my papers. I was now admitted to Children's Memorial once again. My parents and grandparents then said their good-byes, and I did not see anybody from my family until the next day.

For whatever reason, I could not sleep that first night. I remember I had some great nurses, both male and female, who took good care of me while I was there. The staff at Children's Memorial were all very nice and professional.

They answered all of my questions. My visit back to the hospital brought some fond memories for my parents. They talked about what it was like when I came out of heart surgery in '67. As I said, that first night in the hospital, I could not fall asleep. I got up and went for a walk, stopping by the nurse's station, which was right near my room. I saw a large record book that held all my medical records from all the visits to Children's Memorial. The nurses let me read this book, and that is when I saw her name for the first time. I am guessing it was a copy of a birth certificate that I was looking at.

Maybe I had never paid much attention to my birth certificate before, but now I was fourteen years old. I could understand what some of this information was about. Then I saw my father's name on the document: Thomas E. Dowd. That name I already knew. Then I looked at the name listed as my birth mother: Alexandria L. Jones. From this point on, I started to wonder who and where she was. This event—late one night at Children's Memorial—is what triggered this long quest to locate this mysterious woman. I look back at this now and think that I was just thirteen years old when I read my birth certificate. My journey took me thirty-three years more to the age of forty-seven when I would finally get an answer...thirty-three very long years. That was a lifetime in itself. It was after this visit to the hospital that I began to ask questions.

I made it through the stress test and heart catheterization during that week in July 1977. Having only heart-related tests made me feel fortunate that I was not there for something more serious. I remember the hospital chaplain telling us that there were kids on other floors who were very near death. There was one kid in my ward who had been in the hospital for several months. I forget what he was there for, but his parents had quit coming to the hospital to see him. They just left him there. It was a sad situation because he had several surgeries in order to get healed. I remember there was a nurse on my floor who became his adopted mother. She was now able to care for this child. It was kind of like my situation. There was a person in my life who did not want me at birth and made sure that she was not to be found. But there was my father, my grandparents, and my great aunt and uncle, who I now call my parents, who made certain that I was cared for. Along with my two cousins, daughters of my great aunt and uncle, this was and is MY family.

I'll say this again—If it were not for these and other family members, I wouldn't be here to write about it today. I don't know where I would be without them in my life. With my medical procedures completed at the hospital, it was time to go home.

That experience at Children's Memorial was educational, to say the least. Not only did I get a stress test and a heart catheterization, but now I had the name of my birth mother. It was the following November that I found out my grandfather had cancer. You would not have known he was even sick. I mean, at least in the beginning of his illness, he did not look sick. A lot of times, cancer patients lose a great deal of weight. It was not until the very, very end that Grandpa looked weak and frail.

During the time span from when he found out that he had this terminal disease in November 1977, until he passed away in March 1979, my grandpa and I spent about as much time together as possible. We were so very close. I think that because of this situation, we grew even closer. I found myself spending more weekends with them.

The summer of 1978 was when Grandpa bought his last car. What an experience that was! Grandpa normally bought Chrysler and Dodge products. He went to the local dealer in Valparaiso to check out a new car when his 1976 Newport was giving him trouble. He was not able to get a good deal on a Chrysler LeBaron, so we went to Knox, Indiana, to look at a Buick LeSabre. I never thought he would buy the car. He had been loyal to Chrysler, Dodge, and Plymouth product lines. But maybe it was time for a change. Grandpa seemed to like green cars. He had maybe four or five green-colored cars in a row. So we went to this dealer in Knox and, lo and behold, when my grandfather told the salesman what he wanted, the salesman showed us a brand new 1978 Buick LeSabre four-door…green, of course.

The car had a lot of nice options on it, like power windows, door locks, cruise control, and other goodies. After the test drive, then the fun began. If there was one thing I did not know about my grandfather it was that he was a tremendous negotiator. This dealer in Knox had offered him a decent price for his trade, but I never saw Grandpa get so animated. It was not until I worked at a Toyota dealership when I first came to Orlando, Florida, that I ever saw people get so consumed with buying a car. I can see why there are so many of those "no haggle" dealers now. If all customers were like my grandpa when he bought a car, those salesmen would all now be in a mental institution.

I saw my grandfather wheel and deal. I saw him haggle and negotiate. Then, after a number of folks from the dealership agreed on a price, Grandpa agreed to purchase the car. I never had seen anything like it. Of course, Grandpa told me later he paid too much for the car. But he figured this would be the last car he would ever own, so it was a nice one to have.

As Grandpa's condition got gradually worse in the summer of 1978, he asked me what we could do together before he got to the point when he would not be able to travel. I mentioned the idea of going to New Orleans to see my father. It was now the summer of 1978.

Grandpa had bought his new Buick, and neither my grandfather nor I had seen my father in many years. I was fourteen, and my father was now thirty-six years old. This would be an opportunity to see him and talk to him about my birth mother. Combined with that was the fact that I really wanted to see New Orleans. I wanted to see the French Quarter. I wanted to see where my father lived. I also wanted to see the Superdome that my father and grandfather had talked about. It seems that I have a family history connected with the Superdome. Back sometime in the late 1960s or early seventies, my father's older brother, Chuck, got my father a job working and helping build the Superdome.

I'll talk about the Superdome and New Orleans, as well as my experience in the French Quarter later. But it was what Grandpa and his older brother, Everett, used to talk about that made it so mysterious to me. As it turns out, my grandparents, along with my Uncle Everett and his third wife, Mabel, went on vacations together. One of those trips they went to the French Quarter to see my father. My grandparents used to bring me back souvenirs from New Orleans, and one of those gifts was a tourist book on the city. I still have this book somewhere. Anyway, Grandpa used to talk about the French Quarter and how much fun it was. (It was not until my first trip to New Orleans in 1985 that I realized just how much fun it was.) Anyway, Grandpa and I discussed going to New Orleans. We planned to fly down and stay for three or four days.

Then, for some unknown reason, Grandpa pulled a complete 180. Someone must have talked him out of taking the two of us down to the Crescent City. To this day, I don't know who it was that made him decide that my father should come to Valpo instead. This decision made me upset for several reasons. Not only did I want to go to New Orleans, I wanted to spend time with my father for a change. Grandpa assured me that if my father would come to Valparaiso, there would be plenty of time for visiting with him. So, we got on the phone and called him in New Orleans, and he reluctantly made the decision to come home.

My father did not really want to come back to Valpo. He was not pleased with Grandpa's request, but I now know why he asked him to do this. He was protecting me, just like he always did. About seven years later, I figured out why.

Grandpa had been to New Orleans already, and he knew what went on in some of those nightclubs on Bourbon Street and other places. He did not want me to see it. Also, he did not want me to see the way my father lived. He was a BIG drinker. He loved martinis, and he loved scotch and soda. He also smoked like a chimney. I suppose that my parents did not want me to see that, either, so it was the only decision my grandfather could make.

My father, Tom, did not want to come to Valpo, for a number of reasons. I am not sure who he was more afraid of—my grandfather or my mom. Grandpa and Mom saw eye-to-eye on a lot of things regarding my upbringing. These were the two main people in my life at that time who pulled all the strings. If there were clothes to be purchased, that agreement would be between the two of them. If I needed money for this or that, it would be up to Grandpa to decide because he paid my bills.

My mom was not a big fan of my father, Tom, either. She always kept her eyes on me— what I was doing and who I was doing it with. When my father came to town, the two of them actually got along fairly well. But my father had other bad memories of Valparaiso. He was still upset at the loss of my Granny Fran, his mother, and he was not happy with the fact that Grandpa had remarried. I did not know this then when he came to Valpo, but he told me on the phone later and when I visited him in New Orleans several years later about how he was not happy with her.

I think my father was jealous more than anything…jealous because he knew that when Grandpa passed away, she would get a big portion of his estate. He was always thinking ahead. One of the other things that my father was really good at was spending money. He would go through money like it was water. When he passed away in 1996, I remember there was just enough money in his account to pay for some of his final expenses. The rest, as I remember, was split up between my Aunt Bonnie, my cousin Shawn, and myself, and there was not much for us to split.

I remember Grandpa and I, along with one of his best friends from the steel mill, went to O'Hare Airport in Chicago in July 1978 to pick up my father. My father was flying into Chicago from New Orleans, and we took the new Buick to the airport. Grandpa had just had chemotherapy earlier that week, so he was not feeling 100 percent, and he didn't feel like driving. Grandpa asked his buddy, Wally Huber, who he knew for many years, to drive us up there.

Wally and Grandpa worked together as ironworkers for many years. They had the same work ethic and a language all of their own. Rarely did my grandfather ever talk like this around me, but when he was in the company of his mill buddies, all rules were off. I found out later there was a language known as "mill mouth." Not only could my grandfather speak the language, but I think that he might have written the book on it.

For some reason, this one example of a "mill mouth" conversation I can remember like it was yesterday that has stayed with me. With Wally Huber driving Grandpa's car and my grandfather sitting in the front passenger seat (I was in the back seat), we were enroute to O'Hare to pick up my father. We were out on the Tri-State Toll Way, also called Interstate 294. I think we had just passed up a new conversion van that seemed to be a big trend in the late 1970s. For whatever reason, my grandfather did not like vans. I don't know why he did not like them, but he HATED them. You have to remember that my grandfather was old school—very old school. He did not like men with long hair and beards; he did not like loud rock and roll music; and he was a big fan of the television show, *All in The Family*.

Archie Bunker was his favorite. The conversation continued. Grandpa said something like, "I don't know, Wally, why all of these people have to buy these vans." He went on to say, "I was at Miller's Market grocery store the other day, picking up a few things. I was putting my groceries in the car, and as I got into my car, I heard a woman next to me in a van say, 'All you want to do is f**k, f**k, f**k!'"

My grandfather went on to say, "I mean it, Wally, this guy and girl got into this van next to me and she told him that." Then Grandpa said, "I think that people are buying these vans just so that they can drive around and screw in their vans, like it's some kind of convenience." To this day, I still remember that conversation. This story makes me laugh out loud every time I think about it. I think I was in tears laughing in the back seat of Grandpa's car. I can guess that it was not the kind of thing a fourteen-year-old grandson should hear. But, like the rest of this book, that is a true story. My grandfather told it like it was. That was one of the many memories I have of him.

The three of us got to the airport and found a place to park. If you have ever flown in or out of O'Hare, you know that it is a very big place. HUGE. The one thing to know about O'Hare is you have to know where you are going and you will do lots of walking, unless you need assistance. We had my father's flight number and airline. We went to the Delta area and found one of those television monitors that had his flight number on it. When we found it, I was starting to get nervous. Something you could do back then was go back through security and go out to meet your party at the gate. When the plane pulled up to the gate, you could watch all the passengers unload. So, all three of us went through security and walked all the way down the long hallway to the gate, where we would meet my father.

It always seemed that when you went to meet someone at the airport, you could figure they would arrive at the gate farthest down the corridor. We finally arrived at the gate, and now we were waiting for my father's plane to arrive. I was getting more nervous. I had not seen him in several years, so this was a homecoming, of sorts. The last time I remember seeing my father before that was when he was working on the Superdome. He had been in Northwest Indiana to get a deal done with one of the steel mills that had been contracted to build the outside shell of the stadium. This was the time I remember seeing actual blueprints of the Superdome when it was under construction. My father later sent me Polaroid snapshots of the Superdome as it was being built.

The plane soon arrived at the Delta gate. Passengers started to get off the plane. It must have been a crowded flight because it seemed like it took forever for my father to get off. Finally, he did, and we were reunited, and I was no longer nervous. After a long hug, he was here. You know, up until now, I had not realized it, but this scene in the airport that day in Chicago was kind of like the day I said good-bye to my father in New Orleans. It was that emotional. I didn't know it at the time, but that was the last time I would see him alive.

We went down to get my father's luggage at the carousel and then out to find the car in the huge parking lot. We left, paid the parking fee, and were on our way back to Valpo. There was a lot of traffic going back home, but that was fine with me because now I had the chance to catch up with my father, who I had not seen in years. It was good. I was happy, at least for the time being. My father was here with me and that was all that mattered. I can remember one of the things my father and I talked about on the way back: the death of Elvis Presley. His sudden death was surprising to both of us.

His music going all the way back to the 1950s was enjoyable. When we got back to my grandparents' house, it was late in the afternoon and time for dinner. The four of us went to the Lucky Steer in Valpo for a nice meal. It was a restaurant, like Ponderosa, with an AWESOME salad bar. It was there that my father saw my growing appetite. He was impressed because I think I ate more food than he did. My grandfather said I was a growing boy. I was just hungry.

If there is one thing my father, my grandpa, and I would do is talk about stuff. We got to talk about man-to-man stuff. My father had heart surgery, too, at an early age like I did. He had his first heart attack at the age of thirty-four or so. That's kind of sad when you think about it. But, as I said, he was a very heavy drinker and a really big chain smoker. My father had bypass heart surgery, as well. We had a conversation about what it was like to have a heart catheterization. He told me about how he got sick to his stomach when the doctors injected the dye they use for those procedures. I told him about how they injected that stuff into me during mine. My doctors also knocked me out for most of the procedure.

It was during some of these conversations with my father that I found out some interesting things about him. He told me about his first wife and my half-sister. Up to that point, I had only heard about her from others. My father told me that when my half-sister's mother got remarried, she and her family left Valpo and moved to Florida. Now I was getting curious. Not only at this point in my life (fourteen) did I have a sister I had never met, but a birth mother who I did not know.

It was just the next year, the spring of 1979, when I saw a picture of my sister for the first time. It was her senior photo that had been sent to my grandfather's house with the announcement that she was graduating from high school. It was about two years later, in 1981, when I was able to track my sister down and visit her for the first time. I'll save that story for another chapter.

I finally had the opportunity to ask my father about my birth mother. My grandfather was present for this conversation, as well, but he remained silent. I told my father about my visit to Children's Memorial in Chicago, that I got to look at my birth record, and then mentioned that I saw my birth mother's name. I asked my father to explain what happened. He had a scotch and water in his hand, and it was then that the song and dance started.

For some unknown reason, my father always thought my birthday was on November 19 instead of 17. He then realized why and told me that November 19 was the day he and his mom, Granny Fran, had arrived to pick me up at the hospital in Las Vegas. He didn't tell me much after that...at least I don't remember that he did.

I do remember my father commenting on my rather thick head of dark hair. He stated that my birth mother also had this long, dark, thick hair. At the time, I was fourteen years old and thought I had looked somewhat like my father. My voice had changed and gotten much deeper, too, thanks to puberty. I did not know it then, but I really look more like my birth mother than I do my father. I had no photos of her. My father only stayed about four days on his trip to Valparaiso. I think he couldn't wait to get back to New Orleans.

We did try to go to see our friend, Mrs. Hacker. We went to her house outside of Knox, but she was not home. She usually didn't go anywhere, so for her not to be home was strange. We then went over to Uncle Everett's house just a few minutes from Mrs. Hacker's near Culver. Strangely, they were not home, either. So then the four of us went over to see some old friends of my grandfather's. We went to the outskirts of North Judson to see George and Wauneta Sanders. They knew my father, too. I remember when we pulled up to their house on the farm. Wauneta answered the door, while the four of us got out of the car. They had not seen my father since Granny Fran passed away. It was a good visit. They had known Grandpa for a long time, as he born and raised in North Judson. His boyhood home and farm were not too far from their house and, on occasion, we would go and drive by the old farm. But going to George and Wauneta's house was kind of creepy, even when I was a young kid. Their house was far from the road and on a hill that went from the road to the house. It was heavily wooded, too. There was a big, red barn not too far from the house. But it was the house that was rather strange. It was a really long, ranch style house that had rather large rooms. Coming into the house from the breezeway, you came up through the steps at the back of the kitchen. I don't remember the kitchen being very large, but the house was very wide, as well as long. You walked through the kitchen and the dining room and then on to the living room. Maybe because I was just a young kid, this house seemed so large, and the bathroom was huge. I think I might have even stayed there one summer for a few days when Grandpa had something going on. He asked them to keep me for a short time. I remember their house had these huge windows, too. You could look out and see their farm and the surrounding area. You could always see who was coming up the driveway, too. I don't think that I went back to George and Wauneta's house too many times after that visit…maybe I never did. As my grandfather's condition got worse with his cancer, he ran out of time. I can remember that visit very clearly as I write this. I remember hearing my father talk about New Orleans and Wauneta talking about my grandmother's funeral and how sad it was. Of course, any funeral is sad, but with Grandpa and Granny Fran and these friends, George and Wauneta, their friendship had a long history. I learned that the four of them used to go square dancing together quite a bit. My father told me that Grandpa had even been a square dance caller on occasion. I think we stayed to visit for about two hours or so. It was always fun getting to see old friends. Funny thing is, I don't remember seeing George and Wauneta much after that time. It was only a short while later that my grandfather died and things in my life really changed.

There was one other conversation my father and I had while we were visiting during his stay. He was adamant about not ever coming back to Valpo again. I knew he did not want to come to visit us in the first place; he would rather have had us visit him. For whatever reason, that did not happen, so here he was, back in the hometown he hated.

I mean, he hated Valparaiso with a passion. He used to talk about the so-called "Valpo mentality" and what it was all about. I never understood it then, but I do now, after all of these years of living away from it. You can almost talk to anybody who grew up in Valpo and then moved away like my father did. This so-called "Valpo mentality" is not anything you can truly define. What the phrase really refers to is how people who live in the Valparaiso, Indiana, area really think and react to certain situations. I guess it is a frame of mind. Valpo used to be an extremely conservative area. It is not so conservative anymore since the rapid influx of Illinois folk who have moved into Northwest Indiana when property taxes in the state of Illinois just got to be outrageous. Valpo has changed a lot since the late 1970s, but my father hated it for this reason and this reason alone. The two of us had arguments about this later when I went to visit him in New Orleans. I asked my father if he would come back for my grandfather's funeral if and when he passed away. My father said no and that it was not up for discussion. I suppose it was the best decision for all parties involved. On the last day of my father's visit, Aunt Bonnie and Uncle Roger from Grand Rapids were going to take him to the airport. As it turned out, my cousin Shawn and a friend of his were going to New Orleans, as well. I thought, "Okay, why does my cousin, Shawn, gets to go to New Orleans and I don't?" However, Shawn was already eighteen and so was his friend, and you had to be eighteen to drink in New Orleans. I was only fourteen. I had some time to go before that time arrived, and when it did, there would be no way I could go there. But I hated it when other people got to do things like that and I did not. I was pissed off. I am STILL pissed to this day about this. I am not mad at my cousin, Shawn, for going to spend time in New Orleans, but what I am upset about is that my grandfather had no control over that decision. I mean, with me, my grandfather had control, and so did my parents. The three of them liked having parental control. But with my cousins from the same family, it was like, yeah, go to New Orleans and have a blast, and Mike, you stay here and stay on this leash. I'm like, what just happened here? Then what made me even more pissed off was the fact that my aunt and uncle would not take me to the airport with them.

My aunt said, "Oh, Mike, yeah, we are not going to stop on the way back from the airport. We are going straight back from O'Hare to Grand Rapids."

Although I was unhappy about my not being able to go with them to New Orleans, today it makes some kind of sense. It was always difficult for me when others were able to do things that I could not. In addition, I could not go to O'Hare with them because Aunt Bonnie and Uncle Roger would be driving straight back to Grand Rapids, not back to Valpo. So here was one more disappointment for me. Little did I know that would be the last time I would see my father for seven, long years. I saw him next on his turf in the French Quarter of New Orleans. So, they all left for O'Hare without me. I remember waving good-bye to my father and seeing them drive down Roosevelt Road and over the railroad tracks.

It was now the late summer of 1978, and I was getting ready for tenth grade at Valpo High. Grandpa was all worked up about me going to such a large high school. I did not know at the time that I would be graduating with 437 other classmates in 1981. That was a big school in those days. Valparaiso was a growing community then, and it still is.

But my grandfather was concerned about some of the social issues that were going on inside the high school. To this day, I don't know who he had a conversation with, but whoever it was seemed to scare the crap out of him. This concerned Grandpa, so we had a man-to-man talk while he sat in his favorite chair. He was concerned about all of the so-called drug use at the high school and about all the pregnant girls who attended. It was several weeks into the semester that I was able to tell him that this was really not the case. I mean, he made it sound like drugs and "dope," as he referred to it, was as common as a soft drink. I assured him that if there were drugs at the school, they would not find me. Then I addressed the situation about "all of the pregnant girls." There were two, as I remember at the time. One of them worked in the lunch line at school.

Then, some time later, one of my classmates got pregnant. She was somebody I knew because she was a neighbor to my older sister. I assured my grandfather that I was not going to school to get involved in drugs and get girls pregnant. This may have calmed him down somewhat. Then he told me that since he knew he was going to die soon, he had changed his will. It was during this conversation that Grandpa told me he was cutting my father out of his will and leaving me as one of his heirs. Although I did not know it then, this would forever damage my relationship with my father. I mean, really damage things. I know why Grandpa did this. However, my father felt that his dad was just mad at him and cut him out of the will.

Grandpa also stated that he was going to make mom my legal guardian in the event of his death. He said that this was the best thing for me and, in the event he passed away before I turned eighteen, this would have to be the arrangement. I agreed to it because it was the best choice. Again, Grandpa protected and raised me, and with my great aunt and uncle and their daughters, I was included as one of their own. He was protecting me from my father now, and in so doing, he would really make my father angry with him for the rest of his life.

It was after the Christmas and New Year's holidays when my grandfather's health started taking a turn for the worse. Grandpa was in and out of the hospital for chemo treatments and such, and it took longer to recover after each one. Finally, one day after being there, he announced that he was done with having chemo. He was done with radiation treatments, as well. Grandpa had just had enough. The end of February 1979 was the last time I stayed at my grandparents' house for the weekend. He complained all weekend that he was in pain and just did not feel like himself. I remember when he dropped me off at my parents' house at the end of that weekend, he said, "Please, say a prayer for me." I told him I would and said my good-bye to him. This comment from Grandpa made me feel badly. I just couldn't think about it. But I realized then that the end was coming quickly. That evening I called my father, and he was not much help, either. I remember him saying that he knew the end was near. There was just nothing anybody could do. My father was right, as much as I hated to admit it.

The next day, my grandfather was admitted to the hospital for gall stones. This cancer was spreading and was messing with his gallbladder. Grandpa would need surgery, and the next day, he was going to have his gallbladder removed. After his surgery, I went to see him in the hospital for the last time. I remember that Uncle Chuck (my father's older brother) came from Pittsburgh, PA. He knew that the end was near, and he took off work, so that he could be there. I remember seeing Grandpa for the last time. This visit really upset me. I could tell how sick he was. Grandpa always wore glasses, but now he was not even wearing them. He really did not feel like talking. This hurt because he always took time to talk to his grandson. I was his favorite.

I was the one he raised as one of his own. I was trying to ask him things, but he was just falling off to sleep. Sometime after that, I said my goodbyes and left. My parents were waiting for me down in the coffee shop. I had a talk with Uncle Chuck that day in the coffee shop, but he was no help, either. He had his own concerns. He knew that the end was near with his father. I think he just wanted to get everything over with and get back to his wife, family, and his job. He did not care about me. He knew what was happening to me once my grandfather passed away. He knew what all the arrangements were. Nice and neat, just the way he liked it. He would not have to deal with me ever again. I think he was glad to get me out of his life, as well. I felt like I was just pissing him off. Maybe because my father lived in New Orleans and worked for him on the Superdome project. By now it was clear that for some time, my father and his older brother had not been on speaking terms. I am sure that my uncle hates him to this day and is glad to have me completely out of his life. Period. There might be a difference of opinion about this, but this is my side of that story.

As a young child, I used to play with Uncle Chuck's kids, Curt and Christy. We had fun back then, and things were simple. But things changed as I grew up, and certainly my life really changed with my grandfather's death. I realized then that I couldn't go back to the way it was.

I remember that day when Grandpa died: March 12, 1979. Like most normal days, I went to school and remember coming home on the bus, as usual. I was at my sister's house, just around the corner from Grandpa's. It was a bright, sunny day, and the snow was starting to finally melt after a brutal winter. I remember that I was staying with Sharon and Bob because Grandpa was in the hospital and Mom and Dad left for Indianapolis to go to the annual Indiana Gas Convention. I didn't know what was about to happen. Everything was going to change, and change immediately. I just didn't know it yet. I had the key to my sister's house and went in. I shut the door, took off my coat, and turned on the television. My brother-in-law was at his local rent-a-car and truck business. My sister was teaching school in nearby Chesterton.

The phone rang. It was Uncle Chuck. He wanted to know if my sister was home. She was not. I asked him how my grandfather was doing. There was silence. He then asked me if I knew when my parents were coming home from the gas convention. I didn't think that they were coming home right away because they were going to Florida for an extended vacation. Again, I asked him about Grandpa. I knew that I would not see him until he started to feel better after the surgery. Now he asked if I knew when my sister was coming home from school. I said not until four-thirty or so. Then Uncle Chuck gave me the news I was not expecting. He said, "I hate to be the one to tell you this, Mike, but your grandfather passed away earlier today." He went on to say, "Please, tell Sharon to call me when she comes home from school."

He said he was at my grandfather's house and to call him there. I asked him if my father had been told and he said yes, he had already talked to him and told him the news. I asked if my father was coming to Valpo for the funeral, and he said he did not know for sure. So, then I hung up the phone, and I did not know what to do. My body was numb. I could not think. And I just could not imagine life without my grandfather. But now he was gone. The first thing I had to do was get hold of my sister. I grabbed the phone book and called the school. I asked to speak to my sister, Sharon. When she came to the phone and said hello, I said, "Sharon, I am sorry to call you at school, but I just got a call from Uncle Chuck, and he told me that Grandpa just passed away."

She said, "I'll be right home." She did come home quickly, and then we had the task of calling Mom and Dad at the hotel in Indianapolis. They said that they would pack and leave immediately and be home as soon as possible. They asked my sister how I was doing, and she told them that I was holding up fine, at least, as well as could be expected. I was just numb from all of the news, and I had nothing to say.

Later that night, Mom and Dad came home and picked me up from my sister's house. I did not know at the time, but I found out later that my family was worried about what was going to happen with me. I remember my parents talked to a lawyer, and they were going to go to court if they had to, and that was to make sure that I was not going to be placed with the wrong people—like with my father in New Orleans. I didn't know at the time, but he didn't want me, either. He just wanted his money from my father's estate. Was he going to be in for a big surprise!

I went to school the next day,, even though I really shouldn't have. I didn't sleep well that night, and I was still emotional from the news of Grandpa's death. I remember talking to my friend, George Moncilovich, who was one of my best friends. I was in tears. I was a damn wreck, and the first hour in high school had not even started. I then wondered how I was going to make it through the day, but somehow I did. I managed to tell all of my teachers and the attendance office that I was not going to be at school the next day due to my grandfather's funeral.

When I got home from school, I had to get ready to go to the wake. That was not going to be easy. I didn't like funeral homes—they were scary and creepy. Seeing dead family members and family friends just made me uneasy. I guess it was from watching too many of those *Dark Shadows* episodes with my sister Susan. Anyway, we got to the funeral home, which was down by the old Porter County Jail. It was ironic because just a couple of days before I had a business class in school, and we went to the jail and the Porter County small claims court for a field trip. I remember thinking to myself, while we were waiting for the bus outside of the jail, just across the street from the funeral home. I had hoped I would not be there anytime soon. As usual, I was wrong. The weather had turned really cold again, and it was almost the middle of March. I remember we got to the lobby to take off our winter coats, and I had on my new, three-piece suit. It was light blue in color, and I had on a dress shirt and a tie. My grandfather had just bought me that suit, and I was proud to wear it. All of my family from the Dowd side was there. Aunt Mabel and Uncle Everett had flown up from Fort Meyers, Florida, where they had a winter home. Uncle Bill was there with his wife, Aunt Lola, and Grandpa's other brother, Glenn, was there with his lady-friend Olive. My cousins were all there too: April, Mark, Shawn, and Francie with Aunt Bonnie and her husband, Roger. Uncle Chuck and his wife, Joanne, were there with my cousins, Curt and Christy. I remember we walked up and took off our coats, and it was then I could see Grandpa in his casket. It did not look like him, either. All I could do was stare. I was still in denial and shock. It made me nervous to be there.

I had been to a large number of wakes and funerals for friends and relatives who had died prior to my grandfather. It is never easy to go to one of these things, even for me today. I really feel sorry for the families who stand up there, by the casket, and accept condolences from everyone who comes to the wake. You talk about how sick the person was and how much better off they are now that his or her life is over.

As I get older, I strongly believe that you never really die. It is your spirit that leaves your body, and it is that spirit that goes on to heaven or hell—or maybe in between, if that is what you believe. I never said this before now, but I am a strong believer in the Christian faith (raised a Methodist). I believe in the Father, the Son, and the Holy Spirit. I believe that Jesus Christ died for my sins, as well as others, and I believe in heaven. I don't go to church as much as I should, but I am still a firm believer in God. I believe in the power of prayer.

As I found out later in life, when I had my second heart surgery at the age of thirty-eight, there were people praying for me that I did not even know. Many people from other faiths were praying for me then, and I will never forget that. If there is one thing always difficult for me about life, it is that people and animals die. I DO NOT LIKE DEATH. I DESPISE IT. Whenever I meet the Grim Reaper, I'll have a hell of a time with him. Or, he will have a hell of a time with me…one or the other. It is especially difficult for me when it is a family member or a good friend. I remember all of the people who I spoke to at my grandfather's wake. I got to see Grandpa's next-door neighbors, Dottie and Ed. There was Joe and Pam, who had lived next door and took care of Grandpa's snow plowing when the weather got bad. His ironworker friends were there. There was no "mill mouth" talk going on now.

I had forgotten that Grandpa was a Shriner. When my dad and I walked up to the casket for the first time and paid our respects, Grandpa was wearing a sort of apron. I am not sure what you call this, but it is a special tribute to someone when they die as a member of the Shriners. It was then I learned that later in the evening, there would be a special service that would take place for my grandpa. It would be a service that remembered their fellow Shriner. It was a nice tribute to him.

I think it was sometime that night, too, that my Uncle Chuck told me that my father would not be coming to Valparaiso for the funeral. I never got the chance to talk to my father after I heard the news of Grandpa's passing, so I never heard his reaction. I was at the funeral home when a large number of flowers arrived. I went around and looked at all of flowers that had been delivered. There were some very large bouquets that were on a stand and in a wreath shape. My father had sent them. He put my name on the card, too. What a tribute, I thought. It was too bad he could not come to the funeral, but I figured he was sick or something. It turned out he was not sick. It was years later I found out there were some relatives that did not want my father there. I heard this from one of my cousins. There were a number of people who thought my father was going to cause trouble and even try to take me back to New Orleans with him.

So, out of peer pressure, somebody called my father in New Orleans and told him not to bother coming. I do not know who it was who did this, and I don't know If I should have thanked them or kicked them in the teeth, but for whatever reason, my father was not at the funeral. When I learned this news,

I suddenly felt empty. When someone dies who is really close to you, not only do you feel bad about them dying, but you feel empty. You feel alone. You feel like no one can help you, and you feel sorry for yourself. Then the depression sets in. I just felt that I didn't know what was to be in my future. How was I going to get along without my grandfather? Who was going to be there for me? I JUST FELT LOST. I FELT LONELY. It was like an Elvis Presley record. It was so bad for me.

The Shriner memorial service was a nice tribute, and I made it through that okay. I was nervous when thinking about the next day. As I said previously, I don't do well at funerals. This funeral would be the most difficulty one that I had ever attended. My family and I arrived at the funeral home about a half hour before it started.

At home I remember getting up from bed and going downstairs to get ready. Dad had already been up earlier than usual that morning. He was at the kitchen table writing what looked like some sort of letter. I asked him what he was doing, but he didn't answer me. I went downstairs to get dressed. Normally, we would have had out-of-town relatives staying with us, but not this time. Mom, Dad, and I had the whole house to ourselves. It was much more efficient that way. I was able to sleep in my own bed and get ready in my own bathroom. I put on my suit again, this time with a different dress shirt and tie. Dad always fixed my tie for me. We all got ready, and I remember my parents being so nervous, as well. I did not know what they were concerned about. We saw my Uncle Chuck first. This was not exactly the way I cared to start the morning of Grandpa's funeral. He had been in charge of things his whole life, so he was, once again, in charge of the funeral. He was the one who decided who the pallbearers would be. I think about five or six of my cousins from the Dowd side of the family were selected. They were my cousins Glenn, Kenny, and Ray Dowd, plus three others I don't remember. I thought it was kind of strange, though, that the pallbearers used Grandpa's Buick LeSabre on the day of the funeral. I wondered why I was not asked to be a pallbearer for my grandfather's funeral. I wish that I had done that for him. But my Uncle Chuck was in charge, and he never asked me. I was very disappointed.

Would I ever have the chance to ride in Grandpa's car again? It was even strange to see someone else, like my cousin, drive it. It was even worse when I was at Grandpa's house the first time after he died. The house now belonged to my grandmother and she owned it. That was all made official after my grandfather's will was read. Before the start of the service, we were talking to Uncle Chuck about the arrangements. He said that I should ride with my cousins, Curt and Christy, while my aunt and uncles and their spouses rode in the limo. He did not want me in that car, either. I felt as though he was sticking me at the end of the procession. I think if my father had been there, Uncle Chuck no doubt would have told him to get a ride from someone else to the cemetery.

The service seemed to take forever, and it was crowded, too. I did get to sit up front with the family, not far from the casket. The minister who gave the eulogy was the minister Grandpa had chosen for his funeral. He was the Reverend Franklin from the Round Lake Church, just outside North Judson. My grandpa was not going to be buried there, even though his parents were there, along with a host of other Dowd relatives. Many more of Grandpa's friends were in attendance. I mentioned George and Wauneta from the North Judson area, and also Kenny and Mary White. My grandfather's three brothers were all there, too. For whatever reason, Mrs. Iva Hacker was not in attendance. I heard she was not feeling well. My sister Sharon was there also. I saw her in tears, too. The funeral service came to an end and, just like Grandpa's life, it was over. I remember seeing everyone paying their final respects. When the crowd left the room, the funeral home staff closed the room off.

It was only immediate family now in the room. We got up from our seats and saw Charles McKinley Dowd for the last time. I was in tears pretty hard at this point, and I had nobody to hold on to. Nobody to hug. I felt so alone in that room at that moment. Watching my grandmother weep, my Aunt Bonnie in tears, and my cousins, all with tissues, and even Uncle Chuck wiping his tears away. I felt cold and nervous, as well as sad and lonely. I had never felt worse at that moment in my life. To this day, even with all of the funerals I have been to, that day in March 1979 was the single worst day of my life.

I remember when we left that room, we all went to get our coats to depart, and we were still in tears. Sharon, Mom, and Dad all came by to see me, and they were in tears, as well. I just thought they were sad for my grandfather, but little did I know that they thought I was no longer going to be a part of their lives. I found that out later in the afternoon. I made it through the service at the cemetery and cried even more. This was it. My life would change forever at this point, and I had no idea what was going to happen. At that point, I guess I really didn't care. I remember riding in the car with my cousins. It was all tears and silence. I remember Curt lighting up a cigarette and stinking up the car with smoke. My cousins did not want to talk, and I didn't, either. I don't think they really wanted me in their car anyway, but their dad told them to take me to the cemetery, and they did what they were told to do. That did not mean they had to talk to me, either. It was bad enough that we buried our grandfather that day, but I could not stand the silent treatment. That just pissed me off.

Although the weather was cold and rainy, I made it through the cemetery service. It was only fitting. Late winter in Valparaiso, and at Grandpa's funeral the weather was cloudy, dark, and bitterly cold. Afterwards, we went to a Lutheran church across from the high school for the post-funeral luncheon. Most everyone who had attended the funeral was there, and the mood was much better, too. I know I was rather hungry, but as emotional as I felt, I certainly was not starving.

The luncheon was sponsored by the Valparaiso Women's Club, a social club that my grandmother belonged to. There were a couple of women I recognized at the luncheon who were preparing the food on the tables. I knew one of the ladies that was there: my brother-in-law's mother, Mrs. Anne McCasland. She and my grandmother had known each other for a long time through this social club. It was fitting that she would be there to help out. After I was done eating, I wanted to thank people who came to the luncheon. I went around and thanked everybody I could, including all of my cousins, aunts, and uncles. Many of Grandpa's friends were there, too, and this might have been the last time I saw them, as well. With the luncheon over, my mom and dad and I left the church in the cold rain and went home. I was so tired and ready to go home and not be bothered with anything. It was time for some peace and quiet.

However, before we left the church luncheon, Uncle Chuck asked my parents if the four of them could get together and talk privately. That meant without me. So, my dad suggested the two couples meet down at my dad's LP gas store and plant, down on US 30 at 7:00 P.M. They all agreed, and we went home. Little did I know what Uncle Chuck was up to now.

I remember when we got home, Mom, Dad and I were really tired from the day's events. I went downstairs to watch television and relax, while Mom went to read a book and Dad took a nap on the couch upstairs in the living room. I could not sleep, as I was either too tired or too wound up. I was watching some old scuba movie on T.V. After my dad woke up, we had a long, serious talk. I had no idea what was on their minds, and I thought I had done something to make them angry. I was not the best-behaved teenager back then, so I had no idea what they wanted to talk about.

My dad started the conversation. He said that he and Mom had no idea what was going to happen with my custody, and he said that they had consulted a family attorney. He stated that they would hire this attorney if they had to. I felt it was a stupid question, but why would they want to do that? My dad responded that he and Mom had no idea what was going to happen with my father and didn't know if my father might put up some sort of battle for my custody. I told them both that I had no idea what they were doing and why they were doing it. Mom and Dad did not know that my grandfather's will stated that my guardianship would go to Mom until I turned eighteen. Both of them seemed to think my father would put up some sort of fight, so that he could take me and my possible inheritance. They knew if my father did that, I would be left with nothing.

I told Mom and Dad they really shouldn't have anything to worry about. My grandfather had told me about this long before he died, and he also told me that he would leave my father $1,000. So, in all respects, he left my father with next to nothing. I was to get his share of the estate. My parents did not know this because apparently my grandfather had not told them. I then reassured them that they should not worry about it, and it would all come out after they read Grandpa's will.

My parents and I talked about the funeral, too. We talked about all of the people who were at the funeral and why Sharon and my parents were all upset after the funeral was over. My dad said something to the effect that they were all worried about me and what was going to happen to me after this was all over. He then went on to say that Sharon was upset, too, about the same thing, and she was the one who found the family attorney who would represent them in court if it came to that.

The other thing my dad also told me was that Sharon was pregnant with their first child and that I was going to be an uncle. I was told to keep it a secret because she had not told her school principal yet. Then my dad said something I will never forget. He went on to tell me why he wrote that letter the morning of the funeral. It was some sort of proof that they had been taking care of me and no one should take me away from them. Again, I told them that they really should have nothing to worry about, and that Grandpa's will should take care of everything. But they were willing to fight for me, if that is what it came to. They were willing to take it to court if they had to. Then, my dad told me something else. He was proud of me for being the kind, young man I was at the funeral luncheon. I said I did not know what he meant. He said how proud he was that I went around to everyone at the luncheon and thanked them for coming and attending my grandfather's funeral.

I said to him, "You saw that?"

He said, "Yes, I did." He went on to say that he never saw anybody from my cousins to Uncle Chuck and Aunt Bonnie ever do that, and he noticed it right away. I said to them that I thought it was the right thing to do.

Little did I know, it would be a long time before I would see my father's family again. It was almost like the start of the Cold War with them, including my father. It was a long, cold March that year and, as I said, 1979 would go down as the absolute worst year of my life. It still is…

CHAPTER 4: YET ANOTHER NEW BEGINNING

It was about 6:45 P.M. when my parents and I finished our conversation. I was in tears, once again, after all of the day's events. Now with this conversation over, I was wondering just what my future was going to be. My parents realized what time it was and that they were going to be late for their meeting with Uncle Chuck. I had no idea what was up with him and really did not care. Mom and Dad made a phone call, one to Uncle Chuck to let him know that they were running late, and then another call to my sister Sharon to ask if they could drop me off at their house while they talked to my uncle. Normally, I would have just stayed home by myself, but after everything that had happened that day, and as emotional as I was, my parents just did not want to leave me by myself.

So, I went to Sharon and Bob's house.

Mom and Dad must have been gone for at least two hours when they finally returned to pick me up. While I was with Sharon and Bob, I thanked them for all they had done for me, as they were the ones who found the attorney who would have gone to court in the event that things had gone sour. I also congratulated them both on the news of their first child. Sharon said the baby was due in September.

As my Dad said, Sharon wanted me not to say anything to anybody yet because she had not told anyone at the school where she taught. I said I was fine with that.

Then, sometime after 9:30 P.M. or so, Mom and Dad returned from their meeting. I asked them how things went. Dad said everything was fine. He said that there was no need to worry and that everything was in my grandfather's will. I guess these were words of reassurance: I should have nothing to worry about. I did not know it then, but that was not the conversation they had. It would be about seven or eight years later that I would find out the truth of that meeting. We then went home, my parents and I, and I went to bed because I had to go back to school the next day. It was tough to go back so quickly. Everything was a blur. I could not really concentrate on anything. I was just going through the motions.

A few days later, my parents received a call from the attorney's office who was handling Grandpa's estate. It turned out the attorney was an acquaintance of Uncle Chuck's. In fact, it was my uncle who had recommended this attorney to my grandfather when he decided to rewrite his last will and testament. My parents made an appointment with the attorney, and within the next day or two, they went to the law office located in the old Indiana Federal Bank Building in Valparaiso. This building is still there today and is located on the corner of Lincoln Way and Washington Street.

I had been in the bank a number of times, and even had a savings account there, but had never gone to any offices upstairs. I remember that after the meeting, my parents told me that this attorney, James Bozic, wanted to have a meeting with me. They didn't tell me what he wanted to discuss; nonetheless, he wanted to speak to me. A few days later, it was my turn to go to the law office and talk to my grandfather's attorney. It was after school, so it must have been around 3:00 or 3:30 P.M. Dad waited for me outside the office while I went inside.

He introduced Mr. Jim Bozic to me, and then we shook hands. He was a very nice man and seemed quite friendly. He said that he was here to help and that is why we were in his office. He wanted to tell me what to expect and then offered me a seat across from his desk and asked how I was doing. I told him I was fine, considering everything I had been through. He said he understood because he saw this sort of thing on a daily basis. He also knew I was very close to my grandpa. My grandfather had told him about me. He also knew that I had to be protected in the event that Grandpa's son, Tom (my biological father), decided to take things into his own hands. This attorney knew everything and just what my situation was all about. He was smart, very smart. He was protecting me. He knew that it was not only his job, but in my grandfather's best interest, as well as my own. After he told me about how he got involved as my grandfather's attorney (through Uncle Chuck), he then went on to talk about why I was in his office.

The lawyer said that it was important to know why my grandfather had named me a beneficiary in his will. It was important to Grandpa to see that not only would I finish school at Valparaiso High, but he also said that it was even more important that I go on to college and get a degree.

"You will be inheriting about $20,000 in the next year or so, and it will be up to you and your great aunt and uncle to make sure that you use this money for a college education," he said.

"Your great aunt will soon officially become your legal guardian until you turn eighteen. She will also oversee and make sure that your grandfather's wishes are carried out and that you get a quality college education."

He then stressed to me just how important it was to get an education from a good college and told me it would be much easier to get a good job that provided me with a quality life down the road. I agreed with what he said. I was in my sophomore year in high school, and I had made a promise to my grandfather before he died. That promise was not only to finish high school but to also graduate and go on to college and get a degree. My attorney understood that I understood that, and so did my parents. He then asked me about my grades. I told him they were not the best, but I was on a mission to get my diploma and that I would not quit until my diploma was in my hands.

I also told him that I was fifteen years old and that I was going to be taking driver's education next summer. I was looking forward to getting my driver's license and having a car. He agreed with that and said that there would be money for me to go to college after high school and that whatever was left was mine. I said okay, and our meeting was over.

I thanked him for all of his services, and he said, "No problem. That's what I am here for." He also said that if I had any questions about my situation, or questions about my grandfather's estate, to call him. I asked him about my father's situation. The attorney said that he would be sending a copy of my grandfather's will to my father and that he would be receiving something like $1,000 from his will. I shook my head. He said, "What is your concern about your father's part of this?"

I said to him, "He is only getting $1,000? Why is that?"

He went on to say that my grandfather believed that my education and proper upbringing were more important. I said something like, "This won't cause trouble?"

He said, "Once a will is written and gone through probate court, the will is then considered law."

My father really had no money. He was living on disability income at the time, and I knew he was looking forward to this money. He was virtually being cut out of the estate. The attorney assured me that my father would not cause any problems, "and if he does, let me know." He'd like to be informed.

I told him I would, and our first meeting was over. He added that it would be about six to eight months before my grandfather's estate was finalized because, by law, there had to be that much time allowed for bills and other issues to be paid prior to the beneficiaries being paid. I said thanks and went out to meet my dad in the lobby. We then went home.

I guess it was either that night or sometime during the week that I got a phone call from my father. He was calling from his apartment in New Orleans, and I could tell he had been drinking. In fact, I am sure he was just plain drunk. I could tell from the way he acted and spoke on the phone. I was at home, watching television in the family room in the basement, and it was after 9:00 P.M. He asked how I was doing, and I said fine.

I realized that I had to be careful what I said to him. After all, I had been to the attorney's office, and I knew what was in store for him. I didn't want to be the one to spill the beans to him about my grandfather's will. I was not going to be the one who told him that he was only getting $1,000 from my grandfather's estate. Let him find out when he gets a copy of the will. It was not for me to tell him, even though I knew and he did not. He went on to ask me how the funeral was. I told him that there were a lot of people there: friends and relatives who had come to pay their respects.

He really did not care who was there. He asked me if I had seen the flowers he had sent from both of us. I told him I was there when they were delivered, and I told him thanks for putting my name on the card, as well. It was then I asked him why he was not here for the funeral.

He said, "I do not travel well, and I was home sick with the flu." He said it would have been really difficult to be back in Valpo when he was not feeling very good. At that time, I thought he was telling me the truth, but later I found out that he lied about it. He was not sick, and it was not that he did not travel well. It was because someone called him and told him *not* to be there at his father's funeral. He was told he would be nothing but trouble. It was long after my father died when I found this out. My father sounded drunk, and I didn't like talking to him when he was under the influence. He was never angry with me on the phone, but I could tell he was upset about something. He said that he was thinking about leaving New Orleans and moving to Brownsville, Texas. I asked him why he wanted to move there, and he said there might be new opportunities for him there. I did not know what that meant. All I knew is that he always talked a lot of garbage. He talked liked he was going there to do something, but I had no idea what it was going to be. I hung up the phone that night, feeling really uncomfortable. I really didn't want to talk with him anymore if he was going to be drunk and call me. It wasn't right for me to talk to him if he was going to behave like that.

About two or three weeks later, I found out that Mom, Dad, and I were going to Macon, Georgia, to see my sister, Susan, during spring break. We didn't get the chance to see her very often since she moved to Macon and was teaching school there. It was good to get to warmer weather, too. It had been a cold, wet March, and with my grandfather's funeral and all, so it was just nice to get out of Valpo for a while. I was tired of winter. We stayed at Susan's apartment.

This was 1979, the year that Michigan State was playing Indiana State for the National Title in NCAA basketball. This was also the year of the famous game between Larry Bird and Magic Johnson—one of the most historic games in college basketball tournament history. Both men would go on to be awesome players and rivals, and later friends in the NBA. A few years later, a guy named Michael Jordan (who is my age) would come into the league, and the three of them would take the NBA to a whole new level. I enjoyed basketball and have always been a big fan of the sport. My high school usually had good teams, too. I have always loved watching. Dad and I, along with my sister's boyfriend, Bill Andrews, all watched the game. Unfortunately, Michigan State beat Indiana State. I felt badly for Larry Bird and his teammates as they lost the game.

That day my parents and Susan went shopping. They were going to be gone for a few hours, and I had my sister's apartment all to myself. I was bored; it was early in the afternoon, and I decided to call my father collect. By now he had received his copy of Grandpa's will. Even though it was only one o'clock or so in the afternoon, I think my father had already started hitting the sauce.

I asked him how he was doing, and he said he was "lousy."

I detected some anger in his voice and said, "What is upsetting you today?"

He said he had received his copy of his dad's will and he was "pissed off."

I played dumb and asked him why.

That's when he really got mad and said that he was so angry with my grandpa, and if he ever came back to Valparaiso, Indiana, again, he would take a giant hammer and absolutely desecrate my grandfather's grave.

He went onto say, "I can't believe that dumb S.O.B. did the things he did in his will to me. I mean, most of that money was not really his, and he knew that." He was referring to the fact that Grandpa inherited the money that Granny Fran had worked for and saved when she worked in the ammunition factory over in Union Mills. After she died, I assumed all of her hard-earned money and savings went to my grandfather. That money did not go to any of the kids, I guess. Then he started calling my grandfather just about every obscene name in the book. Talk about a "mill mouth" conversation! He just could not face the fact that he had been cut out of Grandpa's will. Then he said, "It's not about the money!"

Yeah, right, I thought. Then he started blaming people. He started tearing into my grandfather's second wife, who wound up with the house, some of the money, as well as three acres of land Grandpa had bought at Mrs. Hacker's farm. He bought that property a few years earlier before the cancer, and he wanted to build a retirement and weekend home there. He never got the chance. Then, my father started to blame his older brother, Chuck. I always had respect for Uncle Chuck, but he started with the obscenities toward him. He never talked bad about his sister, Bonnie, but then he did something I never thought he would do. He had the nerve to start in on me. He didn't call me obscene names that I remember, but he stated that all of his problems were my fault. He felt that other people convinced Grandpa to do what he did and that things would have been different if he had been there. Then, again, he started with the obscenities at my grandfather. After a few more minutes of this, I just about had enough. He was mad. Angry and just plain pissed off. After I hung up the phone with my father, I decided right then and there I was not going to call him anymore. I had no need to. If he wanted to call everybody obscene names and blame me for his issues, the hell with him, I thought. I don't need him in my life anymore, and I am done with him. I should have told him off on the phone, but I did not have the heart to do it.

I wanted no part of him anymore…I was DONE with my father.

Now, my relationship with my father was over at this point in my life. It was time to get on with my own life. It was time to continue high school and get ready for summer. But first there was one thing I had to do. I wanted to complete my confirmation classes I started the previous fall at the First United Methodist Church in Valparaiso. The years of '77, '78, and '79 were some of the worst years of my life. Not only did I lose my grandfather but also a host of other relatives. People say that death is a part of life. I don't like that statement, but I guess it's true. During those three years, our family lost an assortment of relatives from the Johnson side: aunts and uncles from the DeHaven side, as well as family from the Dowd side. It was a rough time for all of us.

But going to confirmation classes, learning more and more about God and the Bible, and all things religious, plus getting baptized—well, this meant a new beginning for me. I was baptized in May 1979. Now, I was a confirmed member of the First United Methodist Church of Valparaiso, Indiana, and forgiven of my sins! About ten billion of them…give or take a billion or so. I now felt better about myself. I felt like a new, young man at the age of fifteen. Somehow, at that moment of my life, I did not feel confused anymore, at least for the time being. It truly was a wonderful feeling. I have a lot of fond memories being a part of this church. I knew several people from high school who attended church there, also. Some of these friends I have known my whole life.

It was the summer of 1979, and I was glad that the 1979 school year was over. It was the worst year of school I had ever had; just glad to be done and finished with it. My sophomore year was over, and it was now time to take driver's education during the summer session. A number of my classmates (the class of '81) had already taken driver's ed, but because I started school when I was four, a lot of my fellow classmates were older than I when it was time to get their driver's permits.

There were some classmates in the summer program, but a lot were from the class of 1982. It was kind of fun to be in their class, as well. I really enjoyed the driver's ed class. My teacher was Mr. Tom Stokes, the former head football coach at Valpo High. He was the coach of the team that won the state title for Valpo in football back in '75. We never won a state title in football again. But that's another story. My driver's ed teacher in the car was Mr. Dale Ciciora. I did not know it at the time, but Mr. Ciciora would go on to be my all-time favorite teacher in high school. I would have him for a history class in my senior year, thanks to flunking a history class in my junior year. I liked the way he taught. He was personable and loved by most all of my classmates. And he was funny, too. He was not afraid to tell a joke when you were driving the car in class. He was the kind of person and teacher you could really learn from. Many of the driving skills that he taught me back in 1979, I still use today. Of course, now I just drive a lot faster! But the most challenging thing about driving a car was learning to parallel park. But, Mr. Ciciora was skilled at that, too, and he passed it onto us. He made it look easy, and he made it easy to learn.

I got through the summer of '79 with help from my parents, my sister, Sharon, and her husband, Bob. They had just bought a Hertz-Rent-A-Car franchise from Bob's former boss and now the operation in Valpo and

Michigan City was theirs. That summer I started my first job as a garage-man. This is when I learned to professionally clean cars. This is when I learned to professionally clean rental cars. I learned to wash, rinse, sweep, and clean the inside of the windows. I learned how to work hard, and I also learned to change the oil in both cars and trucks. It was a job I had throughout high school. I worked for my brother-in-law until the day before I went off to college. I worked seven days a week, and even though it was only a few hours a day, this job taught me responsibility. I'll never forgot those days in the rental car business. Yes, I wrecked a couple of cars, too. They were accidents, and in the rental car business, that happens.

The fall of 1979 was my junior year. It was time to take the SAT test. What a joke. I mean, I was not a good student in school as it was, and now I had to start taking all these tests to get into a good college. And speaking of college, I had no idea where I would go. I remember Grandpa had told me he wanted me to go to Angola Tri-State, over near Fort Wayne. This was the school where Uncle Chuck had gone, and so it was always a dream for my grandfather for me to go there. Tri-State was a private school, and it was expensive.

I did not have the grades or the SAT scores to go there. Now that my grandfather was no longer living, I could kind of choose the school where I wanted to go. I wanted to go to school as far away from home as I could. As a teenager, my relationship with my parents had gone down the tube. They were just putting up with me. But now it was my junior year of high school, and I had to find a college to get into and find a program that I would like. After taking the SATs, I learned from my guidance counselor that I would not have the grade point average or the SAT score to get into a college like Indiana University, Purdue, or even Ball State or Indiana State. That was bad for me because I knew that I had to make my end of the promise that I had made with my grandfather. I was afraid that if I did not graduate from high school and get into a college, I might lose my inheritance money.

God only knows that would have been fuel for my father to just take from me. But back then, I was always worried about a lot of stuff that could not happen, and this was one of those things. It was after another conversation I had with my guidance counselor, Mr. Jim McMichael, that seemed to help me find the school I might be looking for.

He suggested Vincennes University, a junior college. After that then I could transfer to another school. It was easier said than done, but it sounded like a good plan at the time. I started looking at catalogs of Vincennes University. They offered a lot of programs of study, and they had on-campus dormitories. It was during my junior year that I was preparing myself to go there. It was a four-hour-plus drive from home, and that sounded good to me—away from my parents and away from Valpo. That is what I wanted. More freedom for me.

After many discussions with my guidance counselor, my SAT scores were sent to Vincennes University. I was also getting my driver's license in January 1980. In the state of Indiana, you had to wait six months after you turned sixteen before you were eligible to get your license. I had saved most all of my paychecks in a savings account. I had to do this because I would need to pay my parents for my share of the car insurance, so that I could drive their '77 Buick Electra 225 Coupe. They had purchased this car after owning that '77 Pontiac Grand Prix, which they had custom ordered. Now, a Pontiac Grand Prix from that year had no leg room in the back seat. I always made it a point when I was riding in the back seat to sit with my legs on the other side of the car or sit behind my mom because she was very short and had the front seat moved up. That was the only way I fit in that car, unless I was sitting in the front seat. I was getting tall. When I was on the ninth grade basketball team, I was approaching six feet tall. I had very long legs. I just did not fit easily in the back seat of the beautiful Pontiac Grand Prix, which I wanted to drive when I was old enough. After having this car for only three and a half months, my parents traded the Grand Prix for a brand-new Buick Electra 225 Coupe. The Grand Prix was a gorgeous white with red landau top and a red pinstripe down the middle of it. It had red crushed velour seats, and it was good on gas because it had the 301 V-8 engine in it. But now my parents had gone and traded it for something different. I never got to drive that Grand Prix, but I put it on my bucket list; if I ever had the chance to buy one, I would get one like the one that my parents had owned. I have to admit, this Buick

Electra 225, or as it was called "the deuce and a quarter," was also a really nice car. It had power everything: windows, locks, and cruise control, and it rode solid. This red-colored Buick with a white padded top had a red interior, and it would be the car that I would take to get my driver's license. My parents always had very nice cars as far back as I can remember, and my dad was a stickler for keeping them spotless. He never liked anything dirty. When working for my brother-in-law at the rental car agency, I would take my dad's car over to work, wash it, and clean out the inside really well as a favor to my parents. On occasion, even after I got my license, they would let me borrow the car and take it out for the night, if they were not using it. Washing and cleaning the car was also good practice. The next car my parents bought was even nicer than the 1977 Buick.

I got my driver's license on a cold, sunny day in January 1980. The so-called 1970s were over, and it was a new decade. When I got my license, the bureau was over on Napoleon Street in Valpo. It was next to a place called Buck's Shoe Repair, which is a restaurant today. This bureau was in an old, small building. You had to go there for everything—to get your driver's license, plates, registration, titles, and other assorted auto related things, so you could drive your car legally in the State of Indiana. I remember the day so well. I had heard from other classmates about the process, so I was well-informed. I heard about the lady who gave the driving test. Some people said she was rude and nasty. But one friend told me to be a gentleman to her: open the door like a gentleman would, and show her respect. If she gives you an order to do in the car, don't ask...just do it. Before I did the actual driving test, I had to pass the written test.

The license bureau had just gotten these state-of-the-art machines, kind of like a slot machine, only it was multiple choice. No one-armed bandit here. The question would come up on the screen in front of you, and you had to answer it by pushing one of the buttons below the screen. I only missed one question on the test, and it was about driving with your lights on in the fog. The question was, "Can you use your high beams in the fog?" I didn't remember that from the manual, so I guessed and got it wrong. I missed one on the written test but still passed it with flying colors.

Now it was time for the test drive. I was not really nervous for the written test, but I was now nervous for the actual driving part of it. Failure was not an option here. I had to have my driver's license for my job at the rental car agency. I had to have it, so I could have my own car. It seemed like my whole life depended on me passing this test, and now it was about to happen. I had flunked many tests before, mainly because I did not study for them, and I did not pay attention in class like I should have. Enough excuses about why I was not successful in school.

But now this was different. This was my driver's license. I don't know if it was luck or just being at the right place at the right time. I was introduced to the lady who I was going to test with. I have forgotten her name, but she was the person everyone talked about in high school when they took theirs. As I remember, she was a tall, intimidating person, when you saw her face to face, but as I found out, she was strictly professional. I remember what a friend said about this: "Be a gentleman, Mike."

He was right. I introduced myself, and we then went out to the Buick for the test drive. I opened the door for her and then shut it when she got in the car. I got in the car, we put on our seatbelts, and then I was told to start it.

I asked her if she wanted the radio on, and she said it did not matter, but I decided I did not want to be distracted. She told me to pull away from the curb, and we then went to a familiar area of Valpo that I knew like the back of my hand. Now, one of the things I have not mentioned is that there was a large amount of snow on the ground and on the streets. We just recently had a heavy snowfall before my test drive, and the streets were still being cleaned off. Fortunately, I had a lot of practice on driving in the snow, thanks to my brother-in-law and my dad. They both told me if I was going to learn how to drive, I had to know how to drive in the weather elements, which included driving in the snow. This practice seemed to pay off. We were driving in the area of our old house near Oak Street when my tester said for me to parallel park the car. I drove up to the car I was supposed to park behind and found that I messed it up. She let me try again, and this time, I got it right, and the parallel parking was flawless. The driving test went on. I had to watch my speed and stop signs because in the snow, I had to give myself plenty of room to stop. The rest of the drive went fine, except for a snowbank I thought I ran over. However, my tester told me later that I ran over a curb when I made a right turn. I was docked for that mistake.

The entire drive lasted about forty-five minutes. She told me in the car when we returned to the bureau that I had passed. She told me everything I had done wrong, which was not very much, and then we went into the bureau, where my parents were waiting. I had passed both parts of the test. She even stated that I was a very good driver and that my marks on the test were very positive. Mom and Dad were pleased. I was elated! After talking with my parents, my picture was taken, and my Indiana State driver's license was issued. There was a fee, and my mom took care of that. I was now sixteen years old, and I had my driver's license. Look out, world!

The next day, I showed all my friends what my license looked like. Up to this point, I have not really told much about my close, personal friends. I'll write about my friends, George, Norman, Bill, Jay, and many others in the next chapter. I never had any girlfriends in either junior high or high school. I didn't date until my senior year and that was a set-up date for the prom.

There was a couple of girls I was really interested in. The year I transferred to Thomas Jefferson Jr. High I became reacquainted with a girl named Debbie Watson. I haven't said much about her until now because our friendship never really amounted to much back then. In an early chapter of my life, when I was in kindergarten at Banta, there was a girl sitting across from me, and we were celebrating Halloween. We were about four or five years old, and we were having our treats and drinks when, all of a sudden, this man dressed as a male witch (a warlock, I guess) came into the room. Debbie had no idea what was happening. This man, dressed as a witch and more than six feet tall, came into the room behind the door where Debbie was sitting.

With her back to the door, Debbie did not see him at first. This guy was loud and scary looking. Like any witch, he had a broom, too. He came toward Debbie and, right in front of me, he took his broom and swept it across Debbie's back. She was really scared and ran out of the room in tears. Later, my mom told me that Debbie ran all the way home. Her house was only about a block away, but the funny thing was that her mom was right there in our room, helping with the kindergarten party with my mom. Debbie stayed at Banta until we were in second grade together, and then she moved across town. I never saw her again until seventh grade.

A couple of days after starting seventh grade at TJ, I ran into Debbie again. She was always shy, quiet, and soft spoken. However, I was loud, rowdy, very immature, and full of crap. It is no wonder girls did not want to be my friend. The problem with me in those days was that I had a very big mouth. Most of the time, this is what got me into trouble. This is what got me into fights with fellow classmates at TJ and why I think Debbie never cared for me.

I think she despised me back then. I found the house where she lived, and I stopped by on my bike to see her. After a few, short visits, she did not want to see me anymore. But I had no idea why. I found her phone number in the phone book and called her. Sometimes daily. After a few calls, she did not want to talk to me anymore. Again, I had no idea why. I asked her if she would go to a junior high school dance, and she said no. I asked Debbie if she wanted to go see a movie at the premier movie theatre in Valpo. She said no. I tried a lot of things to try to get her to be my girlfriend back then, but she was not buying it at all. After my first arrival at TJ, I had a couple of really nice conversations with her. It was really nice to become reacquainted with her again after so many years of not seeing her.

To this day, I don't handle rejection very well. It was not until I was in therapy many years later that I realized I could not handle rejection. I think this all stemmed from my birth mother leaving me in the hospital back in Las Vegas. Rejection. What a brutal word! Like being cut from the seventh grade basketball team at Ben Franklin Junior High School and being told by a friend from my past that she had no interest in me. That was tough. It is not easy being a teenager, I guess. I had a friend next door with an older sister, who gave me one of those "mood rings" that were so popular in the 1970s. They were a big deal then, and I was going to give one to Debbie. I didn't have to buy it from my friend's sister; she just gave it to me to give to Debbie. I wanted to give it to her because I thought she would come around and be my girlfriend after that. Was I ever wrong!

Every time Debbie and I saw each other, we did what we could to avoid it. It was a rather small school, and you saw most of your classmates on a daily basis. You saw them in classes, you saw them in gym class, you saw them at lunch, and sometimes you saw them at school events, like basketball games. I tried to impress her in all sorts of ways. I had taken piano lessons for about nine years or so, and I auditioned for a variety show during the spring of ninth grade. I remember spotting Debbie there after the show, so I knew she saw me perform. Did she say anything? No. When I played for the ninth grade basketball team at TJ, Debbie was a stat keeper. Even though I didn't play a whole lot, she saw me when I did. We rode the team bus together but, of course, we never sat next to each other. Was she impressed? No. I was a manager for the football team in ninth grade with my friend, Norman. Was she impressed? No. I even remember getting an award in grades seven and eight for perfect attendance. Did Debbie ever say anything to me? Hell, no! I do remember after we picked up our junior high school yearbooks, the school always threw an autograph party. I remember Debbie did sign my yearbook, and I thought, "Wow, she actually signed it." She didn't say much to me when she signed it, but I thought maybe this was a start.

During that time in junior high school, it was not easy growing up. About the time I got to ninth grade, I tried to care about my studies more. But that did not work, and after all of the rejection, I just did not care anymore.

When I started high school, I left Debbie alone. I finally got the message. She wanted no part of me, and I just had to accept that. She would not be my girlfriend. I never gave her the mood ring. I could not face being rejected by Debbie again. I figured if I tried to give her the ring, she would just throw it back in my face. I remember one Saturday morning, my dad was sweeping the floor in the dining room in our new house on Hastings Court. My friend, Jeff, from next door had come over, and he did not know I was keeping the ring a secret from my parents. Jeff had been given the ring by his older sister, Julie, and I was going to give the ring to Debbie. My dad was there when Jeff came over, and when he heard what I was going to do with the ring, he went through the roof. He even threatened me with bodily harm if I gave Debbie that mood ring. I had to give the ring back to Jeff and ask him to give it back to his sister, Julie. A few days later, Julie gave me the ring again when I was at their house after school. I took it with every intention of giving it to Debbie. But this was junior high school, and if your classmates saw you do this, you'd never hear the end of it.

The story would be all over school. Then I would really never hear the end of it because my mom worked in the junior high cafeteria. She was the part-time cashier. Anytime I got into trouble and was in the office being disciplined, my mom, who was a cashier in the cafeteria, had a direct pipeline from two of her personal friends, who also worked at the school. If I had been in a fight, she knew about it.

I once got into trouble for throwing spit-wads and was sent to the office. It was just a few minutes later that my mom heard about it from her good friend, Madelyn Brown. Outside the school, I called her Aunt Madelyn. But while I was at school, I had to call her Mrs. Brown. If that was not enough, another of my mom's close friends worked in the principal's office as a secretary. This was mom's knitting club friend, Mrs. Anderson. If I were called to the office for anything, and I mean ANYTHING, good or bad, my mom knew about it. I think it was about as bad as being related to the Sopranos—maybe like the mafia or something. I look back on that experience and now realize that all I had to do was stay the hell out of trouble and keep my big mouth shut and nothing would get back to Mom at school. If I had been more mature back then, maybe I would have gotten better grades, too. Now, I realize why my behavior was so bad. First, I was a teenager. I didn't like being told no by anyone, and I was told no by my parents a lot then. This led to arguments with them and fights with my mom. Most of these fights were about the most stupid things, too. For me it all started when we moved from Oak Street to Hastings Court. I did not like leaving the house on Oak Street. It was a big, warm house with a built-in pool and a six-car garage. But after my dad's heart attack when I was in fifth grade and his health concerns after that, my parents decided to try to find a house that was a ranch style, all on one floor.

At that time, I was in seventh grade (1975). I was attending Ben Franklin Junior High School and getting good grades. No Ds or Fs on my report card then. I was enjoying school. The only disappointment was the fact that I had been cut from the seventh grade basketball team. But my grades were acceptable to my parents and my grandfather. It was around October of '75 that my parents found a house that had been featured as a model home in the 1975 Porter County Parade of Homes. There were four homes built for this home show. This ranch house had many of the options my parents wanted.

The house was also built with central air. It had a full basement that was partially finished. Also, with three, nice-sized bedrooms, it came with a natural, wood-burning fireplace and a two-car, attached garage. The yard was huge. My parents fell in love with the house and, yes, I liked it, too. The problem for me was that if my parents bought this house, I would have to change schools. I tried to convince them that I could still go to Ben Franklin Junior High School. They both said no to that idea, and it was off to TJ after we moved. I did not like being told what to do, so now that I had to go to this school, nothing was going to matter anymore. Little did I know that in just a few, short years, my grandfather would die. Little did I know I would be rejected by Debbie. Little did I know that I would find trouble at just about every turn in my new junior high and then have to hear about it every evening over dinner. That was just the first issue for me.

It seemed to me then that just about everything I did was criticized, scrutinized, and either rejected or told to stay out of it. This was the beginning of more fights and arguments with my parents. When we moved to our new house on Hastings Court, we had to make sure that the beds were made every day of the week. My parents became neat freaks, too, and every Friday was cleaning day. Every Tuesday was laundry day, and every day of the week I had to practice piano. Piano lessons were on Tuesdays, and even after we moved from Oak Street to Hastings Court, I had to continue taking piano lessons from Mrs. Eick.

This went on until my senior year, and then I even had to pay for these lessons with my own inheritance money. This was because of my mom. She forced me to practice at least fifteen minutes a day. And if I did not practice for those fifteen minutes, I had to make it up the next time. It got to be so bad that during my senior year, I was about four to six hours behind. It took me about two weeks or so to catch up. Then after my practice time was complete, Mom "let me" finally quit. There were times when I got into trouble and had my bike taken away and the keys put away. Then, when it came time to get my bike back, Mom and Dad had no idea where the keys were. Then, on Christmas, here was a small box about the size of a jewelry box. I thought it was a necklace or something cool like that. No, guess what? It was my keys to the bike. Somebody had taken them away from me and put them up on the top of a bookshelf and had forgotten where they put them. I opened up the Christmas present, and I was so excited to have my keys back. I realized that the damn joke was on me. Everybody started to laugh. I didn't find the situation very funny, but it was Christmas. Ho, Ho, Ho. At least I had my missing keys back.

I don't want you to think that I am bashing my parents, even though it may sound like that. They were very good to me. It just took me a long time to understand it. I am just explaining that these were some of the problems I had when I was a teenager.

However, I want to apologize to my parents for a moment. I feel sorry now that they had to put up with me and my issues for all of those years. For the longest time, I thought my parents were against me. I was wrong, of course. They were always there for me, whether I was in trouble or not. I was just too immature to realize it at the time. They tried to teach me valuable lessons at an early age. Also, I must admit that I was always a chronic liar. I had a problem telling the truth as far back as I remember—all the way back to grade school at Banta. And lying has cost me a lot over the years, including a marriage and several jobs. It has cost me friendships with people, as well.

A therapist told me I cannot change the past; I can only change the future. I will also say that I have lied to just about every family member, as well as my close, personal friends and my parents. Plain and simple, for me, it was easier to lie than to tell the truth. That is just how wrong I was. I now know where all of this came from. When I was younger, I was severely punished for lying (on many occasions), and they were trying to break me of this awful habit. It just didn't work. I lied to teachers in elementary, junior high, as well as high school and college. If you knew me from the time I was born and started talking to the time when I was forty-seven years old, I have no doubt I lied to you, too.

It was not until I discovered who my birth mother was at the age of forty-seven that I found out how much I was also lied to. This story will be told later. But with the lying came the fact that I could not keep a secret at all, either. I can't begin to tell you how many times somebody would say, "Please, do not tell anybody anything about this." Yeah, right. I can't tell you how many times this happened. I would just tell people things that they shouldn't know. It seems to me that there are three kinds of people in this world: those who can tell the truth, those who can accept the truth, and those who do a really good job of hiding the truth. They are the folks who can keep a secret but choose not to tell anybody the whole truth.

So, now at this point in time, I wish to apologize to everyone I know or knew in this world. To all of my family (both past and present), close friends (both past and present), and anybody I used to work for or with. I now know that telling people the truth is the only way to be. Even if it is not what people want to hear. Like the great Perry Mason used to say, "The truth, and nothing but the truth." It will get you out of trouble, at least most of the time. I now realize who I have hurt over the years. You might be thinking that none of the stuff in my book is true. I swore in my introduction that everything in this book is true, as well as the stories and circumstances.

That is why I am writing this story. It is my story and it needs to be told. There is nobody else in this world who knows me better than I do. My readers, please be assured this is the WHOLE TRUTH. I had a problem with telling the truth. I did not like to be rejected, and I was immature. Well, given my inability to be honest, it is no wonder that there were no girls in junior high or high school who wanted anything to do with me. I'm surprised I had friendships that lasted as long as they have. I am not surprised, after being divorced for more than three years, that my former wife and girlfriend divorced me for being a chronic liar. We were divorced for other reasons, too, but if I had not been a chronic liar, maybe, just maybe, my wife and I might still be married today. However, I am not a criminal. I DO NOT have a criminal record and do not intend to have one. I do not smoke, I do not consume mass quantities of alcohol, and I DO NOT take illegal drugs. I don't do that stuff. But what I have been guilty of is lying. The only thing I can do now is ask God for forgiveness, as well as my family and friends. I am sorry to all who I have offended over the years, and I am sorry for spilling the beans when I shouldn't have. Let me say this one last thing about lying. It gets you nowhere in life, and nobody will trust you. For those family and friends who do not trust me anymore, I understand. I am truly sorry for it all. My confession is now complete.

The year is now 1980, and I am a junior in high school. I have my driver's license. I am considering a college: Vincennes University. I have a part-time job and several, close friends. But no girlfriend. At this time, I was wondering…just who am I? I was actually enjoying school, too. We had an awesome varsity basketball team my junior and senior years. Both years we went to the Fort Wayne Semi-State. I did not make the trip in my junior year, but I did go in my senior year. I really thought that both of those years we could have gone to the Final Four in Indianapolis.

As I mentioned previously, basketball in the State of Indiana is a big deal. Being a student that has a state ranked high school basketball team is a big deal, too. But if there were anything I really enjoyed in high school, it was hanging out with my friends. With Grandpa gone, I was never really welcomed at my grandmother's house anymore. I never or rarely saw Aunt Bonnie or Uncle Chuck, either. That included all of my cousins from that side of the family, and that kind of hurt, too. These were kids from my family. We had this one thing in common—we all had the same grandparents. I had visited in their homes in Michigan and Pennsylvania, and they had been to my house.

I thought that they were all mad at me for one reason: because I had inherited money from our grandfather's estate and they did not. My father was, for the most part, cut out of our grandfather's will, and most of his share was left to me. In fact, my grandfather's will was shared by five people: Uncle Chuck, my grandmother (Grandpa's second wife), Aunt Bonnie, and me. You could say that my father shared in it, too, but only with $1,000. And we were not speaking to each other. As far as I was concerned, it would be a cold day in hell before I ever spoke to him again. It was during this time I found out that I was also being spied upon. It took me a while to figure that out, too. However, now it was time to enjoy high school with my friends and graduate.

I was able to do some really cool things with my friends. I went to the Chicago Auto Show with my friend, Norman, and his family. I was so glad to go because it was something my parents would never attend. That show just never interested them. However, my friend Norman and his family made it an annual trip, and I had a great interest in it. I remember telling Norm on a bus ride home from school that I had never been to the Auto Show. Norm said, "You should go with us." I loved cars then and still do now. There were some really cool ones at the show. Just about every make and model of car was there, and there were some local celebrities, as well. I remember meeting former Chicago Bears running back, Walter "Sweetness" Payton. Walter was not the first Bears player I had met. The first one was a former Bears quarterback named Mike Phipps. Mike just happened to be in Valparaiso one day for a grand opening of a new health club called the Klubhouse. Norm's dad had belonged to that club, and because Mike Phipps was a member of the Chicago Bears, this was a cool thing. I remember getting his autographed picture, and he made it out to me. I remember talking to him about the game he had just played the previous Sunday against the Los Angeles Rams. He was telling me what it was like to play against Rams linebackers, Jack and Jim Youngblood. But meeting Walter Payton was even better. This was the greatest player who ever played the game, as far as I was concerned, and my friend, Norm, and I got to meet him. Walter was always in the Buick section at the Chicago Auto Show at McCormick Place. He was a spokesperson for the Chicagoland/Northwest Indiana Buick dealers, and he made their television commercials. He signed autographs at the Auto Show, too, as well as took questions from the audience. I got to see Walter Payton play in person during the '85 and '86 seasons. I met Walter at the Auto Show on several occasions, and I also met him after he retired from the Bears when he came to Valparaiso University and played for the Good News Bears basketball team.

I guess that would have been after the '87 season. Being able to know this man, even on a limited basis as I did, had a very large influence on me. He stood for hard work, perfection, and retired from the Bears as the all-time leader in rushing in the National Football League. He owned several other NFL records, as well and is in the NFL Hall Of Fame. Then, a few years later, about 1999 or so, Walter died of cancer. Just like that, one of my personal heroes was gone. I'll never forget meeting Walter Payton and seeing him play at Soldier Field. I figured after he passed away, he was no doubt in heaven, playing with his teammate, Brian Piccolo, and being coached by Papa Bear George Halas. I'm sure he is up there now playing with other teammates who lost their lives and played for the Bears, too. I am just sure of it. My tribute to the very best, Walter Payton. God bless.

Anyway, I spent a lot of time with Norman and his family in Chicago and other places, as well. Norm's parents were naturalized U.S. citizens from the Philippines, and they had a huge family, too. Many of them came from the Philippines and spent a month or so visiting. I can remember when I met Norm's grandmother, who came to visit in 1981. She came for Norm's older brother's graduation from the University of Notre Dame. Norman's brother, Nelson, was graduating from the school of pre-med and would go on to become a medical doctor like Norm's parents. Norm's grandmother was also in Valpo for our graduation (Norm and I), which was slated for Wednesday, June 3, 1981. I spent a lot of time with Norm and his brother's, Nelson and Robert, as well as his parents. I spent a great deal time with Norman in high school, in college, and after college. We had met each other in junior high school at Thomas Jefferson when I started there in seventh grade. I have known that man for over forty years now. Norm stood up in our wedding when my former wife and I got married; so did other good friends, as well. We spent a lot of time together, just as good friends did. Norm now lives out near the San Francisco area, and it is always cool when I get the chance to go out there to visit. However, I don't see Norman as often as I used to, but thanks to social media, like Facebook, we still stay in touch.

My friend, Bill, and I did a lot of stuff together, as well. I knew Bill Frank before going into the sixth grade at Parkview School. I met him that first summer before we started sixth grade. We were teammates together, playing little league baseball. Like Norman, I knew Bill's family, as well, and Bill is like Norman in many ways. They both like to eat massive quantities of food, both are incredibly smart, particularly about sports and other topics. When we were well into our twenties, Norm and Bill would come over to my parents' house on Hastings Court and play pool.

We had a pool table in the family room of the finished basement at that house. Both Norman and Bill were in my graduation class. Bill and I also went on to Vincennes University together. I could tell you all of the things we did as friends, but that would take forever. Bill, like Norman, was also in my wedding. I was a groomsman in his wedding, too. And we were both into auto racing and still are. Bill and I have spent a lot of time over many years going to the Indianapolis 500, as well as the Brickyard 400 and The Daytona 500. Ironically, not long after I had my second heart surgery, Bill had heart surgery, too, to fix the same problem. I'll have more on my second heart surgery later on.

Now I'll tell you about my old friend, George. I first met George back in Social Studies class in seventh grade at Thomas Jefferson Junior High about November of '75. I remember the first time I met George in that class. The teacher stated that I needed extra help because I was not doing my homework correctly. She sent George and me out into the hallway outside the room. We sat on the floor with our backs against the lockers. George was very interested in U.S. history, and he knew a lot about it. He was a really nice guy, and it was only a matter of time before we started talking and getting to know each other.

I found out that we had many things in common. We both liked semi-trucks, we both wanted to become over the road truck drivers, and we had both had heart surgery at an early age. It turned out a number of years later, when we were both in college, that George had heart surgery again. I suppose that if there is one thing that is bad when you have had heart surgery, it is being told by a doctor that you need heart surgery again. George and I really got to know each other very well about '77 or so. We began to spend a lot of time together and built a friendship that lasted thirty-seven years.

The film *Smokey and the Bandit* had come to Valparaiso at the old Premier Theatre starring Burt Reynolds, Sally Fields, Jerry Reed, and Jackie Gleason. I think it was a Friday night, and I called George to see if he wanted to go. He said, "Oh, hell, yes," so George and his mother came by to pick me up. We had a blast that night watching the movie, and this kind of fun set us up for a friendship that has lasted thirty-seven years. I'll talk more on that later. I was a groomsman for George when he and Lori were married, and about a month later, George was my best man when I was married. George was a wonderful friend to have, and I got to know his family well, too. I know his parents to this very day. George and I did a lot together as teenagers. We graduated together with Bill and Norman in the great class of '81 from Valpo High. I visited George at Indiana State College and Indiana University when both of us were in college. After that George got a job with the U.S. Government, married his girlfriend, Lori, and they raised three sons. George also was an actor. I remember seeing him in a play at the old Memorial Opera House Theatre in Valpo years and years ago. He went on to have a couple of bit parts in some motion pictures. You don't always have life-long friends. But George, Bill, and Norman were good friends for life.

About the time my senior year started, I made another close friend. His name was Jay Mathews and we met in homeroom the last year of school. Jay and his mother moved from nearby Portage, Indiana, to Valpo, and he was going to graduate with us in June 1981. Jay sat behind me in homeroom. We started talking, and, well, we just became friends. I wish that I could have picked up girls like he did. Jay actually lived in Valpo until he was in second grade, but then moved to Portage. Like the rest of my close friends, he was really smart. In fact, he was a straight A student and a member of National Honor Society. I was a member of the National Flunk Society, if there had been such a thing.

I wrote the book on that club. To this day, I wonder how I became good friends with such a smart group of guys. Norm was not a straight-A student, but he always got good, respectable grades, and he went to Purdue University. Jay, a straight-A student, went to Indiana University in Bloomington and graduated with honors. Jay made it look easy. He told me that in the two semesters he was at Valpo High, he got all A's, except for one B. If I had brought home B's on my report card, my parents would have been very happy. Jay and Norm, as well as George, did well on their SATs and were able to attend good, four-year colleges. Me, I took the easy route, went to Vincennes University, and then on to work in the broadcasting world. They were smart. All of them.

George was a football place kicker and played on the ninth grade team at TJ when Norman and I were managers for the team. He played on the junior varsity football team in our sophomore year and then varsity in our junior and senior years. He was a good kicker, too. Jay was and still is a big baseball fan. After our senior year of high school Jay, Norm, and I would pile into his Chrysler Newport and go to see a Chicago White Sox game at the old Comiskey Park on the south side of Chicago. This was when announcer Harry Carey was still with the team. Harry became the announcer for the Chicago Cubs, too, just a few short years later. I remember Jay was a really good driver. You had to be when driving in and around Chicago. That took a lot of experience. As much as I hate to admit it, I really miss going to that old baseball stadium on the south side. It was only a few years later that the new baseball stadium was built next to the old one, and it was rather painful to see that old stadium being torn down. The building was square-shaped, and I remember seeing a game at the new place. Two sides of the stadium had been torn down. There were weeds growing where the outfield was, and the rest just looked in a state of ruin. How sad. That ballpark, the old Comiskey Park, had been replaced with a brand new one, and there was no going back. One of my fondest memories was when the much-hated New York Yankees were in town. Jay, Norm, and I were there, and we were in the outfield, watching the highest paid player in the game at that time. It was Dave Winfield. During that game, somebody threw a beer on him while he was playing, and some drunk fans were even throwing dollar bills at him because he was making such an incredible amount of money. That was before there were state lotteries and you had to work for your money. Being paid millions of dollars to play baseball just did not make much sense to me back then, either. So much for the old ball park.

As I have gotten older, I realize that the more time you have invested in your friendships, the more those friendships mean to you. I could go on and on about things we did together, but that would take the rest of the year to write. Today my friends are spread out all over the country, but I certainly can't forget the great times we had together, doing all the things young boys and young men do. I could go on and tell you about all of the sporting events we went to see, I could tell you about all of the movies we saw together, and I could talk about all of the food and drinks we all had in Valpo, Chicago,

Milwaukee, San Francisco, and Indianapolis. It was all fun and a great time was had by all. I would not trade those days for anything.

In 1981 I was in the final semester of my senior year. I had been accepted to Vincennes University, and I was getting ready to graduate. I was able to do a couple of cool things in my senior year. One was to drive to school. My parents wouldn't let me drive every day, but I got to drive on a fairly regular basis. The first car I ever owned was a '74 Chevy Nova. My brother-in-law, Bob McCasland, had acquired that car in trade. I had some work done to it, and after it was painted and the shag carpeting went in, it was really a cool-looking car. I paid $325 for it and probably sank another $2,000 into it to get it looking and running well.

I went to the Chicago Auto Show in February of that year with Norm and his family. I also went to Fort Wayne to see my high school basketball team go to the semi-state tournament. Then as we got closer to graduation, I was able to go to King's Island theme park in the Cincinnati area for our senior trip. Bill and Norm and many other people I had known for a lot of years went on that trip. It was a couple of weeks later that I went to the prom. I had never been on a date before, and prom was going to be it.

As I mentioned previously, my date and I were set up by another friend of mine, who was hosting an exchange student from Denmark. Her name was Mona Vesterbeck. I rented a tuxedo, took Mona out in my parents' new Buick Park Avenue, ate a very nice dinner, and besides going to the prom, we also went to the post-prom party. That night was a costly one, but it was worth every bit. It would have been nice to take Debbie, but feeling that I would be rejected, I never asked her.

In the fall of my senior year, my parents bought another new car. They sold the Buick Electra 225 Coupe and bought a really, stunning, luxury car. To this day, the 1980 Buick Electra Park Avenue was, and still is, the NICEST and most comfortable car I have ever driven. I never owned a car like this, and I suppose Buick will never make a car like this again. It was the darkest maroon in color (almost black cherry), and the car came with draped cloth, velour seats. It was so luxurious. I really loved that car. That Buick holds a lot of wonderful memories for me, as well. Not only was it luxurious and comfortable, it was also how the Buick drove. Mom and Dad let me take it to the prom, and it was also the car that took me to college.

After our class trip to Kings Island theme park and after prom, it was now the last week in May—now time to call it "done with high school." I don't remember what day it was, but as seniors, we had finished our last day of classes before final exams. I couldn't believe that thirteen years of school were now over. The last day of classes ended with the six-hour final exam. Then, there were two more days of final exams. School was done...officially. I don't remember what my final exam was, but I almost felt like crying my eyes out. I mean, here I was, Michael M. Dowd, soon to be a high school graduate. It was time for the fun to begin. I don't know what it was about graduating, but it was fun, and I was also nervous. Baccalaureate services were held at the Chapel on the Valparaiso University campus. This ceremony is a tradition for those graduating from Valpo High. My sisters, Sharon and Susan, both graduated from Valparaiso High School in '69 and '73, respectively, and both of them also attended this ceremony. My parents and my sister, Sharon, attended my graduation for me and 430 classmates.

I was only seventeen years of age, and I was now a graduate. Graduation is always an honor and an achievement. I received my diploma with some classmates that I have known since day one of kindergarten at Banta School: Ted Foster, Mark and Eric Berg, Jennifer Scott, Darlene Miller, Rich Roberts, Dean Tricisk, Andre Kratz, and Debbie Watson. Of course, I can't remember them all, but you know when you get older, so does your memory. I now understand why my grandfather was so persistent about my need to be educated. Grandpa never made it past the eighth grade because he had to quit and work on the family farm. It was not until I came home with my diploma that this subject was brought up. It brought tears to my eyes because one of the promises I had made to him was now accomplished. I graduated from high school and would be going off to college.

The day was Wednesday, June 3, 1981. We received our final report cards after reporting to our homeroom to prepare for the final event. I passed by the skin of my teeth. Mom was so worried that last semester of school. I think that she thought I would never graduate. She was so nervous that she actually got the hives on and off that year, and I remember my sister, Sharon, saying during the ceremony when I was handed my diploma that Mom actually sighed with relief. I guess she had been holding her breath. Back in 1969, I sat with Susan and my parents in a hot Boucher gymnasium to watch Sharon march on the floor and get her high school diploma. Now she was there to see her little brother get his.

The weather that night on the football field was awesome. It was a little windy, but we had the most beautiful sunset to the northwest. In the photo of me getting my diploma from Principal Garth Johnson, it almost looks like a fake background, but that sunset was real. The principal praised our class. He wished us all the very best and welcomed us to the "real" world. I took a minute or two to reflect on my graduation at this point. I thought about all of the classmates I was graduating with. I'll never forget my friends, especially Bill, Norman, George, and Jay. Jay graduated with honors. He wore a gold tassel because he graduated in the top fifty of our class. Everyone else wore a green and white tassel. Our class valedictorian was Steve Ikedtta. He was not only an extremely smart and gifted student but he was also on the varsity wrestling team. Steve went on to school at MIT. He gave a speech on how the sport of wrestling was like life itself.

He talked about the fact that life has its ups and downs and it even might pin you against something from time to time. Also, like the sport of wrestling, there are always opponents. Sometimes you win and sometimes you lose. It was a good speech. Our names were now called. The crowd was not supposed to applaud until after all of the names were called. This rule, of course, was never followed. There were a few hoots and screams and lots of applause. I know that I was all smiles when I got up there on stage to receive my diploma. I remember getting a high five from someone I had known for many years at school. I sat down and looked at my diploma. I think I was about ready to cry as my eyes started to well up. Another emotional moment for me was when Mike Bartelmo received his diploma. Mike had been in a very bad car accident in the first semester of our senior year. I had known Mike since elementary school. I'm still in touch with him today, as I see some of his posts on Facebook. This car accident had paralyzed

Mike and confined him to a wheelchair. When his name was called, everyone from our graduating class and the crowd in the football stands gave him a standing ovation. What a cool, nice tribute to our fellow graduate. As I was waiting for my row of graduates to be dismissed, I spotted Sharon in the stands, waving at me. My eyes began to water again as the joy of the graduation ceremony was now starting to hit me. My education from the Valparaiso Community Schools was now over.

Whatever level of school you graduate from, it is always an accomplishment. For some, like my grandfather, it was his dream, as well as mine. I was also thinking about my father, too. Even though he was not at my graduation, we were back on speaking terms. He apologized for all the bad things he said about my grandfather and me, and he was realizing that I was now growing up. He knew I was going on to Vincennes University. Oh, he had remarried, too. His new wife's name was Jacquee. She was now my new stepmother, but I never got to meet her.

When leaving the football stadium, I ran into my good friend, George. He stood there in his cap and gown with a funny look on his face. We hugged each other. Our days at Valpo High were over, and our emotions showed. I think I might have said something like, "Come here, you son of a bitch." I was joking, of course, and we both broke down in tears. It was after George and I were done hugging and laughing that Mom, Dad, and Sharon found me, and there were more hugs, tears, kisses, and congratulations.

On the way to turn in my cap and gown, I noticed that I was walking behind Debbie Watson. I wanted to say something nice to her. Several times in high school I felt guilty about what had taken place between us. Now was the time to take care of that feeling. With my left hand, I kind of grabbed the back of her right arm. She turned around and smiled. I said, "I want to wish you congratulations!"

She then said very softly, "Congratulations to you, too." Then we continued to walk towards the high school building. I did see Debbie at the senior party at the VU Student Union later on that night, but it would be more than twenty-nine years before I would ever see her again. That was like another lifetime.

Norman dropped me off at home on Hastings Court, and I now returned home as a high school graduate. He told me he was going to get me a Houston Astros baseball jersey at Pier 39 because he knew I loved the style of uniform. I still have that jersey, and that is another item, like my ninth grade basketball jersey, that I'll never give away. It just means that much to me. We congratulated each other one last time, and I wished him a safe trip to San Francisco. I got out of Norm's car and went up to the front door of my parents' house. It was then I think I looked up to the heavens and thanked God at that moment.

As I went inside, Mom said, "Hey, there is our high school graduate!" It suddenly hit me that this was so cool to hear. The following Sunday, my parents threw a graduation party/open house for me. We invited all sorts of friends and family, and a lot of people came. There were friends of mine from school, who I had graduated with; friends of our family that I had known my whole life; and family members from the DeHaven and Johnson side of the family. My grandmother (my grandpa's second wife) came, and it was good to have her there.

The Class of 1981 had a lot of graduates in my family, as well. My cousin, Brad Blomberg, graduated from Akin High School in Akin, Minnesota, and my cousins, Connie Huber and Colleen Kipper, both graduated from nearby Chesterton High School. My cousin, Christy Dowd, graduated from Moon Township High School near Pittsburgh, Pennsylvania (Uncle Chuck and Aunt Joann's daughter), and my cousin, Wendy Youngblood, graduated from Wheaton Central High School in Wheaton, Illinois. It was a big year—1981—for me, as well as my cousins. Mom and Dad gave me a really nice luggage set because they knew that I would be traveling to and from school. It was a nice gift, and I used it a lot during my college years and even after that. With money I received from family and friends I bought a nice stereo and a new color T.V. I took these items to college, as well. Sometime after the graduation party, I had the task of sending out thank you notes. To this day, I know that I never sent my parents a thank you for that party, and I still feel guilty about it. It didn't occur to me at the time that I should send one to them. So, now, from the better late than never file…

Dear Mom and Dad,

I am hereby officially saying thanks to you, my parents, for a wonderful graduation party. I had a great time with friends and family at that graduation open house, and I want to take this time to thank both of you for a very wonderful day and for the nice luggage set, as well. I will always owe so much to the two of you, as well as Sharon, Bob, and Susan. It took a lot of blood, sweat, and tears to get me to this stage in my life. Thank you again for all of it!

With love, your son,
Michael

Why I never sent my parents that note before, I just don't know, but now I have officially done it. It's really more like confession. I'm just glad I am able to do it now. With my high school days over and my graduation behind me, it was time to get ready for college at Vincennes University. Little did I know what college life would be like.

CHAPTER 5: Back to School

It is now the summer of 1981 and time to really get ready for college. Since I was already accepted to Vincennes University, I did not bother to apply to another school. My parents did not want to see me attend a big school like Indiana University or Purdue, and I really had no interest in going to Purdue—except the fact that my good friend, Norman, was there. I had considered Ball State and Indiana State, but I just did not have the grade point average needed for those schools.

Also, my SAT scores were holding me back. I won't tell you my actual score, but I will say that my score was crap. The only place I would get accepted with a scores like mine was Vincennes University. During high school, it was my guidance counselor, Jim McMichael, who helped me through a tough and confusing time. He was my counselor during my junior year of high school and also the assistant principal of discipline at Valpo High when I was a sophomore. He was the bad guy then and always watching in the hallways, lunchrooms, bathrooms, smoking lounge area, and after-school activities, like school dances and sporting events.

He seemed like the bad guy because if you were caught doing something wrong—whether minor or severe—you had to deal with him. I was never really in trouble much in high school but, still, you didn't want to have to talk to him about any problems you might have. So, I was rather surprised and scared when I found out that he would be my counselor in my junior year. The fact of the matter was it was just downright intimidating. However, after only a few meetings with Mr. McMichael, I found him to be very understanding. We talked about my bad grades in my sophomore year. I told him that it was a confusing time for me when my grandfather died and all that was happening. He understood, he listened and, most importantly, he cared. I introduced him to my parents, and the four of us sat down together and discussed my education after high school and the possibility of going to college somewhere. It was during the first semester of my junior year that Mr. McMichael recommended Vincennes University. He told us that it was a rather small school (less than five thousand students at the time), and with all of the programs they had to offer, it would be more of a one-on-one kind of education, instead of just being a number at a huge school like Indiana or Purdue. I remember some of my friends from high school telling me about some of the class sizes at Indiana University—sometimes five hundred to eight hundred students in a class.

Not all classes were like that, but the more popular the class was, the bigger it became. My friend, Norman, told me that it was not like that at Purdue; however, he would be in West Lafayette for two years only. Then his plan was to come home and finish his college education at Indiana University Northwest in Gary. My parents wanted me to go to a smaller school, so I would get the attention I needed from teachers and help with anything I did not understand.

After my SATs were over in my junior year and during my first semester as a senior, I applied for admission to Vincennes University. I remember that my mom and I went to Vincennes, Indiana, for a campus visit. Mom liked the campus as we took the grand tour of the place. The campus was small, then, and most of the classrooms were just a short walk from the dorms. I had been accepted just about a week or so before our visit.

I got my letter of acceptance in late September. I remember getting that letter in late September 1980, and the letter was waiting for me at home on the dining room table. Mom had gotten the mail that day, and she put the letter in the middle of the dining room table so that it was standing up against a flower pot. This way I would see it right away when I got home from school. Of course, I opened it immediately. I was rather nervous. It seemed like my whole future depended on this letter. And it was kind of like the film, *Back to the Future*. I have often talked about this film previously when discussing time travel and how I would change my own future if I could. Now I look back on the day that I received that letter, and it felt like my future (whatever it would be) depended on it. Almost everything I had worked toward depended on this message. I opened the letter, and it was the news I was hoping to get. I was accepted to Vincennes University! I now had a college to attend. The only thing I had to do now was finish high school.

As I said in the last chapter, I graduated from high school by the skin of my teeth. But now it was time to start the college process. It would begin in July 1981 with pre-registration and orientation.

About the last week of July 1981, Mom, Dad, and I took a trip to Vincennes, so that I could pre-register for classes and see what my dormitory room looked like. Vincennes is about 225 miles south of Valparaiso, right on the famous Wabash River and located in southwestern Indiana, between Terre Haute and Evansville. The trip took about four hours to drive from Valpo to Vincennes, but I didn't mind the drive. The three of us were going together in Mom and Dad's beautiful Park Avenue. This was the car they let me take to the prom in high school, and now it was my ride to Vincennes. Dad drove the whole way on that trip, and it was good that I did not have to drive. You had to be careful driving that Buick long distances because it was so comfortable that you could fall asleep while driving. It was nicer than any limo I had ever been in. That Buick Park Avenue was just one sweet ride and IT was taking ME to college.

We arrived a day early in Vincennes and stayed at the Executive Inn just, off the main entrance from US 41. It was a nice place to stay in those days, as it had all of the things you needed in a hotel, and we had a room by the indoor pool. There was a huge restaurant, a bar, and lots of rooms all over the place. The hotel was the home of several businesses, too, including two radio stations located on the top floor. I have forgotten what the other businesses were, but there was plenty of room for just about any kind of office. It was just a short drive over to the campus. I was to report there the next morning. Since Vincennes was 225 miles south of Valpo, the weather seemed a lot warmer, too. The summers were really hot and a lot more humid. I also liked that Vincennes usually did not get a lot of snow in the winter. I was tired of the snow and ice in northwestern Indiana and, quite frankly, it would have been nice to go to college in Florida or somewhere more southern, but of course, somebody put the stop on that thought.

The next morning, the three of us woke up early, had breakfast, and headed off to Greene Auditorium for the start of orientation. My college days officially started on that hot July morning at Vincennes University. I forget all I had to do, but this was where I pre-registered for classes for the fall semester. I was to start in about seven weeks, and this was the first step. After pre-registration there was a welcome speech by Dr. Phillip Summers, the President of the University.

Dr. Summers was a man I got to know at the very beginning of my college years, until long after I graduated. He had just been named university president. He was very friendly, not just to me and my future classmates, but he was also a hit with the parents of these students. Even in the fall of 1981, college was expensive. There were so many expenses for all aspects of it. Dr. Summers knew that. He knew that going to Vincennes University was not only worth the money but also a sound, solid investment. He knew that because he spent his first two years of college at Vincennes, as well. Yes, Dr. Summers was a hit with the parents. A housing meeting was going on while I was doing some placement testing. My parents were invited to attend the meeting, which was in the front lobby of the dorm known as Harrison Hall. It turned out that this was the dorm that I was assigned. We drove around and saw some of the historic sites around the campus and along the Wabash River, and then it was time to go back to Valpo and prepare for college.

Mom and Dad told me later how entertaining this meeting had been. Dad said that somebody asked if any of the dorms on campus were co-ed. Dr. Summers said that the only co-ed dormitory on campus was Clark Hall. Then somebody asked if the restroom facilities were co-ed, as well. Dr. Summers said something like, "Oh, yes, most of the bathrooms and showers are co-ed, as well."

Then Mom said, "You should have heard the deep sigh of relief when they realized that Dr. Summers was just kidding." I guess the parents got a big laugh out of it. He had a funny way of keeping the laughter going with those parents of new students just entering Vincennes University. You could always count on a good joke from Dr. Summers with just about any speech he gave.

The rest of the trip was fun, too. After I finished all the pre-college stuff, Mom, Dad, and I drove around Vincennes and looked at all of the historic things there. First there was the George Rodgers Clark National Historic Monument, located right on the banks of the Wabash River. To this day, you can go to this memorial, and when it is open, you can look at all the murals on the inside, as well as displays. There is also a film to see which explains the history of Vincennes, Indiana, and about the people who helped build and became the founding fathers of the Indiana Territory. Second is Grouseland, the former home of President William Henry Harrison. The dormitory, Harrison Hall, which I lived in for nearly two years, was named after him. Third are the historical buildings to the west of the university campus. These buildings were some of the first ones used by the settlers, and a few of these became future buildings of Vincennes University. There are certainly more places to see, and I often thought there was never enough marketing to bring in tourists to see these historic places. After spending a few days on the campus of the university and around the town itself, our trip was coming to an end, and it was time to get back to Valpo. I had to get back to work for my brother-in-law, Bob, and Dad had to get back to work at the LP Gas Plant he managed. Now it was less than seven weeks till the start of college, and the countdown began.

In late August 1981, I was packed and ready to leave for Vincennes. I was rather nervous because this was a whole new world for me. I'm sure my parents were glad for me, too, but even more, they were glad to get me out of the house. Nobody told me that college was going to be a fun time. College is not for everyone. It seems that you hear about people who go to college and wind up quitting or flunking out. I did not do that. I had the patience to keep on until I was done.

Okay, I admit, it did take me seven semesters to get an associate's degree. Once I figured out what the hell I was going to do, I then had a goal. I had no idea it would take me that long to get finished and get a degree, but now I know it was the best decision for me. My first two years (four semesters) at Vincennes, I lived in Harrison Hall. The wing I was assigned to had lots of cool young men who lived there.

I was assigned to Room 31. During the orientation, we had a chance to see one of the rooms from another part of the dorm. This gave us some idea what it looked like and how much room for clothes and stuff I would have. Harrison Hall was an old dorm. Things are much nicer now, but back in 1981, that dorm was a dump. The bathrooms were disgusting, and the rooms looked like ones from a mental institution. I, of course, have never been institutionalized, nor do I ever have plan to be, but for all the money we paid for room and board, it seemed that things could have been nicer. If it were up to me, every dorm room would look like a nice hotel room with your own bathroom and more privacy.

I will admit that at least we had air conditioning and cable television. Some dorm rooms around the state did not have these items. Even at Indiana University in Bloomington, the rooms did not have those amenities. Regardless, it was a room, and it was my home away from home for the next two years. Then there was the food. I don't know what is worse: airline food or college dorm food. I have had other college dorm food, and the best I ever had was at the University of Notre Dame in South Bend, Indiana. I think the worst was at my own college. There were nights that we had what was called "Steak Nights" at Vincennes. Those dinners were good, but I don't know what kind of food they were putting in us back then. When I graduated from high school, I weighed about 120 pounds. I was extremely thin, and after two years of dorm food at Vincennes, I think I put on at least fifty or sixty pounds. Think how many calories and carbs I must have been eating. There was no nutritional information supplied to us about food then, either, so you really had no idea what the sodium or fat content might be. However, we had to eat. Sometimes it was tough going over to the cafeteria and standing in line to eat awful food. It did get to the point by the end of the school year, we got so disgusted with it that we just could not stand to eat there. Thank God there was McDonald's.

There were other places, too, but for the money, fast food was it. Living in the dorm also meant there was little privacy. I was the kind of person who liked to keep to myself, and that was not possible living in a dorm; no privacy and sometimes no regard for any of your personal items also. You had to be careful when you loaned out a shirt or something. If that guy liked the shirt, you might not ever get it back. For me it was difficult at times dealing with people who did not respect my space or my belongings. There was also the usual host of rowdy neighbors, who kept strange hours and engaged in activities that I wasn't interested in.

If someone liked your calculator, that you did not put away, it would come up missing. You had to watch for other things, too, like your car keys or your eye glasses. People in college can be kleptomaniacs, and if you did not watch your stuff, it was gone before you knew it. Then you dealt with the crank calls and the drunks that made it into the dorms late at night, usually while you were trying to sleep. They would start beating on your door in the middle of the night, wondering where the hell their room was. I have to say, after being ripped off, and all of this stuff going on, it is a wonder I did not lose my sanity back then. If you are not an outgoing person, and you enjoy your privacy, you may lose all of that in a college dorm. Then we also had the marijuana smokers, who always seemed to get away with it. We had neighbors who smoked at night or during the middle of the afternoon. They would pop a ceiling tile and stand on a chair, so that the smoke would come into my room and stink up my place. The R.A. never seemed to understand that the smokers were in the room next to me and never seemed to care. I guess he was one of the people who knew about it and no doubt smoked it with them. After two years of being in a dorm, along with a course of study that I simply did not like, it was time for a change.

In December 1982, as I was finishing my third semester at Vincennes, I had just returned from a mid-morning class and picked up my mail from the front desk. I had a letter from Mom with my allowance check, and she told me that my grandmother (my grandfather's second wife) had been in a bad car accident and was in a coma. I had just received a Christmas card from my grandmother, along with a check as a Christmas gift. It was about four years after my grandpa had passed away from cancer. She was with a friend somewhere in the Chicago suburbs while doing some Christmas shopping. Someone told me later at the wake that the driver of their car pulled out in front of a semi-truck loaded with steel. They weren't wearing seat belts, and the rest is history. I was not able to go to see my grandmother in the hospital because she was comatose. Her sister, Dorothy, called the day after Christmas to tell us that she had passed away. I asked if there was anything I could do, and she said she wanted Dad and me to be pallbearers at the funeral.

We told her that we would do that and to please keep us posted about the arrangements. I was actually glad that I was asked to do this. I had been upset that nobody asked me to be one at my grandfather's funeral, so doing this was an honor for me. The wake and funeral were in the same funeral home. Although it was kind of creepy to be back there again, this time was different. Mrs. Hacker, my grandpa's old friend, showed up and was brought in by wheelchair. Mr. Hacker was living in a nursing home then, and even though she was getting up there in age, she still knew what was going on in the world.

This brought back so many memories of going to see Mrs. Hacker after my grandfather died. The first time I went to see her with my parents was when the three of us were going to Argos, Indiana, to see the Chizum family. It was really neat to take Mom and Dad to Mrs. Hacker's house because after years of describing everything to them about the adventures at her house and those fabulous, home-cooked meals we ate, it was cool to finally show them what her house and property was like.

It was also fun for Mrs. Hacker to meet my parents. Surprisingly, the three of them had never met. Mrs. Hacker had this incredible antique collection. I was able to show them the famous dinner table that we ate at. After that visit and after I got my first car, my 1974 Chevrolet Nova, Mom and Dad let me drive down to Mrs. Hacker's house to visit. That was freedom—going over those country roads with my own car! Mrs. Hacker loved that Nova, too. By the time I took the car to her house, my Nova had been repainted, and the inside now had shag carpeting. She really loved that! I can remember taking her to an ice cream stand in nearby Bass Lake, and I bought her an ice cream cone. We really had fun, were good friends, and remained that way until the day she passed away. Mrs. Hacker died a few years later, when I was working for radio stations WLOI and WCOE in LaPorte, Indiana. She somehow found out I was an announcer on that station, and when she died, she was in the hospital in LaPorte.

I think Mrs. Hacker was ninety-five years old when she died. I did not make it to the funeral, but I did go and pay my respects at the wake. I remember driving over to Hanna, Indiana, to the funeral home. She was then buried next to her late husband, Clarence Hacker, in Knox. What a great friend and what a great life she lived. A number of years later, I found the cemetery where she was buried, and I took some of her favorite pink roses. It was fitting because her favorite color was pink. She grew pink roses at her house in the front yard, right next to the parking area. She was always proud of her roses, as well as her garden. I always missed the times when my Grandpa and I would throw the football around in her three-acre yard. It was the first place I ever used an outdoor bathroom known as the "Odd House." I remember going on the combine with my cousin, Ray Dowd, to harvest the beans and wheat that were grown in her eighty-plus acres he farmed for her. I have so many good memories of Mrs. Hacker's house. I really felt like it could have been a second home. I learned so many things as a kid with my grandparents, like farming and gardening and trimming trees and going for long walks in the woods nearby. There was wildlife in those woods like deer and rabbits. Every now and then, there would be a story about some giant snake that Mrs. Hacker would dust off with her shotgun. She was a good shot. All of these wonderful memories came back to me when I saw Mrs. Hacker enter that funeral home that day, the day of my second grandmother's funeral service.

It was attended by many people. My dad and my grandmother were cousins, so they had grown up together. She knew all of my dad's sisters and most of our family from the DeHaven side of the family, as well as the Dowd side that she had married into. My grandmother had a son and a daughter, as well as other grandchildren. I knew her family for many years. It was sad for them, too, because it was unexpected. My grandmother had been in very good health, and this car accident just caught us all off guard. The funeral was attended by many people, including all three sides of my family: the Dowds, the Johnsons, and the DeHavens. I was a pallbearer, along with Dad and several other men. The dinner after the funeral took place at a church hall and was arranged by my grandmother's sister who lived just down the road from the church. My grandmother was buried next to my grandpa in Valparaiso. I have other aunts, uncles, and cousins who are buried in the same cemetery, so when I visit, I pay my respects to all of my relatives who are nearby. Visiting family and friends in the cemetery can be an emotional time for me when I go there. I feel like Forrest Gump or someone like that. I never like saying goodbye to people at their funerals. I do believe that I will see them again in heaven, but until that happens, I just go and visit and enjoy the peace and quiet. It is like a good kind of therapy for me when I do that. I always try to go and see my family there when I am home in Valpo to visit. It makes me feel good and refreshed; almost like some sort of confession or something. Now with my grandmother's life over, I had to go back to college.

Now in my fourth semester of college, I really should have been ready to graduate. But I did not like my major, and I felt it was time for a change. My grades had slipped. I was on academic probation. I had lost interest in college, and it was just not fun anymore. I had chosen business administration originally as my major because that was what my grandfather had wanted me to study.

But now I needed a major that would give me the skills for a job when I was finished, and business administration was not it. I met someone who was a broadcasting major at Vincennes. They had an incredible school for radio and television broadcasting. This program was known for being hands on because you learned with equipment and facilities that many radio and television stations actually used. The university owned and operated its own public television station, as well as an NPR FM radio station. This friend showed me around the whole place and introduced me to a number of staff members and teachers in the program. I became convinced to change majors and go into a program in which I might be a lot happier. Broadcasting seemed to be it. So, in the fall of 1983, I began my new major.

I had given some thought about going into the hotel and hospitality business like my cousin, Shawn Kenworthy. Shawn had gone to school for hospitality and majored in hospitality when he attended college in Michigan. Also, Shawn was able to spend a lot of time with my father, Tom, in New Orleans, when I was still in high school. This all happened after my grandfather died. Tom and Shawn became quite close during those years, and Tom was still upset with his dad, my grandfather, and others like myself for getting cut out of Grandpa's will. My father got his $1,000, but that was all. I got $27,000, so that I could go to college and have enough to finish, as well.

During the last semester of high school, I was thinking about my father and wondering what he was up to. We were not speaking to each other at this time. Shawn had gone to New Orleans to work at a hotel and restaurant, where my father's wife was working. I became very jealous about this. My parents would never, ever consider letting me do something like that. But Shawn got to spend time with my father and his new wife. He also worked at a fancy French Quarter hotel in New Orleans, and New Orleans was a place I always wanted to visit. It held a certain mystique for me. I thought about the times my grandfather, as well as my father, talked about it. I remember Shawn telling me about it, too. I was told by family friends about the all of the fun they had in the Crescent City—the world famous French Quarter, the Superdome, the music, the food, and Mardi Gras. New Orleans was on my mind a lot until I finally got there. I even dreamt about it. But the fact that Shawn was in New Orleans and spending the whole summer with my father—well, that just pissed me off. Yes, I was jealous! Shawn had been like a brother to me and, thankfully, he was the one who got my father and me back on speaking terms. Shawn came to see me while I was still in high school, and we took a walk away from the house on Hastings Court, where we were living. It was a surprise visit after he had finished working during the summer months in New Orleans. I feel badly now because I realize he was trying to get my father and me back on speaking terms. However, I was still jealous that Shawn had spent the whole summer there with Tom.

We were about a block away from my house and talking about the situation. Then he asked me, "Why are you so upset with Tom?" It was something I did not care to talk about. So, he asked me again in a different way. Shawn said, "Tom told me that he said some really bad things to you."

I jumped in and said, "Yeah, he said some really horrible things after Grandpa passed away. He said things that I never expected he would say, and then he tore into me about them. After a conversation on the phone with him, I decided that it was in my best interest not to speak to him anymore."

It did not occur to me that my father put Shawn up to all of this, but now I realize that Shawn was looking out for me in a way and then getting back to my father in New Orleans and telling him what I had said. I told Shawn that I would never speak to my father again and that I did not need him in my life. This may have caught Shawn by surprise. He must have had a talk with my father about all of this because when I talked to Tom for the first time in two years, my father was a much different man over the phone.

Then Shawn surprised me with something else. Not long after Grandpa passed away, I had told my father I wanted a picture of my sister, Katy. She graduated from high school in Florida in 1978. This was another issue lingering for me. I felt that getting to meet my sister would help me heal the wounds of my grandfather's death. I had a goal to find and meet her. But here was my cousin, Shawn, with a photo of my sister when she was a senior in high school. I think this was a peace offering from Tom because up to that point, if Shawn had not stepped in and tried to sort everything out, my father and I may not have spoken ever again. Shawn gave me that picture of Katy and then he said, "You know, that thing between your father and you will take time to blow over. I'll stay in touch, and I will tell Tom that we spoke; that is, if you don't mind." He went on to say, "You know, you should call him sometime. He would love to hear from you."

I told him I would have to think about that for a while. I told him I really had no interest in doing that if things were going to continue like they had been. And I had no use for Tom in my life if he was going to bad mouth me and everybody around me. I told Shawn that it really just upset me the way my father spoke to me that day on the phone. I was just done with him. Shawn continued to remind me that things like this would get better in time. He thought that when I got older, I would understand things and see the situation better. I told him that I didn't think that was going to happen.

It was sometime in the second semester of my senior year that I finally broke down and called Tom. I had to call collect, so that there would be no record of the call on my parents' phone. I had no idea what his phone number was, so I called an operator in the New Orleans area code. I asked for anybody named Thomas Dowd in New Orleans. There were two listed, and the first one the operator reached was not my father. Then the operator said there was a listing for a Thomas and Jacqueline Dowd, and I told her she might as well try that number. The phone rang, and a woman answered it. The operator said, "This is a collect call to Tom Dowd from Michael Dowd. Do you wish to accept the charges?"

The woman responded "yes," and the call went through. The woman asked me who I was, and when I told her that I was Tom's son, Mike, she immediately brought my father to the phone.

He came on and said, "Hello." The operator confirmed the call, and he accepted the charges. Then Tom said, "Michael, how are you, my son?" I told him I was doing fine and asked him who the lady was on the phone. Tom stated, "Oh, that's my wife, Jacquee." I asked him when they had married, and he said that they had been married for a year or two and that she was working at a hotel in the French Quarter.

I spoke with them for about an hour and a half that night. Tom and I cleared the air, and he told me he was very sorry for all of the things that were said after my grandfather died. He had been bitter about things and I understood. I explained that I just did not like being blamed for issues that were not my fault. He understood, and we moved forward. I guess we finally patched things up, and I owe my cousin Shawn a lot of thanks. Shawn was right. It was only a matter of time before my father and I would be back on speaking terms.

In the next chapter, you will read about my successful search for my sister, Katy, so I am skipping that event for now.

I spent my first four semesters of college living in a dorm, and it was time for a big change in my course of study. After being put on academic probation, I was now going to change majors and live off campus. During that time, I also sold my Chevrolet Nova to a cousin and was now driving a '76 Buick Century Coupe. During the winter of 1983, when I was home for Christmas break, the timing chain broke, and the engine froze up. It was going to take about two months to fix, and since I needed a car to get back to school, I bought a 1982 Ford Mustang Hatchback from my brother-in-law, Bob.

This car was mostly driven by my sister, Sharon, and, since he was in the rental car business, he had to buy and sell cars from time to time. The Mustang was black with red cloth seats and a four-speed transmission. Since it was a hatchback, the backseat folded down, and there was a lot of room for hauling stuff to and from college. After I moved out of Harrison Hall, it was August of 1983, and I moved into an A-frame house with a friend on the other side of town. This house was a fun place to live because it was unique, and we had plenty of room. Not only that, but we didn't have to eat dorm food anymore. The house was a few miles from campus, but it worked out okay. I didn't feel I was attached to the campus anymore. The way it was supposed to work was that I would only be at Vincennes another three semesters. My academic major now changed, too. I was now in the School of Broadcasting, which included classes in both radio and television. When I finished with school and got my degree, I had lots of hands-on experience—skills that got me several jobs, including the one that I currently have. I mentioned earlier in the book that my decision to go to Vincennes University and now, my change to a major in broadcasting, well, it seems now like it changed my whole future. I guess that was a good decision because now I have more than twenty-five years of experience in the radio and television business. It's ironic because it's another episode of my life that reminds me so much of the movie, *Back to the Future*.

You have no doubt noticed that I often refer to the *Back to the Future* films as a way to document time in my life. Writing this book is a lot like time travel for me. If I only had the phone booth from the television show, *Dr. Who*, or the DeLorean from the *Back to the Future* movies, and if just one of those items really worked, my, oh, my, would I make some serious changes in my life. But since I can't travel in time, at least not yet, I can still relate it to my life.

I see my life in two parts. There was the earlier time when I was born in November 1963 up until the time my grandfather died in 1979. Then there is the time from '79 after my grandfather dies until the present. I have documented most of my life up to this point, and now the year is 1984.

In August 1984, I was finishing my very last semester of school at Vincennes University, and I really felt burned out, too. From August 1983, I started my new major of study: broadcasting and completed my first, second, third, and final semester. That last semester went by quickly, too, because I had so much work to do, so that I could finish and get my degree. But that last semester of college was fun, too. This was the year I turned twenty-one! To celebrate, my friend, Bruce, had come up from New Albany, Indiana, to visit. Bruce and I were freshmen together in the old Harrison Hall dorm. We were roommates in our second year there and spent a lot of time together. He used to go with me on weekends to Chicago and, with my friend, Norman, we'd go out for deep dish pizza at Gino's East.

That weekend my birthday was on a Saturday, and the Friday night before, we went to a place in Illinois called Crackers. When we got there, we were all carded at the door. Since I would not be twenty-one until the next day, the bouncer stamped my hand, so that the bartender would not serve me. However, the bouncer said, "Since you'll be twenty-one at midnight, come back, and I will stamp your hand again, so that you can have a drink at midnight."

When the clock hit 12:00 A.M., I went back to the bouncer, and he stamped my hand. I was now legal to have an adult beverage. I'll never forget my first drink, too. It was a very dry martini, and it was supposed to be "shaken and not stirred," like the famous James Bond drinks, but the bartender just made it stirred. That was one strong drink as I remember; thank goodness I was not driving back to my apartment in Vincennes. It would only be now a few, short weeks before I was done with school, and I could hardly wait.

The first week of December 1984, I took my last final exam at Vincennes University. I remember that day, too, because I already had my stuff packed and was ready to move home from school. This time it would be for good. Right before I took my final exam, my friend, Norman, had gotten tickets for us to see Rodney Dangerfield at the Star Plaza Theatre in Merrillville, Indiana. It was great to see him in person because he had been on television and in feature films like *Caddy Shack*, *Easy Money*, and one of my favorites, *Back to School*. Rodney was on his Rappin' Rodney Tour, and Norman and I just laughed until we fell out of our seats. My final day at Vincennes University was also the day I took my last final exam. I finished it in my Advanced Radio class, and when I handed it to my instructor, Mr. John Hitchcock, I told him, "This is it for me."

I was done, finished. I was out of school at Vincennes University. We shook hands, and I thanked him for all of his help and instruction. Mr. Hitchcock was one of my favorite teachers at Vincennes, and it was only fitting that I take my last exam with him. I went back to my apartment and loaded everything into my Mustang and decided it was time to say good-bye to one final teacher, Mr. Jack Hanes. Jack was one of my television instructors and a favorite one, as well. I worked with him pretty much all throughout my college days in broadcasting. So, I made one, final stop at Davis Hall, where all of the broadcasting facilities were, and since now he had been promoted to Chairman of the Broadcasting Department, he had a big office in the front of the building. I went into the lobby where his office was. His door was open, so I asked if I could come in. He said yes, and I walked in and sat down in front of him. I told him that I had just finished my last final exam and that I was packed, loaded, and ready to go home. Jack then said, "So, I take it you are all done here at Vincennes University?"

I replied, "Yes, I just wanted to stop and say good-bye for the last time as a student here."

Jack then asked me what kind of job I was going to look for. I told him that I was not really sure. I knew that there would be a short list of possibilities, but exactly what those would be was unknown to me. I then asked him if I could use his name as a reference, and he said I could. It would only be a short time later that with Jack's persistence and help I would get my first paid radio job in Michigan City, Indiana.

I must have been in Jack's office for about twenty minutes or so, and I really was not in a hurry to leave. I had just finished college, one of the most important steps in my life, and I just wanted to enjoy the moment. Afterwards, I did say good-bye to Jack Hanes and to other staff members of the Vincennes University Broadcasting Department. I went out to my loaded Mustang and left Vincennes University as a college graduate. It didn't hit me until I was north of Terra Haute, Indiana, that I realized I had just completed the second part of what I promised my late grandfather. That made me tear up and cry. I now was going into the real world, and I wondered just what was ahead of me.

Then, on that last drive home from Vincennes, I started to think about other things. I wondered where my career was going. I wondered if I would ever leave Valparaiso and live out of state. I wondered if I would wind up in the French Quarter with my father and work in the city of New Orleans. Then I started to think about my birth mother. I wondered where she was, what she looked like, and if I might have any other siblings. I wondered what it would take to find her. I thought if I had her social security number, I might be able to do a search for her somehow. And I wondered if I would have to get a private investigator to find her.

Just what was ahead for me in my life? I knew this—I was ready to go back to Valpo, and I was ready to celebrate the completion of my college degree. I was twenty-one now and a college graduate. It would be several months before I got my first job and before I received my degree in the mail. Then it would be official. I made my grandfather two promises before he passed away. I'd kept them both, just as I'd promised. First, I had to finish high school, and second, I had to go to college and get my degree. I kept my word and I completed my education—just like I promised.

CHAPTER 6: FINDING MY SISTER

I am backing up here 1981 because it was no doubt one of my favorite years. That year signaled accomplishment on a number of levels. First, I graduated from Valparaiso High School. And I received a high school diploma, which my grandpa was never able to do. Second, I bought and paid for my own car: a 1974 Chevrolet Nova—that car with the shag carpeting in it. Third, I started college at Vincennes University, fourth, I finished the first semester of college with decent grades, and fifth, it is the year I started looking for my sister, Katy.

I have mentioned Katy in previous chapters. My father and his first wife, Doreen, lived in Hammond, Indiana, when Katy was born three years before me. I came along about three and a half years later in Las Vegas, born to another woman. Over the years, while growing up in Valpo, my grandfather, father, and my mom's family told me about Katy, my half-sister. Mom told me on several occasions that she remembered seeing Katy and her mother in the grocery store. Mom had me in the child seat of the grocery cart, and she said that might have been the first time Katy and I had seen each other.

I don't remember that, of course, but I do remember Mom telling me that story. Katy and her mother moved back to Valpo after the divorce from my father, Tom. Doreen told my mom that she was going to work at the U.S. Post Office in downtown Valpo. That post office building is still there today, but it is now the city hall. While Doreen worked there, she met and later married Thomas Michaels. It was ironic because my father's name was also Thomas Dowd, and he was from Valparaiso, as well. Later they moved from Valpo to Naples, Florida. Naples is some 1,500 miles south of Valpo, and they left with their family to start a new life.

Now, I am no detective, but if I had known how to find people, maybe I could have gone into the people-finding business. Finding Katy was rather like a puzzle. Up through my junior year in high school, I had heard things about my sister from my mom, my father, Tom, and my grandpa. But I really did not have much to go on, except that she had moved from Valpo to Naples, Florida, and graduated from high school in Naples in 1978.

As I said before, here is how I found Katy. It was in my English class in high school that I caught a break. I was sitting next to a guy about a year older than me, Brian Wikle. Brian was a funny guy and had a sense of humor like no other. He was always good for a dirty joke, dirt on a fellow classmate, or anything that was going on in the rumor mill. Brian was the class clown. He used to crack me up laughing in class until I was in tears, and then the teacher would wonder what was so funny. She said I should share the joke with the class. Of course, it was off-color and could not be repeated.

However, the girl sitting in front of Brian caught my attention. One day this girl came into class wearing a shirt that said "Naples." Her name was Rhonda Stone, and she was nice, and I was really shy around girls then. So, Rhonda comes into the classroom wearing this t-shirt that says, "Naples." I said hello to her and asked where she got the shirt. She told me it was a gift from a family member who lived in Naples, Florida. My friend, Brian, who was in rare form at the time, made some funny remark about somebody having "big Naples." Of course, this caught me off guard, and we all got a good laugh to start the class, and again I was getting a dirty look from the teacher.

Later on, I told Rhonda in the Naples T-shirt that I might have a sister living there. She said she would try to find out what my sister's phone number was the next time she spoke to her relative. A few days later, after I had given Rhonda all the information I knew, she came into class with a slip of paper and said, "I think that this might be the phone number you are looking for."

The piece of paper had Tom Michaels' name and his apparent phone number on it. I told her thanks and said now maybe I can talk to her.

I carried this phone number in my wallet for about two years. While living in the dorm, I became friends with a guy from Morgan Township named Gregg Dewey. He lived down the hall from me, and we met not long after classes started in August 1981 and became good friends. Gregg introduced me to his roommate, and they lived down the hall in Room 13.

We went to lunch and dinner together and also a certain movie named *Porky's*. But most importantly, Gregg helped me do something I had not done yet—talk to my sister Katy. I had told him about not being able to speak to her and the circumstances as to why my sister and I had not seen each other for all of these years. Gregg understood and let me use his phone credit card to make that call. One day after the third or fourth try, I finally got through. Katy's mother in Naples answered the phone. I think that she was blown away when she heard my name and my voice on the phone. In those days, I had a deep voice like my father, and she said that I sounded like him. She told me Katy was in college up in Washington, D.C., and that she had gone to Florida State for only one year. I remember when I saw her graduation announcement in 1978 that Katy's intentions had been to go to FSU in Tallahassee, Florida.

Doreen, Katy's mom, and I had quite a nice conversation on the phone. She encouraged me to call my sister in Washington, D.C., and said that Katy was really busy and that it might take several phone calls to get through to her. Later that evening, Gregg and I tried calling her. It was after 10:00 P.M. or something like that when I got an answer to my phone call. I asked if this was Katy Michaels on the phone, and she said yes. Then I said, "Katy, my name is Michael Dowd. My father's name is Thomas Dowd, and it is my understanding that your mother and he were married a number of years ago." I went on to say, "I think that you and I are brother and sister."

There was silence on the phone line, and I thought that she was going to hang up on me. But then she spoke. "Who is this? Is this some kind of crank call?" I had to explain things again, and fast. Quickly, I repeated our common family history and waited for her to respond.

I said, "If I am not mistaken, you were given the birth name of Katy, and you were born in Hammond, Indiana. After your mom divorced Tom Dowd, you and your mother moved back to Valparaiso, Indiana. Then your mom met Tom Michaels in Valpo, and they got married and moved to Naples, Florida."

After she heard me give this information, she then calmed down. She said she had had a number of crank calls lately and that she was not sure who I was. We talked some more, and Katy went on to tell me why she decided to go to school in Washington, D.C. Apparently, Florida State University was more of a "party school" and not as academic as she wanted. What she wanted to do was public relations in the Washington, D.C. area. I told her about my upbringing and how I happened to grow up in Valparaiso. I told her that I had graduated from Valpo High School, that I was now in college at Vincennes University, and that I'd been raised by my great aunt and uncle.

Also, I told her that I was raised by my grandfather and my great aunt and uncle. She asked me where my birth mother was, and I had to say that I did not know. I told her about how she had given me up at birth in Las Vegas, Nevada, and that I had no idea where she was. I told her how Tom's mother, my grandmother, brought me to Valpo and that she died suddenly when I was a year and a half old. After I told her how I was raised by my great aunt and uncle, along with my grandfather, Katy asked me where our father was now. I explained that he was now living in the French Quarter of New Orleans and that he was one of the people who help build the Superdome stadium there and that he was now remarried.

Katy and I talked on the phone for about an hour or so that night. We had so much to catch up on. And it seems like every time I speak to her even now, we are always catching up.

That has been a good thing. During that fall semester at Vincennes University, I spoke to Katy on several occasions. It cost me a fortune in phone calls. On one of those occasions, I asked Katy what her plans were going to be for Christmas. She said that she was going to be in Naples for the holidays. I asked her if she ever came to Valparaiso for the holidays because I knew she had family there, too. She said no, she was not coming to Valpo, and I asked about the possibility of me going to Florida for the two of us to finally meet. She thought that sounded like a good idea and that it would be great to visit with each other.

Now I had to explain to Mom and Dad about how I found Katy and that I wanted to go to Florida over Christmas vacation. They were very understanding and allowed me to go to Florida to see my sister. It turned out that my grandpa's oldest brother, Everett, and his wife, Mabel, had a winter home just outside of Fort Myers in a community called Cape Coral. Uncle Everett and his wife were going to be at their winter home during the holidays, and so I called them. I told them the story of how I found Katy, that she was going to be in Naples over Christmas, and that it would be neat to finally meet her. They asked what they could do to help, and I asked if I could stay with them while I was there. I explained that I might need a place to stay while I was there and wondered if I could stay with them. They said it would be fine, even if they had family down there at the same time. I made my travel plans, got my airline ticket, and called Uncle Everett with my travel arrangements.

It turned out my sister, Susan, came home to Valpo for Christmas that year, and we both had the same flight going back to Atlanta. Susan would be going to Macon, Georgia, and I was taking a connecting flight on to Fort Myers. Susan and I were flying on Delta Air Lines. It was going to be so nice to go to Florida to some warmer weather. Susan and I flew out of O'Hare Airport in Chicago the Saturday after Christmas.

Our flight was on time, and I remember getting a big meal on the way to Atlanta. It was great to be flying with Susan because we just did not get the chance to talk about stuff like we used to. We landed in Atlanta and then to my connecting flight. After checking in at the gate and getting my seat assignment, I was supposed to have about an hour between flights, but by the time we walked down to the gate, the gate attendant was already calling seat rows on the flight. Susan and I said our good-byes, and I boarded my flight to Fort Myers.

It was about a ninety-minute flight there, and the time went quickly. Before I knew it, we were landing. At that time, Fort Myers had an older airport. This airport did not have the jetports for the planes to pull up to; you had to get off the plane outside and then walk into the terminal. But it worked out pretty nice because when I got into the terminal, Uncle Everett was having a cup of coffee at the small restaurant while waiting for my plane to land. And Aunt Mabel was waiting for me at the end of the secured area. She was there to take me to get my luggage. It was now time for the second part of my Christmas holiday vacation, as I was now in warm, sunny Florida.

The flight that I was on was crowded, and because of that, it took a while for my luggage to arrive. My suitcase was finally there, and the three of us went to the car. Uncle Everett was, for as long as I can remember, big on Oldsmobile cars. And I came from a family of Buick lovers, and I even owned a Buick Century for about a year and a half. But Oldsmobile was still a great car, and Uncle Everett had owned many of them. The car they had brought to the airport was an Oldsmobile Delta 88 four-door diesel. The color of it was light tan with tan cloth, velour-type seats, and the price of diesel was much cheaper than it is now. When you got the diesel engine with the car, you also got a bigger fuel tank. We put the luggage in the trunk of Uncle Everett's Oldsmobile Delta 88 and, with Aunt Mabel at the wheel, we left the airport. I could not believe how warm it was in Florida at that time of the year, as I was wearing a dark blue sweater and was starting to sweat. It was late December 1981, and I was close to seeing Katy for the first time.

After about an hour's drive to my aunt and uncle's winter home, I realized that I would spend the next several days there. We got out of the car, and Aunt Mabel explained that I would be sleeping on a cot for a few days because my cousins, Don and Shirley, and their family would be staying for a few more days, as well. I told Aunt Mabel and Uncle Everett that I had no problem with sleeping on a cot for a while, as long as it was comfortable. That night I had a nice conversation with Don and Shirley. Cousin Shirley was Uncle Everett's oldest daughter, and Don and Shirley had been married for a long time. I knew some of Uncle Everett's family, but I did not really know Shirley that well. Like me Shirley was born a Dowd. She was raised on a farm near Culver, Indiana.

Shirley's husband, Don, was a very good bowler. I remember that he showed me a ring he was wearing, which was a huge bowling ring he got for Bowling 800 or more in a three-game tournament. While talking with Don and Shirley out on the screened-in porch, I explained to them how I found my sister, Katy. Shirley, of course, knew my father, Tom Dowd, because the two of them were first cousins.

It is kind of amazing when I think about it now, after all these years. I hear from some of my cousins from time to time and what I am always told is how smart and charming my father was. Then, after talking about my father and sister, the conversation moved to talking about my birth mother. In 1981 I was eighteen years old, and I knew that my birth mother was out there in the world somewhere. But I had no idea where she might be. Shirley asked me if I had ever looked for my birth mother, and I said I had no idea where to start. My cousin then asked me if I had a picture of what she looked like, and again, I said no. I didn't even have a picture of her. Shirley seemed to think that maybe my father had a picture of her, but after talking with him on the phone some time later, he told me he did not think he had one. I never gave it much thought, at least for a while, as to her whereabouts. At the time, the only thing I had was her name on my birth certificate. I had no picture of her, and I did not even know what her last name was. In those days, there was no internet, so I was quite limited as to what I could do. It was only later in life I learned that if I had gone to the right organization, I no doubt would have found her.

The next morning, we were up early for breakfast. We were not going to Naples until the next day, so it was time to enjoy the fun and sun of Fort Myers, Florida. Aunt Mabel always made a big breakfast. They enjoyed their big meal at noon and then had a light meal for dinner. After a hearty breakfast, I asked Aunt Mabel if there was anything I could do to help her out.

She said, "Yes, if you don't mind, it would help me out a great deal if you could clean our car for us." Of course, I agreed to do that and took a bucket of car washing stuff and headed out to the side of their mobile home to clean their Oldsmobile. Since I had worked for several years as a professional car cleaner for the car rental agency that my brother-in-law and sister owned, I was pretty good at what I was about to do. It took me about an hour or so to clean it, and it was spotless when I finished. I cleaned the inside and outside of the windows and the white walls on the tires. I swept out the inside of the car, too, and wiped down the dashboard that was dusty. After I was done, several of us took off for the mall in Fort Myers. I thought it would be neat to do some souvenir shopping and see some of the area. We got back sometime late in the afternoon, and I called my parents to let them know I was doing fine. About that time, I realized I would finally get so see my sister, Katy. I told Mom and Dad how nice the weather was in Florida as it was in the low eighties. Florida was fun and warm. I was enjoying my vacation very much.

The next morning, after breakfast, along with Don and Shirley, Aunt Mabel and Uncle Everett and I headed out for Naples. Before we left, I called to get directions to Katy's house. The ride took a little over an hour, but that part of South Florida was really nice.

If you ever have been to Naples, Florida, and the surrounding area, you know that it is a really nice and a very wealthy area. One area of Naples is called Millionaires Row. Some of the most awesome homes are located in this section of town. The closer we got to Naples, the more nervous I was getting. I remember we got into town, just off of US 41, turned by a Kentucky Fried Chicken restaurant, and went into this nice subdivision. Since we had the address, we were able to drive right to the house. Aunt Mabel dropped me off and said that they would come back in an hour and a half or so. Now I was really nervous. So nervous, in fact, that I was starting to shake and sweat. I stepped up to the front door and rang the doorbell. A young man about my age answered the door, and I asked if Katy was there. He said, "Yes, Mike, we have been expecting you. Please, come on in."

At the time, I was kind of glad it was Katy's brother, Tom Michaels Jr., because I was such a nervous wreck at the door. He and I shook hands. It was nice to meet him, too. We started to talk as we both walked into a family room in their house. Then it all happened. I was looking off to my left while talking to Katy's brother. We were discussing the weather, and I was telling him that I thought it was warm and humid. Tom seemed to think it was a little on the cool side. I guess now I realize why I was sweating—I was so nervous. Then I saw someone out of the corner of my eyes off to my right. I turned my head to the right, and it was Katy! We both smiled and hugged each other. I was almost in tears. I know that my eyes watered up at that point. We must have hugged for a couple of minutes or so because I just could not believe that I was with my sister at last.

I will always remember that first visit with her. It was so good to get the chance to meet her and find out what she had been doing after her family moved from Valpo to Naples. A little while after I was there, Katy's mother, Doreen, came home from work. Both Doreen and her husband, Tom Michaels, worked at the post office in Naples. It was nice to be able to meet my father's ex-wife after all these years but even more exciting to meet my sister, too. Since Doreen was from Valparaiso and Tom also had family still in Valparaiso, it was great to answer questions from her about all of the famous places in Valpo—like the old Premier Theatre on the corner of Lincoln Way and Lafayette Street, just down from the courthouse. Doreen asked if the Big Wheel restaurant was still there, and I told her it was. It was a popular spot in Valpo in those days—a restaurant my grandfather had taken me to as a young child. We used to sit up at the counter and eat a hearty meal. My grandpa told me that before he got remarried, he would go there for dinner just about every night of the week after he got home from work. He never cooked, and the Big Wheel was just down the street from where he lived. That restaurant meant a great deal to me and still does. How sad I was when the decision was made to close it. The Big Wheel in Valpo opened in 1963 and closed on Halloween 2007. So many memories there!

I told Doreen about other places that were still there, too. I mentioned the old A&W Root Beer Stand that was out on the west side of Valpo, near the campus of Valparaiso Tech, and one of my favorite places in Valpo, Hannon's Drive-in. Then Doreen said she was sorry to hear about the death of my grandfather. She said, "Your grandfather's second wife sent a letter after he passed away with a copy of the obit." She went on to say, "I knew you two were close, and I am very sorry for your loss." She asked me how it happened, and I told her about the cancer and how it took him quickly. She went on to say what a nice man my grandpa had been and how good Granny Fran and Grandpa were to her when she met my father and married him. Doreen also said that they continued to be on speaking terms, even after the divorce.

I felt a little uncomfortable with her telling me that, but it was reassuring that she meant what she said about my grandparents. Despite the fact that she and my father had divorced, Doreen spoke highly of them. Then she asked me about my father. I told her that he was living in the French Quarter in New Orleans, and Katy was paying close attention to what I was saying. Suddenly it occurred to me that it was her father we were talking about, too. I told both of them that he was doing as well as possible, despite all the heart issues that he had—that Tom (Dowd) had his first heart attack at the age of thirty-six and that he had open heart surgery for a bypass not long after that.

I had told them that he helped build the Superdome in New Orleans. Then I mentioned that he had remarried. Doreen didn't say much about that, but she did wish my father the best. She did not badmouth him or bash him like she could have. Doreen was, in fact, exceptionally nice during the whole conversation. Katy did not say much or ask a lot about our father during that first visit in Naples. It was several years later that my sister would finally get to meet our father.

Not long after Doreen had come home from work and the three of us had finished our conversation, the doorbell rang, and it was Aunt Mabel. She was there to pick me up. Before I left Katy's house, I gave her a Christmas present. Mom and I had picked out a woman's necklace, and I liked being able to give it to her. The necklace was a gold chain with the letter "K" as the pendant.

Also, during the visit, I got to meet one of Katy's good friends, Janet. She was from Naples, as well, but was going to college at Butler University in Indianapolis, Indiana. Then it occurred to me that a fellow graduate of Valparaiso High School Class of 1981, Kevin Murphy, was also at Butler. I asked Janet if she knew Kevin, and her response was, "Oh, my God, I know Kevin!" Janet went on to say that Kevin was playing football at Butler. I told Janet that I knew Kevin all the way back to ninth grade, when my friend Norman and I managed the freshman team at Thomas Jefferson Junior High. I also was a manager for the sophomore team a year later at Valpo High, as well as a manager for the varsity team in my junior year. So, my visit with Katy was fun, and it was great to know that my search for my sister after all those years had now come to such a happy conclusion. Now I look back on that visit and realize that this visit happened over thirty years ago. Over those thirty years, both of us grew up, finished our college education, got married, and Katy would eventually have two sons, Brent and Eric. It would be about fourteen years before I would see her again, and a lot would happen in our lives during those fourteen years.

CHAPTER 7: FROM 1985 UNTIL 2008
—A LIFETIME FOR ME

Is there one time in my life that is my favorite? This is a hard question to answer. I'm not even sure that I know what decade of time in my life I would choose as my favorite: the 1980s, the 1990s, or the first ten years in the new millennium. There were highlights and lowlights from each decade.

During this time, I started my career in the radio and television business, found a girlfriend, and eventually married her. I was a big fan of the Chicago Bears, Bulls, and Blackhawks, Sox, and Cubs. From 1981 until 2010, the City of Chicago won several world titles in sporting events, and since I grew up near the Chicago area, it was great for me that several league titles in different professional sports were won in the "Second City." First, the team known as the Chicago Sting won the NASL title in 1981. Then, in 1986, my beloved Chicago Bears won Super Bowl XX. Third, the Chicago Bulls, along with Michael Jordan, Scottie Pippen, and a host of other great players, won six NBA titles in '91, '92, and '93. Michael Jordan left the game for a time, and when he came back to the Bulls, Chicago won three more titles in '96, '97, and '98. Fourth, the Chicago White Sox won the World Series in Major League Baseball in 2005, and fifth, the Chicago Blackhawks won the Stanley Cup in 2010. I am a Chicago sports fan! I use this as a comparison, if you will, to my own personal timeline.

I have mentioned that the second phase of my life started after my grandfather died in 1979. Less than two years later, I graduated from high school and started college. I also found my sister, Katy, and got to see her for the first time. The comparison I make with my life to the Chicago sports scene is that in 1981, Chicago won its first pro sports title since 1963. Ironically, that was the year I was born. What is also ironic is the day I was born: Sunday, November 17, 1963 is the day my beloved Chicago Bears beat the Green Bay Packers at Wrigley Field in Chicago. Thus, it is only fitting that I am a Bears' fan. Between 1979 and 2010, I was able to meet several former or current Bears' players. I met quarterbacks Mike Phipps and running back Walter Payton. Over the years, I met Mike Singletary, Ron Rivera, Gary Fencik, Doug Buffone, and Bob Avellini , as well as Neil Anderson. I even met former player and coach, Mike Ditka. He owned two restaurants: one in Chicago and another in Merrillville, Indiana.

Comparing my life to the Chicago sports scene, the City of Chicago was starving for a championship then, and I was starving for a job that paid me a decent wage. When the Bears won the Super Bowl, it was mayhem. The Bears only lost one game that year to the Miami Dolphins, on a Monday night at the Orange Bowl Stadium. I had three jobs working in the radio business, in Michigan City, in LaPorte, and two jobs with the same radio station in Valparaiso. Every station, except the one in Michigan City, had fired me for whatever reason. I couldn't seem to hold down a job. Program directors or general managers let me go, sometimes for no real reason.

However, I did meet some nice people in the business: Program Director, Chuck Van Cure, in La Porte, and some really nice folks in Michigan City, but I only worked for them on a part-time basis. Even when I worked on a full-time basis, the wages were below the poverty level. I remember that my first full-time job in radio paid me a salary of $180 a week. It was a good thing I was still living at home at that time. Several years later, I saw the film *Private Parts*, the story of Howard Stern. It amazed me how Howard survived working for all of those tiny radio stations. I was reminded of some of the places where I had worked. Some of these radio stations were even located in a house.

Although I never worked at a radio station in a house, I did talk to a guy about a job at a radio station in Knox, Indiana, that was in a house. What the film pointed out was that there were a lot disgusting people working in small time radio. Most radio stations in the northwest Indiana market were family owned and operated. These people often did not treat their employees well. First, there were the cheap wages, and paydays were every other Friday. What was wrong with that, you say? I worked at one place where we were supposed to get our paychecks by 3:00 P.M., but there was not enough money in the payroll account. The general sales manager had to go and collect outstanding accounts, so the station could meet payroll. Paychecks arrived four or five hours late. This meant that employees often had to run quickly to the bank, so they could deposit their paychecks quickly to avoid bouncing any checks.

I know there were times I had to pay my rent late with additional fees because of these late paychecks. These same general managers often drove expensive cars, had expense accounts, and made very good salaries. Some did not care about their employees, and if those employees left because of disagreements with management, so be it. Often, general managers would have cut the corners out of the building if they could have. It was all about their own paycheck and not taking care of the building, equipment, or paying reasonable wages.

When you worked part-time, you received minimum wage until you quit. If you were promoted, you were paid what we called "welfare wages." Most employees had to get their own health insurance or just did not have insurance because it was too expensive to get insurance through the station. So, after working in and out of radio for about three years, I gave it up. I wanted no part of it anymore. There were a few good people in the business, but most were not. I only put up with small-time radio in northwest Indiana for about three years. I don't know how Howard Stern put up with it for all the years he was in that business. Now, of course, he makes more than $100 million a year in satellite radio. I have to give him credit for what he has personally accomplished. Here is a guy who worked in these small-time markets, rather like I did, but he had the patience to make radio work. He stuck with it and moved into bigger markets of Detroit and then to Washington, D.C. After D.C., he went on to WNBC in New York City. Howard Stern fought with everybody. He angered many people, but he was entertaining, too. People listened to him, they loved him. Eventually he went to work for CBS Radio Network. There he fought with critics, program directors, general managers, and the Federal Communications Commission. Howard took them ALL on and really, if you think about it, he won. He is now on satellite radio and making a fortune. He calls himself the "King of All Media" and has earned people's respect. "Howard Stern is not for everybody." I agree with that statement. "Maybe Howard is just misunderstood." All I can say is, I was glad to be done with small-time radio. Perhaps someday I could hit Powerball and go back to purchase one of these small-town radio stations. I would love to put those people on unemployment lines.

I was done with small-time radio, and it was time to move on to something else. About 1986 my good friend, Tim King, lost his job at the radio station where he was working—must have been around mid-August of that year. I missed working with Tim, as he was a good friend. He went with us (Norman, Bill, Jay, and myself) for late night dinners at Gino's East and would then go drinking out on the town at the corner of Rush and Division Streets in Chicago. But after all of the fun and glory, Tim lost his job for no apparent reason. It was time for something different. Tim moved back to the Pittsburgh area with his parents.

It was about two weeks or so after Tim left town that I was asked to play on the Deadliners coed softball team. The team was headed up by a good friend, Chris Isadore. Actually, he was a good friend of Tim King's, as the two of them covered lots of city and county government meetings for different media outlets. Chris and Tim were responsible for getting me on the team the prior year, so after Tim left for home, I was asked to be on the team again.

I didn't know how playing on this team would change my life again. By this time, I was living in a studio apartment in Valpo on Chicago Street. It was a fun, little apartment with a small kitchen, a walk-in closet, and a decent-sized front room. I went to our first game of the year at Kirchhoff Park in Valpo. My apartment was right behind the park and when we had a game there, it was in walking distance. I was introduced to a young lady who eventually became my girlfriend and later my wife.

Her name was Pam, and she was on the team as a pitcher. She worked with Chris Isadore at the Post-Tribune newspaper in Gary. I never had a girlfriend and never really dated. Girls I wanted to go out with were not interested. Pam was different. I don't know why, and even to this day, I often wonder what she saw in me. Here I was, out of a job, had no money, and trying to get a job of some sort. Pam was single, attractive, and athletic. She was a graduate of Valparaiso University with a degree in journalism, and she was now working as a sportswriter for one of the local papers. Her job was union scale, and she was making good money. She drove a nice, red Buick Skyhawk. She lived with her parents and supported herself.

We were introduced before the game started. One of her best friends, Julie, came with her that day, and I found out later that Julie was a bit of a psychic. Several years later, she told me that she actually predicted that Pam would meet her husband on the night we met. That husband turned out to be me. By the end of our second game, I had the nerve to ask her out. After years of rejection by other girls, I was amazed that Pam said yes. We went out to dinner about a week later to a restaurant called Round the Clock in Valpo.

Earlier that day, Mom invited me to come over for spaghetti that night. I said, "No thanks, I have a date." I think that Mom almost dropped the phone, or maybe she thought I was kidding. I told her about Pam and how we met playing softball together.

She said, "Well, have fun!"

And we did. I wound up having spaghetti at the restaurant. Pam and I dated for several years after that until I popped the question. I finally got a job at US Cable of Northern Indiana in Merrillville, not long after we started dating. I worked at that place for seven and a half years.

Pam and I were married June 23, 1990. Our ceremony was at St. Andrew's Catholic Church in Merrillville, and the reception was at a Catholic church gymnasium in Portage. More than two hundred people came to the reception, where we were surrounded by family and friends. It was so nice. When I look back on it now I think about my grandparents, my father who was still alive at the time, and my birth mother. I know that my grandparents were there in spirit. But my father said that he was not in good enough health to travel. So, he did not come to our wedding. In October Pam and I went to New Orleans, and we told him all about it. I also thought about my birth mother. She was missing out on my life. Here I was, twenty-five years old and now a married man.

After our honeymoon in the Bahamas, Pam and I made our first home in a two-bedroom apartment in Valpo. Pam and I were only there a couple of years because in 1992, we bought our first home. We found a nice, well-cared-for, ranch-style house outside of Valpo in nearby Washington Township. It had three bedrooms and was on a rather large lot with a fenced-in yard. It was also nicely decorated inside. The sellers had taken really good care of the place, and it came with a lot of nice features. It was our home for the next seven years.

Over the course of about eleven years, from 1985 to 1996, I made about ten or eleven trips to New Orleans to visit my father. Earlier I said that I would never speak to him again; however, I got in touch with him when I was a senior in high school. We kept in touch while I was in college, and during that time, my father and his second wife, Jacquee, moved to Memphis, Tennessee. It was a shame that I did not visit them in Memphis since it was only a two- or three-hour drive by car from Vincennes. Tom decided he did not like Memphis, for whatever reason, and he moved back to the French Quarter; a short while later, he and Jacquee were divorced. For a while, my father was in business with another guy, and they opened a night club on Bourbon Street called Cajun Country.

The club served alcoholic drinks only and no food, which was common practice in New Orleans. My father, as a managing partner, supervised the bartenders, servers, and others. What his business partner did was drugs. I don't know what his real name was, but he was nicknamed "Stormin Norman" in the French Quarter. Unfortunately, the more this guy did drugs, the more trouble came to the club. After my father received threats, he decided that he'd had enough. He left New Orleans and went across the state line to Biloxi, Mississippi. He hired a lawyer and had his name removed from the entire partnership. which was a smart move on Tom's part. It would only have been a matter of time before the drugs would snuff out the profits, and the place would have closed. My father left New Orleans for about a year. When he heard that the club was closed and his former partner had left town, my father then returned. It was then that I made my first trip to New Orleans. That trip, and several other trips to New Orleans, would be life-long memories for me.

This first trip was in October 1985. I was out of a job in broadcasting and working part-time for my brother-in-law at the car rental agency. I needed to leave Valpo for a while, and the month of October seemed like a good time to do that. My friend, Tim King, took me in his Ford Pinto to Chicago's O'Hare Airport. I remember taking Ozark Airline from Chicago to Lambert International Airport in St. Louis, changed planes, and went on to New Orleans. I had wanted to go to New Orleans for a long time, and now I was on my way. Tom told me that he would not be at the airport to pick me up but explained how to take a shuttle to the French Quarter. For the price of $7, the shuttle driver dropped me off at Brennan's Restaurant. My father had this gorgeous apartment just down the block from this world-famous restaurant. I'm sorry that I did not bring a lot more money because I would have loved to dine at this place. In the French Quarter, all of the buildings look somewhat alike, and it is very easy to miss where you are going. The driver dropped me off at 417 Royal Street, so I thought it should be easy to find 431 Royal Street. I must have walked past the darn door five or six times, then I had to find a pay phone to call my father and ask where his door was. I finally found it after walking past it one more time. I rang the buzzer to his apartment, the return buzzer rang back, and I was able to go inside.

The entry to this apartment building was spectacular. The marble floors were shiny and looked spotless in the reflection of the light from the huge chandelier in the hallway leading to the stairs. I had at least two, loaded suitcases and had to climb a flight of what seemed like more than one hundred steps to the top. By the time I started up, I could hear Tom shouting out, "I'm up here. Come on up!" I found his apartment. It had been many years since I had last seen my father, and it was great to see him again. Maybe it was 1978 when my father, Tom, came to Valparaiso for the last time. That was just before my grandfather passed away the following March.

It was now October 1985, and we had seven years to catch up. It was great to finally see him. He had just turned fifty the month before and, as it turned out, I only had ten more years with him. I'm sure if I had known that, I would have spent more time with him. But now I was in New Orleans. I was in the French Quarter! I was in one of the most traveled cities in the United States, here to see my father and look for a job. Tom's apartment was very nice, and it was rented by friends from Houston who had a computer company. His friends had this apartment in the French Quarter, so that they had a place to stay whenever they came to visit. In order to write it off as a business expense, they had my father stay in the apartment, so they could work out of the front room "office" when they were in town.

This computer business dealt in computer hardware. Back in the mid-1980s, there were no laptops or servers. There were disks and data recorders, as well as computer terminals and huge machines; all of this ran the software for the companies they worked for. It was a "buy and sell" kind of company. They bought old, used computer equipment that companies were disposing of and stored it in a warehouse. They had a list of companies that might need spare equipment in the future. It was a good thing for my father.

He got to live in this really nice apartment and be right in the heart of the French Quarter. That night my father took me out to a bar down the street at one of those fancy hotels. It was a place where he hung out because of the location of the bar. We had fun that night, and I remember being rather hung over the next morning. That first trip to see him was fun. I spent about three weeks with Tom, and we really got a lot of our issues out on the table. We talked about my grandfather, but I warned him that I wouldn't listen to him bitch and moan and complain about what happened with my grandfather's estate. Instead, he ended up joking about the fact that I got the money and he got nothing. But we did cover a lot of stuff—like my visit to Naples, Florida, when I got to see my sister, Katy. My sister told me once that she was engaged to a French count. My father got a good laugh out of that. I remember his remark: "What does that make us, a count-tee?" He must have had too much to drink, but we laughed a lot about that comment.

We also talked about my birth mother. I asked Tom if he had a picture of her. He didn't think so but he would look through some stuff he had moved over from Biloxi. A couple of days later, he did look through some photos he had but didn't find any of my birth mother. I asked him what she looked like. I remember he said she was really attractive, kind of tall with a slender build and really dark black hair. Now, my hair is dark brown, but not black. But it is thick, and he said her hair was a lot like mine. I asked him how they had met. He had been working at a bar in Lansing, Illinois, after his divorce from his first wife, Doreen. The story was, according to my father's recollection, she either came into the bar as a patron, or she worked with my father at the bar. Knowing what I know now, I think that she might have actually worked at the place. It just made sense after I figured and sorted everything out. I then asked Tom if he knew where she might be, but he had no idea. My father said he lost track of her long before I was born and, in reality, he did not even know that she was pregnant with me at the time.

I did find this rather hard to believe, but it's what my father told me. Just about every visit I made to the French Quarter included a discussion about my birth mother. It was during one of those discussions that I got one of the biggest clues that would help me find her. But I still had no idea where she was or even if she was still alive. Tom brought up the possibility that she may have had other children. He didn't know how many for sure, but he was certain that there were other kids born to my birth mother even before I was born. This intrigued me because this was the first time I had heard that. I really didn't know what to think.

It was on another visit to New Orleans and another discussion about her that I received the first real clue I would need to start my search. I was in New Orleans in 1995, so that I could take Tom to a procedure he was having to remove cancerous polyps from his mouth. The procedure was successful for the most part, and a couple of days later, my father and I were having another discussion about my birth mother. The discussion started with me asking Tom why he hadn't been at the hospital for my birth. Then Tom responded, "Look, you know your mother and I were not married when you were born. The fact is, the two of us had split up, for whatever reason, and

I heard through the grapevine that she was already married to another man when you were born."

I then asked Tom if he happened to know the name of this man. He looked at me with a puzzled expression. I actually asked him something that seemed to stump him. He then responded, "No, I don't remember the man's name. But I think it was a really funky last name."

I asked, "What do you mean, *funky*?"

He explained that this guy's last name was not a common one, like Smith, Jones, Johnson, or Williams. My father tried to remember this mystery man of sorts, but just could not remember. After that discussion about my birth mother, we never mentioned her again. It was the last discussion I would ever have with Tom about the subject because now we had to concentrate on his health issues.

I never found a job worth accepting in New Orleans, but it was sure fun going there. In November 1985, I went to work part-time at a country western radio station in Valparaiso. I was hired to do the overnight shift. This job lasted about nine months, when I was to be promoted to a news reporter and anchor. However, I was let go altogether. As I said before, small-town, family-owned radio—well, what a scam it is to work in that business.

Regardless, it was the next year, 1986, that I met my girlfriend and future wife, Pam. After the two of us married and bought our first house in Washington Township, we made several trips to New Orleans. One trip was to the French Quarter after we became engaged. Then a couple of months after we got married in 1990, we made a return trip. We spent a lot of time all around the city. We ate some very nice restaurants and enjoyed the great food there. For lunch we would get a muffuletta at either Central Grocery on Decatur Street, or we would go to the place called Café Maspero. Then, for dinner, we would go to one of our favorite places for seafood: Ralph& Kacoo's. By the time Pam and I were married, I had left radio and was working for US Cable of Northern Indiana in Merrillville. That was a *real* job. It had real benefits and a paid vacation. I was there for about seven and a half years. After US Cable, I went to work for TCI. It was located in Gary. It was during this time when my life started to fall apart.

The year was 1996, and in January, I got a phone call from my father. He said that he had been to the doctor at the VA Hospital in New Orleans, and they found a spot on his lung. During that year, I made at least three trips to New Orleans to be with Tom. During one conversation with my cousin, Shawn, in late September 1996, he recommended that I get down to New Orleans and take my father to see his doctors at the VA. Shawn could not go because he had other commitments, so I called my travel agent and booked a trip. This time I would stay in a hotel. There was a nice one next to my father's last apartment on Chartres Street in the Quarter. It was called Hotel Le Richelieu and was a gorgeous place. I went back and stayed at that hotel at least three more times. The month was October, and the weather was still warm. After I checked into to my hotel, I went next door to see my father. It was late in the afternoon, and he was usually at the corner pub by this time of the day.

But not this day. He woke from a nap and answered the door. My father looked terrible. His hair was all messed up; but even worse, his chin was missing as the result of a surgery he had a few months before. He let me into his apartment and started back to bed, but he fell over a hard, steel object. I got over to help him up and got him into bed. He was in bad shape, and the fall didn't help, either. Because of his last surgery, he was now talking through his trachea. It was really tough to see my father like this, not only because it reminded me of the death of my grandfather, but because Tom's condition seemed so much worse. He really looked bad.

The next morning, I got up early and was at his apartment by 8:00 A.M. Tom was already up, dressed, and shaven. I was impressed because after the way he looked the day before, I was surprised at his mobility. He finished getting dressed and asked me to hang on to his wallet and money. I told him I had money for a cab and so forth, but he insisted. He gave me a wad of cash that must have been about $400. He had to see two different doctors: one at the VA and the other at the Baptist Hospital, across the street. It was at the VA when reality set in. I talked to one of his doctors and asked her what his outlook was. The news was not good. The doctor said, "I suppose if your father has six months to live, that would be a lifetime."

Late that afternoon, I dropped Tom off at his apartment and decided right then and there I would ask him what he wanted me to do. I said, "Look, I was paying attention to what the doctor said this morning. I hate to ask, but I need to know what you want me to do."

Tom replied, "I want you to put me on a plane, one-way, to Waco, Texas. Then, after I pass away, I want you to have me cremated, and you can spread my ashes."

I asked him where he wanted me to spread his ashes. He always talked about the Florida Keys because he used to live there. But he surprised me by saying, "I want you to spread my ashes on the football field at Valparaiso University. I have some terrific memories there, and I would like to have my ashes spread there." I told him that I would see what I could do.

The next day, with a friend of my father's named Captain Ziggy, we went to the New Orleans International Airport. I had already called and gotten my father a plane ticket on Continental Airlines. I packed everything that would fit into his luggage. Captain Ziggy (who looks like a spitting image to actor Sam Elliot), my father, and I were off. My father was, for the most part, silent on the way, but when we went through Metairie, he remarked about the apartment he had had here. That was back when he worked on the Superdome. It was only fitting, I guess, that he would show me where he lived when he worked on that Superdome. He was always proud of that work. I think that working on the Superdome was always a big part of what he accomplished in life.

We arrived at the airport and decided to go with curbside check-in. We asked for a wheelchair for my father. Since this was pre-9-11, Captain Ziggy and I were allowed to go back to the gate with Tom while he waited for his flight. An attendant wheeled him back to the gate for us, and it seemed like the longest wait in the world for that plane to arrive. It began to hit me that this might be the last time I would ever see Tom alive. I mentioned to my father that he would not be allowed to smoke on the plane. He knew that, but I felt I should remind him.

Finally, they called his flight. Since he was in a wheelchair, my father was boarded first. The airline personnel were really nice and let Captain Ziggy and I go onto the plane and make sure Tom was secured in his seat. After he was secured, I turned around and saw Captain Ziggy say his last goodbyes. It struck me then that I had better do the same because as things looked, this would be the last time I'd see him alive. It was my turn to say my tearful goodbye. I told him to have a nice flight, and I would talk to him when he got to Texas.

Captain Ziggy and I waited until the plane took off, and then the two of us took a cab back to the hotel. My flight home to Chicago was not until Sunday, so I had some time to kill. We were dropped off in front of Harry's Corner Pub at 900 Chartres Street in New Orleans. We went inside and had a drink. Harry's, as it was known, was my father's hang out. Maybe not just a hangout; it was his life. Since Tom had lived on that side of the French Quarter for several years, I met him there many times. He knew everybody in the place, including the current and previous owners. The late Benny Barker owned the place when I first visited Tom there. Then, some years later, Benny passed away, and the bar closed for a while. Then, a couple from Alabama bought the place and did some remodeling and cleaning up and re-opened it. I met some of my father's friends at that place. Most of them were the bartenders. One of those bartenders was Ron, a well-known bartender in the French Quarter. Ron's last name is Maravich. If that name sounds familiar, it's because Ron is the older brother of the late "Pistol Pete Maravich." I got to visit with Ron just about every time I visited my father in New Orleans. He was such a nice guy, and he lived upstairs from my father in the last apartment he had. Almost every Monday, Ron would take my father grocery shopping in his car and make sure Tom had food for the week. When it got to the point that Tom could no longer do his own shopping, Ron did the shopping for him. Ron always looked in on him. Even when I visited my father, Ron would come by, knock on the door, and just say hello. Ron still works as a bartender at Harry's, and every year I say I'm going back to New Orleans. I have now only been back to New Orleans twice since my father's death. I miss New Orelans dearly.

That night it just felt strange that my father was not in New Orleans anymore. He had lived there for more than twenty years, almost like a hermit. I got ready to go out that night, and since this would be my last night in town, I was going to do it up right—eat, drink, and party! Before I left my hotel room, I called and talked to my father and my cousin, Shawn, to make sure that he had arrived in Waco all right. It turned out he did get there just fine, and Shawn's wife, Becky, was helping get Tom comfortable in a recliner that they had bought him.

Shawn remarked on what a great job packing I had done, especially with all of the medicine and medical supplies he had with him. I did not stay on the phone long. It was now time to hit the town and enjoy my last night in New Orleans. I can't remember where I went for dinner, but I know that I put on nice clothes. After dinner it was time to hit one of my favorite musical bars in the Quarter. I always enjoyed going to at least two bars on Bourbon Street: Maison Bourbon, which had Dixieland Jazz music, and another called Cajun Cabin. I went out on the town that Saturday night and enjoyed it. I only wish my wife, Pam, could have been with me. It would have been so nice to have her there. It was just one of those things that I thought would bring us closer together.

I came back to Valpo the next day and brought home a number of souvenirs. It was good to be home. I missed work all of that week, even more I had missed Pam, so it was good to get back into the rhythm of my life. I talked to my father a few times while he was in Waco. I got hold of my sister Katy, as well, and we agreed to meet in November in Waco and surprise Tom. I thought it would be nice for Tom to have both of his kids there to see him before he died. However, about two weeks before we were supposed to go to Texas, I got the phone call I had been dreading. On the morning of October 28, the phone rang while I was getting ready to go to work. Since I was in the bathroom getting ready for work, and Pam was still sleeping, the call went to the answering machine.

It was Shawn's wife, Becky, on the phone. Pam wondered who called because she heard the machine go off. Just as I stepped out of the bathroom, Pam was listening to the message. Becky's message was: "Mike, this is Becky in Waco. When you get this message, please call me as soon as you can. I have some bad news about Tom."

This was a phone call I did not want to return. But I had Shawn's phone number nearby, and I told Pam that I had better call them back. Becky said that sometime during the night, Tom passed away, and the authorities were there at the apartment to confirm his death and take him to the funeral home.

I asked to speak to Shawn and asked him what was happening. He said the deputy coroner was there to pronounce Tom dead, and they were putting Tom in a body bag to take him to the funeral home. Shawn asked me then how soon we could get to Waco. Since it was morning, I would try to get down there sometime that day. Shawn told me that they were taking Tom's body out of the house, and he wanted to say his goodbyes to him before the authorities took him away. I filled Pam in on what had happened and asked if she could get a few days off, so that we could go to Texas and take care of Tom's funeral and estate business. Pam was able to make those arrangements. After I called work and let them know I would not be coming in for a while, I called Mom and Dad and told them the news. They offered their support and asked if there was anything they could do. I was able to get a flight for us at 3:30 P.M.

Pam and I left for O'Hare Airport in Chicago. We left for Houston and then took a puddle-jumper to land in Waco about 9:00 P.M. that night. The Waco airport was nothing more than the size of a small gas station. We got our luggage and waited for Shawn and Becky to pick us up. It was about fifteen minutes later that they pulled up in their Oldsmobile Cutlass convertible. It had been a very long day, and I had no idea what was in store for us. Shawn told me on the way to their house that he had gone ahead and had Tom embalmed. He explained that by having him embalmed, we would have more time to make decisions, and to make decisions with a clear head and not be rushed to get Tom cremated.

I realized that Shawn was right. I had not thought about having the opportunity to say goodbye to Tom properly. Shawn got Pam and me a room at the Holiday Inn. He was the general manager of this Holiday Inn near his apartment and not far from Baylor University. It was fall, and in the State of Texas, college football was in full swing. The hotel was always crowded during football weekends but not so much during the week that we were there. We checked in and went to sleep. The next day, while we had room service for breakfast, I was trying to get hold of my sister, Katy, and let her know what was happening. I had tried to reach her before we left for Texas, but she was not at home. Remember, this was before cell phones became popular and there was really no good way to reach her. I tried one more time and left one more message for her on her answering machine with the phone number for Shawn and Becky's.

Pam and I went out to the front desk and waited for Shawn to pick us up. Shawn said that his mom (my Aunt Bonnie) and her husband (Roger) had been on vacation to visit Aunt Joanne and Uncle Chuck in Houston. You may remember that Bonnie and Chuck were my father's siblings. Shawn, Becky, Pam, and I waited for Aunt Bonnie and her husband to get to their house. When everybody got there, and we were just about ready to leave to go to the funeral home, the phone rang, and it was my sister, Katy. I told her what was going on. She apologized for not getting back to me sooner. She was sorry for our loss. Katy was in graduate school and also working a full-time job. She said that because of her commitments, she would not be able to get to Texas for a few days.

I told her that we were going to the funeral home in a few minutes and that Aunt Bonnie, Shawn, Becky, Pam, and myself were going to take care of Tom's final arrangements. Katy asked, "What will you do with Tom's remains?"

I said that we were going to have him cremated, as he had asked. We would let her know when. I thought maybe we would have a memorial service for him in another few weeks or so. Katy said that was fine, and that if I could, get back to her about when we could have it. She and her husband would plan to come to Valparaiso, if that is where we had the service. I told Katy that was fine and that I would like to introduce her to Aunt Bonnie. That phone call was the first time that Aunt Bonnie talked to my sister, Katy. It was just a few more weeks before they would finally meet as adults.

All six of us went to the funeral home somewhere in downtown Waco. It was a nice warm, sunny day. We went into an office, and the decision-making process began. Aunt Bonnie, Shawn, and I started talking about all the things that had to be done. We were in agreement that Tom's body should be cremated. We had to decide what newspapers we would have the obituary sent. We decided that *The Post Tribune*, where Pam worked, and *The Times* newspapers would be the two that would get the obit announcements. We thought about sending one to *The Times Picayune*, which was the newspaper in New Orleans, but after consideration about what it might cost, all three of us decided that most of Tom's friends at Harry's Pub knew about Tom's death because Becky had called and told one of the bartenders what happened.

After we made all the decisions we needed to, five of us were allowed to go back to the embalming room and pay our final respects to Tom. He was in this room no bigger than a walk-in closet. We walked in and there, and Tom was lying in a peaceful state on steel slate, where he had been for the last day or so. Considering how sick Tom had been before he died, he actually looked fairly good. He still had some color to his skin, and considering he was not made-up, like they do for funerals, he really did not look as bad as I thought he might. We said our goodbyes and wished him God's blessings. There was not a dry eye in the room. I only saw Shawn cry one other time and that was at our grandfather's funeral. Aunt Bonnie was in tears, too, and so was I. Shawn said, "So long old friend." I think Aunt Bonnie said something, too, but I was in tears and cannot remember. She was probably saying goodbye to her brother, also. Pam was there to comfort me and, I was very glad she was.

I needed a rock to hang on to.

After we all said our goodbyes to Tom, we said a prayer and left the room. I mentioned how I did not like funeral homes. How I was able to walk back and not fall down while being so nervous, I don't know. Probably because I had Pam to lean on. I was thirty-two years old and had just lost my father to cancer. Now he would be cremated. The person handling the arrangements asked where she should send the ashes. I told the lady that she should send them to me, as I would be in charge of the memorial service for Tom. I received his ashes a few days later, along with a copy of a certificate declaring that the ashes were Tom Dowd's.

We went back to the hotel, changed clothes, and went out to eat. I wasn't much in a mood for food. That afternoon Shawn and Becky took us to a restaurant called the Black-Eyed Pea. I had never heard of the place, but the food was good, and it was a lot like a Chili's restaurant. I was not in a mood to eat, even though normally I have a rather healthy appetite. But after we got there, we all started to unwind a little bit. The visit to the funeral home was still on our minds, but with all of us together over lunch, our moods improved. We went back to Shawn and Becky's apartment and were invited to play a few holes of golf. They lived right on a golf course. I never really took up the sport, because, quite frankly, I stink at golf. But, for whatever reason, doing something instead of just sitting around the apartment, playing golf just sounded like a good idea. We played three holes of golf, right behind their apartment, until it started to rain. We all took shelter inside the apartment. Shawn and Becky ordered pizza to be delivered, so dinner was on its way.

That night Shawn and I went through Tom's wallet. Shawn used the money from Tom's wallet to pay the funeral home for all of the arrangements. Then, as we were searching his wallet, we found three business cards of Tom's from the days that he worked at Caesar's Palace in Las Vegas. Tom had told me that he worked at that casino on the Las Vegas Strip as an accountant in the count room. He seemed to think that he was working for Caesar's about the time I was born. It was two days after I was born when Tom and my grandmother (Frances Dowd) came to Southern Nevada Memorial Hospital in Las Vegas and picked me up. Tom had also told me that my mother gave birth to me and then left the hospital. She was nowhere to be seen or heard from again. That is, until I found her many years later.

There is one question that will probably never get answered: Why did they split up in the first place? Some may think that the answer to that question is really none of my business. However, I would like to know. The other question I have is: Why did my grandfather did not hire someone to find my birthmother after she left me in the hospital? To this day, I have no idea what really happened. The rest of the stuff in Tom's wallet was split up between Aunt Bonnie, Shawn, and myself. The next day, Pam and I went home to Valparaiso. It was so good to be home. I was hoping things would get back to normal.

The following Saturday after Pam and I got home from Texas, the mail carrier arrived at our front door, delivering the box with Tom's ashes. Besides his ashes, I was really surprised by the outpouring of sympathy cards and messages of support. The employees where I worked in Gary passed around a card, took up a collection of money, and gave it to me as a surprise. I think we must have received over twenty-five cards.

I was so surprised at the outpouring of sympathy. I had to put together a plan for a Memorial Service for Tom. I really did not know what to do for him, and I had a feeling that Valparaiso University was not going to let me pour his ashes on the football field like Tom wanted. I then had an idea about spreading his ashes over my grandmother's grave in Valparaiso, but the cemetery said that they do not allow ashes to be spread on the graves there. So, after running out of places to do this, I got the idea of spreading them at the Indiana Dunes National Lakeshore Park. My father had told me that he used to go there when he was younger, and it made sense that we put his ashes out into the water of Lake Michigan. After planning Tom's memorial service, Aunt Bonnie and her husband, Roger, along with my cousin, April, Aunt Bonnie's oldest daughter, my mom and dad, and my sister, Katy, and her new husband, Mike Willliams, came together on a cold November day.

It was just a few days before my thirty-third birthday on a Sunday. We all met at our house in Valpo, and then we went in two cars to the Dunes State Park. The weather was cold, raw, and rainy; it eventually turned to snow later that afternoon. Shawn and Becky could not make the trip, and even though they were invited, Uncle Chuck and Aunt Joanne did not make the trip, either. It was great to see Aunt Bonnie and her husband, Roger, again, as well as my cousin, April. But it was also great to finally see my sister, Katy, and meet her husband, Mike. The three of us: Katy, Mike and I were able to go out the previous night and have a really nice dinner in Valpo. I had not seen my sister since she had come to Valpo a few years earlier when her mother, Doreen, had passed away. Katy's mom had died of cancer, as well.

The three of us had a wonderful dinner and a wonderful time. The night before Tom's memorial service, Katy, her husband, Mike, and I toasted a glass of wine to our father, Thomas Dowd. I told Katy about a side of Tom she had never heard before. She had no idea that Tom had spent a lot of time in Florida, including the Fort Myers area, not far from where she grew up in Naples. Tom used to tell me about what it was like working on a fishing charter boat in the Florida Keys. Katy told me about how she and her brothers went SCUBA diving in the Florida Keys. Katy was surprised to learn that her father had been living in South Florida like she was. I told her about what an awesome cook he was, as well. Then Katy told me about the time she actually met her father on a trip to New Orleans. She was in New Orleans for the Republican National Convention when George H. W. Bush was nominated for the Republican ticket for President of the United States. I knew about this visit, and I realize that I should have gone and been there to make sure nothing bad would happen. Katy said she walked into Harry's Pub in the French Quarter and just stood in the doorway, wondering which one of the guys at the bar was her father. Tom was there in his usual place in the chair next to the barber's chair that was by the wall of the bar. Katy told me that after she found Tom at the bar, everything was going fine until he started in on Katy's mother. I don't know exactly what was said, but she didn't want to have much to do with him after that. I don't blame her. He no doubt was drunk. Why he didn't offer to take his daughter to lunch at one of those nice restaurants, I'll never know.

I felt badly because I had encouraged the two of them to get together, and I was the person who arranged for the two of them to meet. The whole visit just backfired. It was *not* supposed to go like that. I felt really bad, and even to this day, I wish that particular visit could have been different. I was surprised after Katy shared this with me that she actually wanted to be at the memorial service. But I think that this is the kind-hearted person my sister is. She forgave Tom for all of the unthinkable things he had done, even when he was married to Katy's mother, Doreen. I think Katy forgave him for all of that. It would be a visit to Washington, D.C., many years later, that I would really know this to be true.

The next afternoon, Aunt Bonnie, her husband, Roger, her daughter, April, my parents, Katy and her husband, Mike, as well as Pam and I arrived at the Dunes State Park for Tom's memorial service. It was fall, and it was football season. My Chicago Bears were playing the Detroit Lions at Soldier Field that day, and when we got to the Dunes, there was a touch football game going on with about six or seven guys on the beach. My parents let us use their van with all of the people we had, and Aunt Bonnie and Roger rode with Katy and Mike. We parked our vehicles near the giant shelter at the park. Not far from the park, just to the north, was a small creek that ran into Lake Michigan. There were a few walkers on the beach, but with the exception of the nine of us and the football players, there were not a lot of people at the Dunes that day. This was a good situation because I did not want anybody to interrupt us while we were in the middle of Tom's service.

As it turned out, the Dunes State Park actually was a nice place to have it. With the exception of the cold, windy, rainy weather, the service went off without a hitch. I got Tom's ashes out of the back of the van. I took the ashes out of the box, and I had a hard time getting the plastic container out of the cardboard box. I remember somebody had to hold onto the cardboard box while I pulled on the urn and said something like, "Come on, old man, get out of the box."

I got the urn out, and we went over to the side of the building at the park and started the service. I led the way with a eulogy, and then Aunt Bonnie spoke. I talked about all of the things my father was: a father, a husband, a veteran of the Marine Corps, and a former night club owner on Bourbon Street in New Orleans. I also mentioned that he was one of the people who helped to build the Superdome in New Orleans, as well. I mentioned that maybe a lot of people did not like or agree with how Tom did things. But since his life was over, maybe we could forgive him and remember him not for his mistakes, or bad decisions, but for who he was.

Aunt Bonnie gave a remarkable speech about what it was like growing up as the youngest with her brothers, Chuck and Tom. She talked about what it was like going to the theatre on an afternoon after watching a scary movie with her two brothers. Tom would hide behind something on their way home and scare Aunt Bonnie after she was already frightened from the movie. She gave a very moving speech. After she finished, we had a moment of silence. Then we said the Lord's Prayer for Tom at that time, which served as a blessing for my father's ashes.

It was then time to spread the ashes into Lake Michigan. The nine of us walked over to the creek that went out into the lake. It kind of reminded me of the James Bond film, *You Only Live Twice*, when Bond was made to look like he had been killed in the line of duty and was being buried at sea. I started the ceremony with the first part of Tom's ashes, and then I gave the urn to Katy, and she spread more into the creek. There were some left, so Aunt Bonnie spread the rest of the ashes. We were done; the ashes were gone.

The nine of us watched as the small current took them out from the beach into Lake Michigan. We finished the service with a song from Jim Nabors singing, "Back Home Again in Indiana." I thought it was only fitting that we play that song because this was Tom's final return to his home state. I was fine with the whole service until this song played. When I heard the words from that song, I just lost it. By the time the song was over, I was quite a wreck. After the song ended, I tried to get my composure back, and I ended the service by saying, "Let us all now go in peace."

We regained our composure and got into our cars and left the Dunes Park. The nine of us were now on our way to Strongbow's Restaurant in Valpo for a post-memorial service brunch. My Dad and I, along with others in the van, rode to the restaurant for brunch and to talk about the service. Pam mentioned the fact that when we were spreading Tom's ashes into the creek, and the guys playing football on the beach actually stopped playing their game. They lined up and bowed their heads while Katy, Aunt Bonnie, and I spread Tom's ashes. I didn't see this happen because I was not paying attention to what was going on the beach at the time. She thought they stopped until we were done. Pam had made us reservations for that afternoon.

I was not that hungry, but after a tearful goodbye to Tom at the service, it was nice to sit down, chill out, and talk to family I normally do not get to see. We drove to our house in Valpo. I was able to show Aunt Bonnie and Katy our wedding video. Neither Katy nor Aunt Bonnie was able to be at our wedding back in June 1990, so it was nice to be able to show them a fifteen-minute highlight video of the service and reception. Then I took out a video I was really pleased to show everyone. Pam and I had been to a resort in Cozumel, Mexico, in 1994, not long after I learned to SCUBA dive. The video was only about fifteen minutes long, but it was cool to be able to show all of them what I had learned to do. Katy was a SCUBA diver, as well, so we got to share stories about our dives. I said that one of the things on my bucket list was to be able to dive with my sister.

Katy and Mike left first because they had to meet with other family members on Katy's side of the family. We took pictures before everybody left and, for the first time, I now had pictures of me with my sister. For the first time since 1981 when I got to finally meet my sister Katy, I now had a photograph of the two of us together. This turned out to be a way to bring this family of mine together and celebrate the life of my father. What a nice tribute to Tom. It would be a very long fifteen years before I would get the chance to see Katy and Mike again.

From 1996 until 1998, things in my life really started to go bad. I must have been going through depression after Tom's death, and I just wanted to be left alone. In 1998 Pam and I decided to split up and call it quits with our marriage. We had filed for divorce, and then I had to wait for Pam to sign the papers. Pam decided to take a job with *The Orlando Sentinel* newspaper in Orlando, Florida. I did not wish to quit my job in Gary at the time, and I did not want to leave Valparaiso and sell our house. I had a good-paying job for once with good benefits and more. I just was not ready to leave.

Now I think maybe I should have. About a month after Pam left for Orlando, TCI was sold. The new company that took over laid off a number of managers. I was one of those managers that was cut. I was so angry when that happened. First, I thought I had been lied to. My boss told me that when the new company took over a few changes would happen. Was he ever wrong! Second, the guys who come in and make sure you clean out your stuff and make sure you leave without incident treat like you like you are some kind of criminal.

I thought I was going to take a punch at this one Bozo because of his big mouth and unprofessional manner. On at least two occasions, people had to separate the two of us because of the poor choice of words he used. I left work with really high blood pressure that day, and it was not funny. It took several months to get all of the money that was owed me from the payroll department, and it took forever to get the checks delivered to me. My final two checks were supposed to be mailed, and when they never showed up, I received a call from the office manager from my old place in Gary. She told me that the checks had been delivered to her at the Gary office. When I finally got my money, I was done. Companies like that are just terrible, and anyone who has been through a major company layoff knows exactly what I'm talking about.

Now my life felt like a wreck. My father had died, and in 1998, Pam and I split up with the divorce unfinished. I had lost my job, and my life was a wreck. However, in some way, I was kind of lucky. It was only three weeks later when I got a phone call from the chief engineer at a public television station in Merrillville, Indiana. I had dropped off a resume at this station, and I thought it might be the right time to work there. I was interviewed, and the job was offered to me. I was going to work at WYIN-TV-56. It was only a part-time job, but there was a chance it could become a full-time one. I took the job because I needed the income to pay bills.

I had a mortgage and expenses to pay, as well as gas, food, and other everyday things of life. I worked in this job for almost a year. In the spring of 1999, Pam came back to the area and wanted to meet with me about getting back together. After a two-day visit, Pam and I decided to give it one more chance. What it came down to was the fact that neither of us really wanted to get a divorce, and the truth was we really missed each other. Pam invited me down to Orlando to see if I would like to move there. I was curious about Orlando, and I think I was one of the few people who had never been to Walt Disney World.

I took some time off from the television station that I was working at and went to Orlando to see what it was all about. When the week was over, I decided to move there. Pam and I were getting back together, and my life was starting to improve, as well. At the end of June 1999, I moved to Winter Park, Florida, from Valparaiso. With the help of my brother-in-law and sister-in-law, Mike and Susan Mucha, we loaded up a big Ryder moving truck and headed out for Florida. I had put the house up for sale, but it did not sell until later that year. I found a job at a Toyota store in Orlando. I worked at that Toyota store until January 2001, when I got the job at my present employer, Central Florida News 13.

I was working at News 13 in Orlando, and things were going well. I had a job back in television, Pam and I were back together, and we bought a house that we built from the ground up. We were living the dream, so to speak, until I found out that I was going to have to have heart surgery again. I was now thirty-eight years old, and a local cardiologist found an aneurysm on the aorta part of my heart. The aneurysm was eight centimeters in size, and because of its size, I had to be referred to a specialist at Shands Hospital in Gainesville, Florida. The surgeon was Dr. Tomas Martin, a thoracic surgeon. During the consultation, my surgeon, Dr. Martin, told me what was wrong. I asked him if he could fix the problem, and he told me it was fixable. He said very calmly, "Yes, I can fix that."

On August 1, 2002, I was scheduled for open heart surgery, now for the second time. I suppose the worst thing about having heart surgery is being told you have to have heart surgery again. I asked Dr. Martin again during the consultation if he was going to be able to get the aneurysm out of me. He then replied, "Yes, we can fix this issue." Dr. Martin smiled and said, "I do this kind of surgery about one hundred times a year or so."

Right then and there, I knew he was the right man for the job. I went into the hospital on a Tuesday in late July 2002. I was operated on the following Thursday in an operation that took nine and a half hours to complete. I woke up the next morning around 9:00 A.M. I remember waking up and realized the nurses had moved me to another side of the ward. My curtains were closed in front of me, and I could not see a clock. Both of my hands were tied down, for safety reasons, so I started to think. Okay, what is my name? I remembered. Then I asked myself: Where do you live? Then I answered. Then I asked myself: What is my wife's name? I remembered. I looked down at my chest, and by the looks of the bandages, I could tell that I had had the surgery, and it was behind me. I was coming out of it and beginning to comprehend things.

I hit the nurses' call button, and a nurse came in to check on me. The nurse's name was Carol, and she was very nice. Carol came into my room area and pulled away the curtains, so I could see what was going on in the room. I asked her what time it was, and she told me that it was Friday morning about 9:00 A.M. Just then visiting hours began, and Mom made her way in. She waved at me and smiled. I waved back, and she stopped by to wash her hands. Every visitor who came into that ward had to wash their hands first before visiting with patients. Not long after Mom came in, Pam came in and did the same.

She was all smiles, especially since she had seen me when they brought me out of surgery. Pam told me later that what concerned her was how big my neck was and how gray my skin looked after surgery. According to Dr. Martin, this was normal. I recovered from that heart surgery and, after being off work for about three and a half months, I returned to work at News 13. I had lost close to sixty pounds. There was a technical staff meeting going on in the conference room of the station, and as I walked in, somebody yelled, "Mike!" Then, for no reason, everybody in the room got up and gave me a standing ovation for coming back to work. That was a humbling experience.

I remember saying, "You all know that all I did was take the summer off."

I got serious for a moment and said, "I want to take this time to say how thankful I am to be back at work. I want to thank each and every one of you for your support, your prayers, and kind thoughts. It was your kindness and support and phone calls, as well as cards and gifts that kept me going in the hospital and wanting to return to work here at News 13. I really did not expect this kind of welcome back to work."

After returning to work, I never missed a day of work until 2011. That is a pretty good attendance record, if I do say so myself. That is something I am proud of.

CHAPTER 8: I STILL HAVEN'T FOUND WHAT I'VE BEEN LOOKING FOR

Throughout the first seven chapters of my book, I have explained some of the situations and some of the people of my life, from about 1958 until I was born in 1963. I have told you the circumstances from the time I was born in 1963, until the year of 2008. I have talked about the people in my life, including my family and very good friends and the people like my doctors in my life who helped save my life. I have told you my likes and dislikes, and I have told you that I have never seen my birth mother, either in person, or a photograph. I have also talked about my references in life to the films *Back to the Future*: parts one, two and three, and how my life has compared to the professional sports scene in the city of Chicago. I have told you about my victories and my failures. I have even told you about my favorite years in life and what my all-time worst year was. I have told you everything; well, just about everything. The year is now 2010, and this year was a year like no other. I did things in this year that I never, ever thought I would get the chance or opportunity to do. As much as I have failed in life, I never thought I would ever get the chance to redeem myself either. That was, of course, after my biggest failure of my lifetime happened.

There are some people who like to party really hard on certain holidays. Some people do this on New Year's Eve or the Fourth of July. Since I have lived in the state of Florida, I have noticed that the holiday, May 5th, also known as "Cinco de Mayo," is a really popular holiday. I never really celebrated the holiday myself; that is, until the year 2010. I had met some friends of mine from News 13 across the street for a party on that night.

That night, while celebrating the holiday, I felt that there should have been a good reason to celebrate it. A few days later, I got a letter in the mail, and that letter explained my reason of celebrating. The letter was my divorce papers from my wife of almost twenty years, Pam. Pam and I called it quits about a month before, and the divorce papers I received meant that yes, indeed, it was really over. The proof was in the pudding.

What I got in the mail were the final papers that had been signed off by a judge that said the divorce was final. I have talked with a lot of people who have been divorced, and the one most common thing I have found out was that divorce hurts. I suppose it can be compared to being kicked in the teeth, groin, and guts— all at the same time. Divorce hurts that badly. Pam and I have been divorced for several years now and, for me, it still hurts. I even went to therapy and, quite honestly, that did just not work. The only really good thing about divorce, for me, anyway, was the fact that I was free from a loveless marriage. This does not mean I don't care. I do care. But, sometimes, when you make a lot of mistakes, like I did, that is just cause for divorce. I did make a lot of mistakes, and I paid the ultimate price for those mistakes. I was a big loser in the divorce, too. There are things I will never have again because of my divorce, either. Again, that is the price I paid. I can never forgive myself for my failure, and this might be the reason I may not ever want to get married again. It is just that painful.

Pam and I were divorced on May 5th, 2010, and now I had to leave the nice home we had together. I also had to leave my chocolate Labrador retriever, Buddy. I moved out a few weeks later and moved into an apartment with a good friend from work, Bill Coughlin. Bill had a two-bedroom apartment in Altamonte Springs, and he was looking for a roommate to help share expenses. I guess it was perfect timing, and since I had nowhere else to go, I jumped at the opportunity.

Bill and I had worked together at News 13 for a number of years. We are very good friends, and still are. Bill, his then-girlfriend, and I get the chance to do things together, like go out to eat and go to see movies. We sometimes go the casino in Tampa when our schedules allow it. It was not long after I moved in at Bill's apartment that I scraped enough funds for a laptop computer. This computer, even though I did not know it at the time I bought it, would turn out to be the computer that helped me find some answers to my life that I did not know. About the time I bought this laptop computer, Bill had wi-fi installed, as well as a landline phone installed in the apartment.

A few months went by, and I was watching television one night. Bill had moved out after he found his girlfriend, and I got a new roommate. I saw a commercial for a website called My Life. One of the other good things that came out of our divorce was the fact that Pam and I were on speaking terms, and Pam allowed me to stop by from time to time and see our dog, Buddy. But as bad as all things could get with me, things were now starting to change.

In November 2010, I got the chance to go to Valparaiso for the Thanksgiving holiday. In all the fifteen years I have lived in Florida, up to that holiday, I had never had the chance to go home for Thanksgiving. Since I had seniority and vacation time now at News 13, I could now have Thanksgiving and the week of Christmas off from work. Having this luxury was an all-time first. But before I made my holiday plans, a couple of other things started to happen. Thanks to Facebook, my sister, Katy, and my friend, Debbie Watson, were now friends of mine on the social website. I had not heard from Katy in a long time, and I had not seen her since she and her husband Mike had two boys now.

I had thought about Debbie for a long time, and that started after I had heart surgery back in the year 2002.

But the real question in my life right now was: Will I ever find my birth mother? I had just turned forty-seven in 2010, and that was a question that just was lingering to be answered. Again, this person left me at birth, for whatever reason. Every birthday I would wonder if my birth mother remembered it. Every Christmas, every holiday, and even every Mother's Day, I would wonder where my birth mother was. I was getting to the point in my life where this question was just getting the best of me.

The question of where my birth mother was or is was just like sticking a knife in my back that I needed that question to be answered. However, first things first—I had re-connected with Debbie and had the opportunity to chat with her on Facebook. After a couple of chats, I had asked Debbie if I could call her. Debbie responded and said yes, I could call her. Debbie gave me her phone number, and one night after I got home from work, I got the courage to call her. I really had thought that she may still have it in for me after all of these years. Debbie and I had not talked in about twenty-nine years or seen each other, so you could imagine how nervous I was when she answered the phone. I thought if I played it really cool, and just could be myself, I could talk to Debbie.

Debbie picked up the phone after the second ring or so and answered, "Hello."

I then responded and said, "Hello, Debbie, this is Michael Dowd. How have you been?"

Debbie responded and said, "I'm fine, thank you for asking, Mike. How have you been?"

I responded that considering everything I had been through, I was fine. I was not sure exactly how long we talked, but it was sure good to hear her voice again. We were on speaking terms, and I was not afraid to speak to her. I just honestly thought that she may still may have it in for me after everything that happened back at Thomas Jefferson Junior High School. That whole ordeal carried over into high school at Valparaiso High School, and, well, we did not speak to each other until the day we graduated together. That was more than twenty-nine years ago, and I guess we both grew up. Even me.

Debbie had told me that she had gone to Indiana University in Bloomington, Indiana, after high school. She said she stayed there for only one year because she just downright hated it. Then Debbie stated that from college in Bloomington, Indiana, she then went on to a job near Dallas, Texas. From Texas, Debbie said she came back to the state of Indiana, relocating in the Indianapolis area. Debbie said she now lives south of Indianapolis, not far from Bloomington, Indiana. She had told me that she had two teenage boys and that she was working in the accounting field.

I had told Debbie about me, as well. I told her that I was divorced, with no children, and was working in the twenty-four-hour news business here in Orlando, Florida. I told her about my second heart surgery that happened back in 2002. Then, to kind of put some fun into the conversation, I told her how long I had been friends with Bill Frank, Norman Madrilejo, and George Moncilovich. At that time, I guess we had been friends for over thirty-five years. Then I mentioned to Debbie that since she and I knew each other since we were five years old, it was over forty-two years.

Then Debbie said, "Michael, don't remind me."

Then we got a good laugh at what she had said, and I then responded and said, "I love it when you use that tone of voice with me." Then we both laughed again. I really had an enjoyable phone conversation with Debbie that night, and I then mentioned that I would be home for the week of Thanksgiving. I mentioned that I would really like the chance to come down to Indianapolis and buy her lunch, if that was all right. Debbie said that sounded like a good idea, and she said for me to call her when I got to my parents' house in Valparaiso when I got home from Florida. I told Debbie I would call her when I got to Valparaiso, and I was looking forward to our visit. I could not wait to see her.

I arrived at Midway Airport in Chicago the Saturday before Thanksgiving. I had to take the bus from the airport to Portage, Indiana, to get to my parent's house in Valparaiso. My parents picked me up at the bus lot off of Central Avenue in Portage, and they were waiting for me there when my bus arrived. It is always good to see my parents. Since I now live in Florida, I do try to get back to Valparaiso at least twice, and maybe three times a year, if I am lucky. My parents are now in their eighties but still live on their own. I am so lucky to have them in my life even now, even at my age. If there is one thing I have learned about my parents, that they are the same people they have always been. People have said you never really ever stop being a parent, and with my parents, that is so true. I just wish everybody was like them. I truly wish that everybody had parents like mine.

They are just *that* good. After my parents picked me up at the bus lot, the three of us went to a Cicis, a pizza place known for its all-you-can-eat buffet.

Mom, Dad, and I were eating at the restaurant, when I gave them the news that I was going to meet Debbie in Indianapolis for lunch this coming week. My Mom then said, "That's the girl you were in kindergarten with when that male witch came into the room at Banta, and he scared her so badly that she ran out of the room and all the way to her house."

I mentioned this episode to you when I was talking about my school days at Banta Elementary in Valparaiso. That incident happened more than forty years ago, and not only I remember it, my mom remembered it like it was yesterday. I responded and said, "Yes, Mom, that is Debbie."

Since I did not have access to a rental car, my parents said I could use one of their vehicles. I called Debbie the next day, and she told me to call her back on Monday night after 5:00 P.M., so that she could give me the directions to the restaurant that we were going to meet at.

We agreed to meet at a Chili's, located in a strip mall on the northeast side of Indianapolis. Debbie gave me the instructions to get to the place, and on that Tuesday, I drove down that morning from Valparaiso and arrived in Indianapolis late that morning. I had got to the strip mall about a half hour early, and because there was a large grocery store in the strip mall, I decided to go into the store and see if they had a floral shop. The store, called Marsh, had a huge floral department right in the front of the store, just as you walk into the place. There were two ladies working at the floral department, and I had asked one of the ladies for some help.

After looking, I found a floral arrangement that looked really nice. I then had four, red roses added to the arrangement to make it look even nicer. While I was at the cash register paying for the floral arrangement, I had mentioned that the flowers were for a longtime friend I had not seen in twenty-nine years. The lady asked if I could come back to the store after I gave the flowers to Debbie to let her know if Debbie liked the flowers. I said if I had the chance to, I would. I paid for the flowers and left the store.

The restaurant was just across the parking lot from the Marsh store. I drove over to the restaurant and parked the truck. I left the flowers in the truck, until I found the right time to give the flowers to Debbie.

I found an empty bench near the front of the restaurant and sat down. I called Debbie with my cell phone. Debbie answered, and I told her that I was at the restaurant. I was nervous! Debbie told me to wait just about ten minutes or so, and she was on her way over. Now, I was even more nervous! I was wondering what she would think of me because I was not the skinny kid she knew growing up in Valparaiso. I had also lost a lot of hair and was wondering what she would think of that. I was sitting there on that bench, on a cool forty-degree-something day, just waiting. Then I saw a gray car pull up and park. I saw her get out of the car. I stood up and ran over to her. She recognized me, and I said, "I thought that was you."

There we were, hugging each other about right in the middle of the parking lot of the restaurant, and I thought I was in tears. I am surprised we did not hold up any traffic in the parking lot. I just could not begin to think how much frustration had just been released.

Debbie and I had not seen each other in over twenty-nine years. I had always wondered what had happened to her. Here she was, standing right next to me. We moved over to a spot near the bench outside of the restaurant, and we talked. I told her how great she looked and how she still looked the way she did when we last saw each other. We decided to go ahead and eat at the restaurant, and we then went in. We got a booth near a window, and I took my jacket off. I then said, "I have to go to my truck for a minute, I'll leave my jacket here. I'll be right back."

Debbie smiled and said, "Okay."

I then went out to the truck and opened the truck passenger door. I took the flowers I had just bought and locked up the truck. I went back into the restaurant, and since Debbie was sitting at the booth with her back to me when I re-entered the restaurant, she had no idea I had a bouquet of flowers for her. As I brought the flowers to the booth, I said, "These are for you, Debbie. Here is to forty-two years of friendship."

I think that she was really surprised when I gave her the flowers. Debbie then said something that I will always remember: "You know, Mike, it has been a long time since a gentleman has given me flowers."

I thought about that, and I was kind of wondering what she had meant. Then I realized that she was talking about me. I guess that was a good thing.

Debbie and I had a very long talk about things, about what she had been doing all of these years, and what I had been doing all of these twenty-nine years. I had mentioned that I had graduated from Vincennes University after high school. I talked about my career in television and how I was married for almost twenty years. I had mentioned about being certified as a SCUBA diver and had told her about all of the places I had been diving. She had asked me what it was that I liked about SCUBA diving so much. I had mentioned the fact that it had to be the beauty and the marine life that you never know what you may see. I had mentioned about how I now live in Florida and live outside of the Walt Disney World complex. Debbie then told me about what she had been up to for all of these years. She said that had told me that after she left Indiana University, in Bloomington, she had gone to the state of Texas, just outside of Dallas. Then, a few years later, she moved back to Indiana and lived in the Indianapolis area for a while. She had met her husband in Indianapolis, and after they got married and had their two boys, they decided to leave Indianapolis and go to a smaller town outside of Indianapolis. Debbie and her two boys now lived within a forty-five-minute drive to Indianapolis. Debbie had mentioned that she and her husband had split up, and she was now raising her two boys. The oldest was a star basketball player and student at the high school he attended. Her youngest son was a standout student at the same high school. Debbie never told me what broke up her marriage to her husband, but she had told me that they were separated and were not divorced. Then, I let Debbie know the truth to our visit.

After the both of us had finished lunch, it was about that time that I told Debbie how and why we were there at the restaurant. I had started by stating that I had heart surgery about eight years ago. I had then told Debbie that I was at home one day recovering from that heart surgery, and I was watching television at home. I had been channel surfing until I saw a Bee Gees concert on one of those music stations. The group then played, "How do you mend a broken heart?" I then went on to explain to her what that song had meant to me at the time I was watching the program. I said, "That song that they were singing made me think of all of the fortunate things that I had accomplished in life."

I went on to tell her: "It made me think of all of the great things that I had accomplished, like graduating from high school and college. It made me think of the fact that I was a certified diver with over one hundred logged dives, and it reminded me of my passion for the sport of auto racing, especially the Indianapolis 500 that I had attended for so many years. It made me think of all of that and how lucky I was to be alive after this heart surgery and how I had such a great wife, family, and long-time, good friends." After I said all of that, I mentioned how I had failed many things, and parts of my life had not turned out well at all. The part that I really failed at was the friendship that she and I could have had and did not.

I went on to say, "Then, when I got to thinking about what happened to us back in junior high school, I really felt badly. I tried to do a lot of things to get your attention, and none of it worked. You weren't buying any of it. Quite honestly, I don't blame you for it, either."

"Now, I don't want you to feel sorry for me; that is not what I am asking for. But what I am asking for is your forgiveness. I am really sorry for all of the stuff in school that I was responsible for, and I just wanted you to know how sorry I was for all of it. I know this may sound strange, but I think that after I had heart surgery, I realized why I was lucky enough to survive the ordeal. I think that God spared my life so that I could be here today and tell you how sorry I am for all of the mistakes I made with you, and I regret the fact that we could have been good friends."

I told her how much I had wanted to be her friend. I wanted to take her to the Premier Theatre to see a movie and to take her to Southlake Mall to shop. I wanted to take her to Hannon's Drive-in and treat her to lunch in my 1974 Nova I used to own. I even told her that I had wanted to take her to our senior prom.

"I was afraid that because of all of the things that happened to our friendship in junior high school, that I never got the courage to ask you to do any of those things. I guess it was the fear of rejection."

Then, after I confessed my guts out on the table, Debbie said something to me I never thought she would ever say: "I was not a nice person back then, and if there is anybody I owe an apology to, Mike, it is you." After Debbie said that, I was suddenly relieved.

I had apologized to Debbie and spilled my guts all over the place, and here she was, the one giving the apology. I responded and said, "What did you do?"

Debbie responded, "Like I said, I was not a very good person back in the days of junior high school. Those days were not all very fun for me. And I'm the one who owes you an apology."

I thought about what she was saying, and then it hit me that it took a bigger person than me to apologize like that, even though I was the one who came to apologize. I had mentioned about the flowers, and I told Debbie that the reason I gave her those flowers was not only because I wanted to, but I did it as a peace offering. I did not want any more bad thoughts about anything between us. It was time to just bury the thing and go on.

After Debbie and I had finished our conversation, she decided it was time for her to go back to work. I told her to enjoy the flowers, and she said that since she was having Thanksgiving dinner at her house, she would be using the flowers that I had given her as her table centerpiece. I was proud of that because now I had done something nice for her, and she liked it so much that she would use it for such a special occasion.

I took care of the bill and tip, and even though Debbie asked if she could pay for anything, I said, "No, thanks, Debbie. I have this one. It has been an honor and a privilege to take you out to lunch, and this sort of thing does not happen very often."

We then put on our coats and went outside to her car. We talked for another five or ten minutes, and I told her that I would call her when I got back to my parent's house in Valparaiso. I mentioned that I had a wonderful time. Debbie said she did, too, and thanked me again for the lunch and flowers. Debbie said that she was really surprised, and she did not ever expect them. Debbie had to get back to work, and I was going to make a stop at the Indianapolis Motor Speedway before I left town. Debbie and I said our goodbyes and wished each other the very best.

I made one more stop back at the grocery store where I had purchased the flowers for Debbie. One of the two ladies who were working at the floral department happened to be working at the store, and I went in to use the restroom before going to the Indianapolis Motor Speedway. After I came out of the restroom, I had to stop and take my afternoon medicine. Before I left the store, I stopped by and told the lady how much Debbie enjoyed the flowers. I think it was only fitting to go back and tell someone who helped in a big way how much someone enjoyed their hard work to put the arrangement together for a special person. It was just the right thing to do.

I left the store and went down the street and hit Georgetown and took it south to Speedway, Indiana, where the Indianapolis Motor Speedway is located. The weather was still nice, and I had wanted to go there and talk to speedway historian, Mr. Donald Davidson. I had talked to him a couple of times on the phone from Florida. I thought since I was there, I would introduce myself to him and be able to talk to him.

When I got to the speedway, I was told Mr. Davidson's office was upstairs by the photograph department. As it turned out, there were some photos that I had wanted to buy , as well, so after my discussion with Mr. Davidson, I was able to get what I was looking for in a couple of photographs. I had found a couple of photographs of Indy 500 Champion Gill DeFerran I had seen online.

I purchased the photos and left the Speedway. I was in the parking lot of the museum and gift shop at the Indianapolis Motor Speedway thinking about today's events. I was so happy that I was able to patch things up with Debbie. That lunch with her on that cool day in November just really put me in a great mood. Then I got to thinking about what was in store for me now. I just did not know what was going to happen, and little did I realize that the single biggest mystery of my life was about to be answered. I got back to my parents' house in Valparaiso, and I called Debbie one more time to let her know I got back okay. Again, she told me what a nice time she had and thanked me again for lunch and the flowers.

I said, "I want to thank you, too, Debbie, because today being able to have lunch and talk was just an awesome thing for me, as well."

I hung up the phone and realized that I had finally done the one thing that I had wanted to do. Ever since that one day after I was home recovering from heart surgery, I realized I had to make it a point to fix things with Debbie. It was almost as important as finding my birth mother. I never thought of it at the time, but maybe my guardian angel was looking out for me.

Maybe that guardian angel or God or somebody arranged for this to happen. Anyway, I was just glad it was over, and now I could live in peace. Just like the peace offering Debbie and I gave each other at lunch earlier that afternoon. Now, the only way I could really find peace in my life is if I could find the one thing that had been missing all of this time: my life's search for my birth mother.

I got back to Orlando after Thanksgiving and thought I would only be here for a short while because I was going back to Valparaiso for Christmas. What a Christmas this year it would be.

In my lifetime, I have had to deal with the good and the bad. The high times and the low times…and even the *very* low times. Now that I am almost fifty years old, life seems to be nothing but success and failure. In my case, I have a real bad habit of failure. I have had success, too, but as I said, the bad in my life has truly outweighed the good. In the two years or so of therapy, I realize that my failures have happened because of the bad decisions I have made. Sometimes in life, you do learn from your mistakes, and sometimes you even learn from somebody else's mistakes. Life is truly a learning curve, and when you discover things about your own life, and even things you did not know, or know for sure, it can somehow make you humble. This is the case for me. You have heard of the expression, "Ask, and you shall receive." Or even the line, "Be careful what you wish for because you just might get it."

Some of you may say, "Why are you so hard on yourself?"

My response is this: For most of my life, I have been the kind of person who is never pleased or satisfied with what or how good things are. I should be proud of things in my life. I was raised by a very loving family. I have a high school diploma, as well as a college degree. I had a wife who cared very much for me, until I ruined that relationship and marriage. I am a certified SCUBA diver with more than one hundred logged dives. I have survived not one, but two heart operations, and I am still alive to tell you about them. I have had a career in television for almost twenty-five years.

I should just be thankful. Not thankful of my failures, but thankful that I survived all of those things, and I am still here to tell you about them. But, as the story goes, I wanted more. I guess what I wanted was perfection. As wise as I have become, even at the age that I am now, I know this will never happen. That is what I thought. I can honestly say, I never really thought that after looking for so long and running into nothing but dead ends, I never thought I would ever find the answer to my single, most-pressing mystery of my life: the whereabouts of my birth mother. Then, one day in December 2010, the truth paid me a visit. Over a span of nine days that December, a series of events started to take place that really became the journey of my lifetime.

The day was Saturday, December 11, 2010. I was working an extra shift at my job in Orlando, at News 13, because someone had asked for the day off. I was on the 1:00-9:00 P.M. shift, and I think that the time was around 8:30 P.M. I happened to check my personal e-mail and saw that I received an e-mail from mylife.com. I had seen a television commercial for the website, and I thought I would give it a try. Back in 2008, I found a public website in Clark County, Nevada. This website had a section for marriage records. I put in my birth mother's name, and a match came back out dated July 23, 1963. This record named my birth mother named Alexandria L. Jones and John P. Winterbottom.

I remembered what my father (Tom Dowd) had told me several years ago, and that was he thought that my birth mother was already re-married by the time I was born. It turned out, Tom was correct. When I had asked Tom on that visit to New Orleans about who it was she was married to, I remember Tom telling me that this man had an unusual different last name. It was not a common name like Smith, Jones, Johnson, or Williams.

The name had a real funky pronunciation to it. I then realized that this could have been the clue I was looking for. Because of this commercial for mylife.com, I thought this might be the search tool I needed to find my birth mother. I went on the website and paid the small fee to join. The night of December 11, of 2010, there was an e-mail for me from mylife.com. As it turns out, when you do a search for someone on this website, the site search will still continue to look for the person, even if you don't find the person right away. Anyway, this e-mail stated that the site wondered if this was the person. I clicked on this e-mail because I thought that every road was a dead end so far, so I guess that I would look at the e-mail, and maybe it would be the information that I was looking for. For once I was correct. The e-mail had John Winterbottom's name, address and, more importantly, a phone number to call. I figured, what the hell? What is the worst thing that could happen?

With about thirty minutes before I was to leave my shift, I wrote the name and phone number down on a piece of paper and called. The address was somewhere in the State of Utah. The phone call was going to the same place. The phone rang a few times, and then a female voice on the other end answered, "Hello?"

I responded and said, "Hello, is this the Winterbottom residence?"

The friendly voice on the other end said, "Yes, it is."

I knew I had to respond quickly and let this person know who I was and why I was calling. I did not want her to think this was a telemarketing call or a crank call of some kind. I introduced myself to this person. I told her that I was not selling any products, goods, or services. I then had to ask the voice on the phone if John Winterbottom was there. The woman said, "You mean Jack?"

I said that I had his name as John P. Winterbottom. She then replied and said, "His legal name is John Preston Winterbottom, but he goes by the name Jack Winterbottom."

I asked her if Jack was there at the residence. She told me no and wondered if there was something she could help me with. The woman on the phone had identified herself as Jack Winterbottom's current wife. I asked Mrs. Winterbottom if she happened to know if Jack had been once married to a person named Alexandria L. Jones.

Mrs. Winterbottom said, "Yes, that was Jack's first wife."

Then I realized that I might be on to something. Maybe, just maybe, this was the correct path to answering this life-long question.

I mentioned to Mrs. Winterbottom about how I found her phone number on mylife.com and how I found out that she was located in the State of Utah. I wanted to tell her everything up front, so that she did not think I was up to something. I had to be honest with her, so she would be honest with me and be able to help me out. I know it is not polite to lie to people, and I did not want to do it then. I told her that I had been looking for Alexandria for at least twenty-five years or so. I told her that I was the one son Alexandria had when the two of them were married. I also mentioned that I had found a marriage record dating back to July 23, 1963.

We talked about different things for about twenty minutes or so. We kind of got to know each other during that time on the phone. She told me that she and Jack had split up, and he and moved on to Bakersfield, California. They had been married over forty years and would probably soon divorce. I empathized with her because I had gone through a divorce myself. I knew what she was feeling. I knew what the pain was. That pain of failure. She responded that she was doing all right with the situation, and she thanked me for my concern. Because Jack had moved to Bakersfield, I asked her if I could have his phone number. Mrs. Winterbottom said that I really needed to talk to Jack because there was so much to discuss. I agreed. She then gave me Jack's phone number and wished me well. I had asked her if she knew where Alexandria might be, but she really had no idea.

About thirty minutes into the conversation, we were done talking, and I thanked Mrs. Winterbottom for her time and all of the great information.

It was *very* helpful. Mrs. Winterbottom pointed me in the right direction. She was very nice to me on the phone. She was honest, open, and helpful. Besides finding Jack Winterbottom on that website for the marriage record, this was the most information I had about finding Alexandria. Before I hung up the phone with Mrs. Winterbottom, I thanked her for her time, and I wished her a Merry Christmas, as well as a Happy New Year. She wished me well and said she hoped that I would find what I was looking for.

I then hung up the phone in master control where I worked, and about a minute later, my friend, Dennis, walked in to work the overnight shift. It was time for me to leave, but I was too excited. I was nervous. I was happy, but yet cautious. I wondered where this was going. It would only be a few minutes later and I would tell Dennis about my situation. Dennis had come in to work and sat down at the Grass Valley Master Control Switcher we operated and asked, "Mike, are you okay? You look white as a ghost."

I explained the situation to Dennis. I explained how I had been looking for my birth mother for over twenty-five years and was unable to find her. I now had a lead. I could not drive home now. I *had* to make this phone call to Bakersfield. I had to do this *now*.

I asked Dennis if he needed anything from me. It is policy at the station I work at to inform the master control operator getting ready to start the next shift what is going on—like if there are any trucks out or equipment issues. That night there was nothing to report, and after telling Dennis what happened, he said, "Mike, I got this here. If you need to go home and make that phone call to somebody, go ahead and make it."

Dennis was right, that is for sure. I had to make that call if I wanted to know more. I just had to do it. But I could not make that phone call at home. No, I had to call from a private room at work. I told Dennis if he needed me for anything, come down the hall and get me.

Dennis said okay, but I knew he had it under control. So, I went out into the newsroom and went down to the newsroom conference room. Since it was Saturday, nobody would be using it. I walked in and shut the door. I turned on the lights and sat down at the phone in the middle of the conference room table. Before I dialed the phone number, I wondered what I was going to say. I was just hoping that he was not going to think that I was some crank caller and that he would just hang up the phone on me.

After thinking about it for a few, short minutes, I then proceeded to call the number for Jack Winterbottom in Bakersfield, California. The phone rang a couple of times, and then a man answered the phone. I was getting nervous each time that phone rang. All of a sudden, I was talking to a man that was once my stepfather.

The man on the other end of the phone said "Hello." I asked this voice on the other end of the phone if this was Jack Winterbottom. He said, "Yes, it is." I think he was kind of surprised by my phone call. Who would ever expect to get a phone call out of nowhere and be asked about something that happened close to fifty years ago? Something that was personal. Something that maybe no one wants to talk about. Something that had to do with your first wife. I then told Mr. Winterbottom why I was calling.

I remember saying, "Mr. Winterbottom, my name is Michael M. Dowd, and I am calling from Orlando, Florida. I am not a telemarketer, and I am not selling any products, goods, or services. The reason I am calling is because I have been given some information that you may have been once married to a woman named Alexandria L. Jones. If I may ask, is this you?"

A long pause came over the phone, and I thought, *Oh crap, he is going to hang up on me.* Jack did not hang up on me. After the pause was over, he said very softly, "Yes, I was married to a woman of that name."

I asked if he remembered Alexandria giving birth to a son on November 17, 1963, at a hospital called Southern Nevada Memorial Hospital in Las Vegas.

Jack's response was, "Yes, I remember."

I then told him something that really floored him. I said, "Mr. Winterbottom, I have a birth certificate that states I was born to a woman named Alexandria L. Jones, on that day of November in 1963. I have reason to believe that I am that son that Alexandria gave birth to."

Again, there was another long pause. Again, I thought he was going to hang up the phone on me—this time for good. But he did not hang up.

I could tell he was really surprised by my phone call. Once again, he spoke softly and said, "Oh, my gosh, I never thought in all of the years since you were born that someday you would be calling me. This is really a surprise."

We then spoke to each other on the phone and traded information. Jack had told me that he was married to my birth mother for about three and half years. He went on to say that my birth mother wanted to give me up for adoption after I was born. Then he went on to say that according to Nevada law, in order for one to put up a child for adoption, both the mother and father had to sign off on the paperwork. This never happened with me, as I know this was for certain. My father (Tom Dowd) and grandmother (Granny Fran) had claimed me in that hospital, and I would eventually wind up in Valparaiso, Indiana, where I grew up.

Jack told me he knew about this. He said that the day I was born, the Child Services Division of Nevada had already taken me from my birth mother and was now looking for my father. When my father and grandmother claimed me as one of their own, my grandmother was the one who said that she was going to raise me as one of her own.

Jack and I talked on the phone for about forty-five minutes or so. During the last twenty minutes of the conversation I was given the information on my birth mother that I did not know. Jack Winterbottom had told me that Alexandria had two daughters from her first marriage. I asked Jack if he had ever met her two daughters. Jack then responded and said, "No, I never met Alexandria's daughters. When the two of us were married, she had told me that her daughters were killed in a car accident or were lost in a house fire."

He went on to say that he did not know if that was true or not. "Alexandria had a bad habit of not telling the truth, so I really do not know if this really happened or not."

I had heard of this story before from other family members, but this was interesting because now a man who was once married to my birth mother was telling me this same bit of information.

Then Jack said something else that caught my attention. "You know, Michael, I remember talking to a man who had been in the United States Air Force back in the 1960s. Alexandria and I had already divorced and, several years later, I got a call from this man telling me that he had been married to Alexandria, as well. This man told me they had two boys together while they were married and working together in the Air Force. If I have my facts together, not only do you have two sisters, either alive or not, you also have two brothers."

When Jack told me this, now I was the one who was floored with information. After a brief pause on my part, I asked Jack if he had any idea where Alexandria might be. Jack had no idea. He had not seen or heard from Alexandria since the 1960s, when the two of them were divorced. He did not know if she was even still living. Jack would never say anything bad about Alexandria, but he would only tell me things about her when I had asked him.

I had explained to Jack how I had found him through a computer search on mylife.com. I told him the whole truth to my life's story and how it began in Las Vegas; how I was brought to Valparaiso, Indiana, and grew up there. Jack, in return, told me the truth as to what the circumstances were when he had met Alexandria and when I was born.

Then I asked Jack if he had any idea who this man's name was who had been married to Alexandria. Jack then responded with an answer that kind of blew me away. Jack said, "Michael, I just moved here to Bakersfield, and I still have some boxes of things to go through. If I find this envelope with my divorce papers from your mother, I just happened to write this man's name on the envelope of those papers. I don't know why at the time I wrote the name of this man on this envelope, but now, after forty-plus years, I think I now know why I did it. I wrote this man's name and listed his name as husband number three on the envelope of these divorce papers."

I said, "Okay, how long will it take you to find these papers?"

Jack replied and said, "I think I can find them in a few days. When I do, I will call you with this man's name."

We exchanged phone numbers, and I thanked him for his time and for being open, honest, and helpful. He was extraordinarily nice about this whole ordeal. Jack said how nice it was to finally get to meet me some forty-seven years later.

I returned the same line, and we said our good byes. Jack said that he was going to call me and tell me who this man was who had been married to my birth mother. I just found out that I had not one, but *two* brothers. I just could hardly contain myself. I was now part of a family that I don't think anybody other than myself and Alexandria knows about. I wondered, from that point on, just what was in store for me. I found a path to answer my question. Was it the right path? Only God knows for sure. Maybe my guardian angel knows too.

I came back into master control after talking to Jack Winterbottom. Dennis was still there, working, and he asked me if I was all right. I did not know how to answer him, but I said, "Dennis, I think I just might be on the right path to finding my birth mother. I honestly think that I just might be down that long road to finally answering that forty-seven-year-old question."

I said good night to Dennis and went home. When I got home, I changed my clothes and sat down on the couch and turned on the television. I just could not believe what I had found out. I really felt that I should tell my parents. Then I thought, not now, I will be calling them when I make my travel arrangements later this week to go home on Sunday. I wanted to call them, but then I thought, No, I will wait until I make my travel plans for the Christmas holiday. I just could not hardly wait for Jack Winterbottom to call me back.

I would only hope that he did call me. Now, I had to wait all the way until Thursday to find out. What was I going to do from now until then? I had to still go to work from Monday until Friday, and I would not be off on vacation until Saturday. I made my travel plans, and I thought I should call Mom and Dad on Thursday. Why I picked that day, I was not sure, but I knew I had to give them notice when I would be home. That Thursday would be the day it all went down. That Thursday would be the day my questions would be answered. I just did not know it just yet.

Monday, Tuesday, and Wednesday of that week went by quickly. I remember having a conversation with Robin Smythe, the station's general manager at the time. That conversation took place on Tuesday of that week. I had told Robin in that conversation about my whole life story, and now I was on the verge of finding out who my birth mother was. Robin was floored by my story. She told me, "Mike, you need to write a book."

I guess that was the first time a book about this journey was ever suggested to me. I did not give it much thought then, but Robin was right. Maybe when I found out the whereabouts of my birth mother, I could then sit down and write something. But if I was to write a book on all of this, I first had to finish the story. That story was nowhere near finished.

Little did I know that there was a lot more to it. Jack Winterbottom had given me a boost with everything he told me on the phone on Saturday. I still had to find out where this woman was. I still had to find out if she was alive or not. Now that I know that I have brothers and sisters, this mystery of my life just got even more intriguing. Now, all that was left to do was to wait for a phone call from Jack Winterbottom to tell me the name on that envelope. That name on that envelope contained the key that may unlock the answer to my forty-seven-year-old mystery. Now, waiting for a phone call was just a matter of time.

Thursday morning came, and I found myself getting up early because I had to go to an appointment to see my therapist. My therapist was located in Winter Park, Florida, and my appointment was at 11:00 A.M. This was a good time for me because I had to be at work at 1:00 P.M. It took me about twenty minutes or so to get to work from Winter Park, and I got to work early so that

I could grab a bite to eat before my shift started. I was getting therapy before Pam and I got divorced. My counselor, Karen Bogart, had been training and working with me for about two years. I needed so much help after we got divorced. I had no direction. Karen helped me a lot during those years, and she helped me get pointed into a direction that I needed. She had no idea about my background, except for what had happened between Pam and me, which eventually led to our divorce.

Karen had no idea that I was born in Las Vegas and raised by relatives. She knew none of that. I spent about thirty minutes or so explaining how I got to that point in my life. Then I explained who Jack Winterbottom is and how I found him. I told her I may have at least two brothers and two more sisters. I just did not know what to expect. I guess during that therapy session, I was overwhelmed. My therapist listened and calmed me down. I left my therapist's office in downtown Winter Park and started to leave to go to work. As most of you are believers in God, like me, you know God has a way of sorting things out in your life. If you are confused, you pray. If you are unhappy, you pray. If you need guidance, you pray. Sometimes, God works in mysterious ways.

On my drive from downtown Winter Park to work that Thursday, just like that, God showed up. I never really thought about this until later, but being Irish-American, I have always enjoyed the music of the group U2. That group did a song on an album a number of years ago called "The Joshua Tree." The song I have always enjoyed from that album, is called, "I Still Haven't Found What I'm Looking For."

Now, I know this song has a different meaning and is somewhat of a Gospel song, but I find this song ironic to me because when the music video was filmed about the time the song came out in the late 1980s, the video was filmed in Las Vegas on Freemont Street; ironically, just a couple of miles from the location of the hospital where I was born. I was familiar with Freemont Street, and I will never forget that U2 filmed that video there.

On that drive in my car on my way to work on that Thursday, I think that God was trying to give me a message. After all of the talk that I had with Jack Winterbottom and my therapist, and people from work, here I was, sitting at a stoplight in Winter Park. And on the radio, that famous song played. Usually, I sing along, but on this day, it was different. This song had another meaning, and it was meant for me to hear it.

I just sat in my car, waited at the stoplight, and thought about the words to the song: "I have climbed the highest mountain, I have run through the fields, only to be with you, only to be with you...I have run, I have crawled, I have scaled these city walls, these city walls, only to be with you. But I still haven't found what I'm looking for...I have kissed honey lips, felt the healing in her fingertips. It burned like fire, this burning desire, I have spoken with a tongue of angels, I have held the hand of a devil. It was warm in the night, I was cold as a stone, but I still haven't found, what I'm looking for, But I still haven't found what I'm looking for...I believe in the kingdom come, then all the colors will bleed into one, bleed into one, well, yes, I'm still running, You broke the bonds and you loosened the chains, carried the cross, of my shame, of my shame, you know I believed it. But I still have not found what I'm looking for. But I still haven't found what I'm looking for. But I still haven't found what I'm looking for. But I still haven't found what I'm looking for."

Little did I know it would only be a few more hours before it all happened, and this song that I had heard in my car on my way to work had to be a clue or message. This just re-affirms why I believe.

CHAPTER 9: The Name on the Envelope

After I heard that song by U2 on the radio on my way to work from Winter Park, I somehow thought that my answers to my questions just may be answered. That song just had a calming effect on me. I got to work, had my lunch, and started my shift like I always do. Then, it was 9:00 P.M. and time for me to go home. I got home to my apartment, and my roommate was home in his room, watching television. On my way home, I thought I had better call Mom and Dad and tell them about my travel plans for Christmas.

Since it was 9:30 P.M. when I got home, I thought I had better call them first. I had decided that I was not going to tell Mom and Dad about finding Jack Winterbottom. I thought since it was detailed information, I would just explain everything when I got home on Sunday. It is kind of funny, though, because when you keep stuff from your parents, they sometimes know that you are not telling them the information you should be telling them. I guess that they know me way too well. So, when I got home from work and I checked the messages on my voice mail, and I had this message from Jack Winterbottom for me to call him back. I thought about calling him right away, but due to the time difference, I thought I should call my parents and talk to them first.

I called Mom and Dad and gave them my travel itinerary. I explained that I will be getting a rental car and I should be at home in the noon hour. They said that was fine, and they should be at home, waiting for my arrival. They then asked me how I was doing, and I told them I was fine. I just so wanted to tell them about Jack Winterbottom, but then I found myself holding back and saying to myself, *Just explain everything on Sunday when you get home.* I did not want to have them thinking about this until I get home. This kind of conversation was just something you don't have over the phone. I knew I would have to explain everything in due time, but because I was going to be home in three days, I promised myself that I would explain everything on Sunday. Little did I know, I would end up having a two-hour-plus conversation when I got to Valparaiso on Sunday. There was so much to do. Little did I know that most everything was going to be explained to me that Thursday, December 16. I just did not know it just yet. I hung up the phone, thinking maybe I should call back and tell them about Jack Winterbottom. Then I reassured myself I did the right thing. I am glad now I made that decision.

I played Jack's message again and then got his phone number and called him in Bakersfield, California. I had no idea what it was he was going to tell me. I guess I just had to wait and see. I got through on his phone, and he answered in a pleasant voice. I said, "Jack? This is Michael Dowd who called you the other day about Alexandria. I hope I am not calling you at a bad time."

He said no and that it was good to hear from me again. As I said before, he was very pleasant to talk to and anything I asked him, going all the way back forty-seven years, he was happy to answer. I am so glad he was so nice about all of this because he could have just hung up the phone and told me to get lost. But Jack was not like that. Jack is the kind of guy who wanted me to find what it was I was looking for. He knew that I had been looking for Alexandria all of these years, and he knew how frustrated I was about all of it.

Jack also told me about my sisters, who Alexandria claimed died in a house fire or a car accident, depending whom she told. I then heard Jack say something like, "You know, Mike, I had a lot of time to think about some of the things that happened back in Las Vegas. I remember paying for some of Alexandria's medical bills while she was in the hospital delivering you."

I then said in return, "Well, Pops, thanks for picking up the bar tab."

We both got a good laugh, and then the conversation got a lot more serious. I could tell he was just about to ready to tell me what I wanted to know.

Jack spoke with meaning when he said, "Mike, I was able to find those divorce papers from your mother and me. On the outside of the envelope, I have a name written down as husband number three. His name is Leonard Mitchell, and I have reason to believe that he was once in the United States Air Force, like I mentioned before when I spoke to you."

Jack continued to say that when I spoke to him some time ago he told me that he'd said that Leonard had divorced your mother like he had, and Leonard and my mother had two boys born to them. So, I had two more siblings that I didn't know about. "This means you have two brothers you did not know you had." Jack went on to say, "Mike, I hate to be the one to tell you this, but you may be in the middle of all of this because if you find your two brothers, chances are you will find your mother,"

I asked him, "What am I supposed to do with this name that was on this envelope?"

Jack then replied, "Look, Mike, go back to your computer of yours and put this man's name in there, and find this man like you found me."

I had explained to Jack how I found his Utah phone number from mylife.com.

Jack said something else I would remember, as well: "If you find this man, Leonard Mitchell, and he is still alive, you will no doubt find your two brothers, as well." Then he said something that kind of floored me: "I really think that your two brothers are just a few years younger than you are. They are no doubt in their early- to mid-forties, and I think that if you find their father, you will find your brothers. I will almost bet you that those brothers of yours know where your mother is. If she is still around, they will no doubt tell you where she is."

I was kind of skeptical at the time, but the more I thought about what Jack said, the more he made sense. This man, named Leonard Mitchell, could be the father of my two brothers I never knew I had. If I found this man through mylife.com, I just might find these two brothers of mine. If I find these brothers of mine, then I could just maybe find where Alexandria is. The answer to all of my questions was just maybe just one more phone call away. Here it was, just after 10:00 P.M. Eastern time, and I was now on the verge of finding out just what in the hell happened.

I just may be one phone call away from blowing this mystery right out of the sky. That is the kind of thing I find unbelievable. I never thought that on a Thursday night in December I was just about to find the answer to this life-long mystery of mine. Just what do I do now? I thanked Jack for his time and all of the things he did for me. He said, "That's no problem. I'm glad I could have helped. If there is ever anything I could do in the future for you, Mike, just call."

So, I hung up the phone and sat back down on my couch, with my laptop right in front of me. The time was 10:15 P.M. or so, but I did not really care. I was on a huge roll now and felt as though I were on a mission. Kind of like the line from the film, *The Blues Brothers*. I was like on a mission from God. Laugh all you want, but it was that message in my e-mail that started it all after I did that search from mylife.com. I almost never read it. I almost deleted that message because I thought it was going to lead to another dead end in my never-ending search for my birth mother.

What were the chances that message got me Jack Winterbottom's phone number in Utah? I spoke with Jack's soon-to-be ex-wife, and she told me what she knew. She gave me Jack's phone number after I explained who I was and who I was looking for. She was nice and understanding about the whole situation. Then, I got a hold of Jack and explained who I was. I had to explain to Jack that I was the son my birth mother gave birth to in Las Vegas. Jack told me he *was* there when I was born and told me what he could about all of the circumstances involved when I was born. Jack was just blown away when I called him for the first time, and he was so nice to tell me anything I had asked about. Jack also had this envelope with my birth mother's name of her third husband. Jack had this envelope stashed away for almost fifty years, never knowing until now why he wrote the name of husband number three on the outside envelope of the divorce papers. It amazes me to this day the way these events fell together across five decades. What would be the chances? I mean, really, what would be the chances of writing a name on an envelope for what you think is no apparent reason, and then almost fifty years later some guy calls and says that he is the son of your wife that was born on that Sunday in November 1963? That kind of reminds me of one of my favorite films, *Field of Dreams.* It was kind of like that scene where Kevin Costner's character steps back in time to find Oliver "Moonlight" Graham. When Kevin Costner's character asks Burt Lancaster's character if that was his nickname when he played baseball for the New York Giants, he never knew why he would be asked that question almost fifty years later why he gave up the sport of baseball and became a doctor. I also find that some of the themes of that film have some similarities to my story. The phrase, "If you build it, he will come" comes a little bit later on in this chapter. Then there is the phrase, "Ease his pain," and the third phrase, "Go the distance." All three of those phrases from that film have a meaning to me with my search. It is just so ironic.

The time is now about 10:30 P.M., and I was on my computer, trying to find some more information. Before I did a search for Leonard Mitchell, I was thinking about what Jack Winterbottom had just said. Jack seemed to think that I was just days, if not hours, away from finding out the answer to my long awaited question: Where is my birth mother? Like I had just mentioned, I was on a mission from God, and a mission it was. I pulled up the name for Leonard Mitchell, and mylife.com gives me two possibilities. There was one in the Rockford, Illinois, area, and another one somewhere in the State of Pennsylvania. I think it was Brookvale. I had never heard of that town, but I had been to the state of Pennsylvania a few times.

As it turned out, I had been to the Pittsburgh area when I was about a year and a half old, before Granny Fran passed away, and I had been there a second time, just before my grandfather passed away. Both times I was there was to see Uncle Chuck and Aunt Joanne, and my cousins, Curt and Christy. Then there were two other times I had been to Johnstown and Franklin, Pennsylvania, to visit my friend George's family when we were in college. Then, when George and Lori got married in Johnstown, I was a groomsman in their wedding, so Pam and I went to Pennsylvania to be there. Other than that, I never really spent much time in that state.

That all changes when you find out you have family there. I was looking for Leonard's name, and when I clicked on his name in the State of Pennsylvania, I clicked on possible relatives. There were two, possible connections: a man named Leonard Mitchell Jr., and Michael L. Mitchell.

Their ages listed kind of gave it away. They were both listed in their early-to mid-forties, just like Jack Winterbottom had pointed out. So, now, the question is: Who do I call? At that time, I did not pay attention as to what time it was, and I had to make a phone call and I had to make one now. So, just for kicks and giggles, I clicked on the name marked on the mylife.com search. That name I selected was Michael L. Mitchell. Why I chose that name I really do not know, but I am guessing that since it was the same first name as mine, I thought it would be ideal. Ideal it was, and then I called the phone number listed. I just never knew it would be pay dirt.

I dialed the phone number, even though I had no idea what time it was. The phone rang, and after a few rings, a young woman answered the phone and said, "Hello?"

I responded and asked if this was the Mitchell residence. The woman said, "Yes, it is." "May I help you?" I asked if Michael Mitchell was there, and the woman's voice said, "Yes, just one moment."

It seemed like a few minutes, but a few seconds later, a young man's voice got on the phone, identifying himself as Michael Mitchell.

I then responded by saying that I was sorry for calling so late, and this friendly voice says, "That's no problem; around here we get phone calls at all times of the day and night."

Then he says, "What can I help you with?"

"My name is Michael Dowd, and I live in the Orlando, Florida area. I am not in the telemarketing business, and I am not selling any products, goods, or services." I then asked this young man if someone by the name of Leonard Mitchell was his father. He said Leonard Mitchell was his father. Then I asked him if his dad had been in the United States Air Force a number of years ago.

The friendly voice responded and said, "Yes, that is my dad. Are you looking for my dad?"

I said, "Not really, no." I told him that I was looking for a woman this man named Leonard Mitchell had once been married to. I told this man on the phone that I was and had been looking for Alexandria for many years. Then, when I mentioned that name, he said, "Yes, that is my mom."

I then went on and said, "I am calling to find out where Alexandria L. Jones might be, as I have been looking for her for over twenty-five years or so."

That's when I mentioned that I told him that Alexandria was involved with my father, Thomas Dowd, and she gave birth to me in Las Vegas, Nevada, in November 1963. After introducing myself to him, he then said, "I guess I'll introduce myself to you, then; my name is Michael Mitchell."

I responded to him and said, "It is very nice to meet you, Michael." Then I had the task of telling Michael the truth. I said, "Michael, I hate to be the one person to tell you this, but we may be brothers." I explained to Michael that I was born in 1963, and my birth mother had been married to a man named Jack Winterbottom. "As it turns out, Alexandria gave birth to me in Las Vegas and left me in that hospital. It was only two days later that my grandmother and father picked me up from that hospital, and I was eventually taken and raised in Valparaiso, Indiana.

"That is where I grew up, went to school, from kindergarten through high school. I went on from high school and went on to college at Vincennes University and majored in Radio and Television Broadcasting. After college I came back to Valparaiso, Indiana, and worked in the field of small time radio, and then went on to work in television news which is what I do for a career now." I could tell Michael was really interested in my story, and I could tell he knew I wanted to know more about our birth mother. Most importantly, where she was or now is.

After finding out that Michael and I were possibly half-brothers, Michael told me about the rest of the siblings in our family. He spoke about another brother, Leonard Junior. He told me that we have a younger sister named Jackie, and then he tells me that not too long ago, he found out that there are two more sisters named Nancy and Natalie that are the oldest in the family.

If Michael's calculations are correct, I could be the missing link in all of this. Michael seemed to think that he had been told there might be other children to the family. He thought there might be another sister named Jennifer. Michael had mentioned that Alexandria's mother and step-father had told him that and there might be others. Michael just had no idea it was a brother instead of a sister.

Then I asked Michael the most important question of all: Where is our mother? I said to Michael, "Please, tell me where Alexandria is. I have to know. I have to know if she is dead or alive, and I need to know where she lives. I really need to know where my birth mother is now."

In the short time that I had been talking to my now confirmed brother, I think Michael understood how frustrated I had been. I did not know it at the time, but he was frustrated, too. My brother would tell me later on in our conversation about how he might have thought he could have been a brother to somebody he did know since he was a teenager.

Michael was frustrated with all of the information he was finding out. The fact that it had only been a few months since our sister, Natalie, had found Michael, Leonard, and our little sister, Jackie. Now there was me, another brother to the mysterious family that he had been born into. Finally, Michael responded to my request. "I know this has to be frustrating for all of these years, Mike, but Alexandria lives here in Brookvale, Pennsylvania." My brother went on to say, "Alexandria lives outside of town in the country, and lives by herself, as she is not married at the time."

Finally, I found out the information I had been looking for all these years. I then responded with relief. "Holy shit, I just found her, my missing birth mother who I had been looking for all of twenty-five years or longer. I want you to know, Michael, that I had just found the answer to a forty-seven-year-old mystery."

I felt badly when I found out that my brother is a minister at a local church, just outside of Brookvale. I really felt embarrassed. I'm not sure if he got a laugh out of that line of mine or not. It was a relief to both of us now that he and I knew the truth as about what had been going on for all of these years. Michael told me that he and our brother, Leonard, had been born in Alabama while his father, Leonard Senior, was in the United States Air Force. Leonard Senior and Alexandria had been married for a number of years, then got divorced.

Before they got divorced, another girl was born into the family, and that was our youngest sister, Jackie. The family lived in the State of Michigan for a while, and then when Leonard got out of the Air Force, the two of them divorced, and Leonard went back to farm in Pennsylvania. Alexandria got the boys and youngest daughter in the divorce, but the boys eventually went to Pennsylvania to live with their father. That is where the boys grew up, and that is where they all call home.

Michael and I talked on the phone for about three hours that night. Michael had told me that our youngest sister, Jackie, still lived in Michigan, just outside of Detroit. Michael told me about our brother, Leonard Junior, who drove a semi-truck. That was a career that I wanted, all the way back to my teenage years. In fact, one of the things I have always wanted to do is drive a Kenworth. The funny thing was about me being a truck driver was that my father (Thomas Dowd) or my grandfather did not want me to be in that line of work. The both of them seemed to have my career all carved out. First, with a college education, which was fine, but then be some sort of big-shot executive like Uncle Chuck. Yeah, right.

If I had known better, I would have said no to college and gone straight to truck driving school. It seemed like a cool thing, though, having a brother as a truck driver because I know with all the stories he must have to share with me about his adventures. The other cool thing was there would be an endless conversation about different brands of trucks; in particular, my favorite, Kenworth.

The conversation with my brother, Michael, continued on, and then I had asked him what kind of work he was involved in. He had told me that he was a non-denominational Christian minister. I never knew I would have a truck driving brother, as well as a brother who is a man of the cloth. Michael had told me that he went to a private school in the state of Virginia and got his degree in the ministry, and he and his family had come back to Brookvale, Pennsylvania, when he was offered a job as the lead minister at a small Christian church nearby.

Michael told me about his own family: his wife, who he knew for many years in Brookvale, and his daughters and his son. He mentioned that our brother, Leonard, had kids, as well as several grandchildren. Not only did I now realize that I had found my birth mother, Alexandria, but I now found out that I am part of a rather large family, as well. I have three sisters, as well as two, younger brothers. Now, for the first time in my life, I just may have it figured out. I figured out a forty-seven-year-long, life-altering mystery of my life. I'm no genius, but I must say, figuring this all out, I feel like a detective who just solved a major investigation. Kind of like *Magnum, P.I.*, but without the Ferrari automobile Tom Selleck got to drive.

Before Michael and I hung up the phone, I had asked my brother if he was on Facebook. Michael said that he was on Facebook, and then I opened up my computer and went to the main page to look for him. I did not have a lot of pictures of myself on my page, but there was one from a friend's going away party that I had put on it. That was going to have to do until I could post more on it.

I found Michael's page and friended him. He friended me back, and I then saw his picture for the first time. It was stunning because the two of us looked very much alike. I was floored! Michael said that he was over six feet tall and mentioned that he was a certain weight. I had told Michael that I was over six feet tall and weighed about the same. He was in his early forties. I was in my late forties. By the looks in his face, you could tell Michael and I were brothers.

As we got closer to the end of our marathon phone call, and the shock of it all, with all of the information about us and our family, as well as our birth mother, Alexandria, Michael gave me our brother Leonard's phone number and said he wanted me to call him. I told him I did not think it was a good time to call him now because it was three in the morning, and I would not want to upset him by calling him at that hour. Michael said that Leonard had a truck driving job that required him to work over night from the hours of 6:00 P.M. to 6:00 A.M.

Michael gave me his phone number and said he would tell Leonard he'd given it to me. The last thing Michael and I did was then say a prayer. We were both happy to find each other and find out that we are brothers. We now needed to pray. That was just the right thing to do. After our prayer, we said our good byes, and I had mentioned that I may call him soon, like the next day or so.

Michael then said that was okay, and if I had any questions to call and ask him. Michael also asked if he could send an e-mail to our sisters, Natalie and

Jackie, and tell them the good news. I responded that he could do that, and it would be wonderful to talk to our sisters in all of this. But, before I did, I had to talk to Leonard first. I hung up the phone with Michael and just kind of sat there on my couch and tried to soak in all in. I could not believe to think how far this had come together in just a week. This all had started with an e-mail and a phone call to Utah. Most of all of the attention had now shifted to the states of Michigan, Arkansas, and Pennsylvania. I now had two sisters in Arkansas, two brothers in Pennsylvania, and my youngest sister in Michigan. Then there is me in the state of Florida. I just sat there on my couch and thought to myself, I wonder where this is going? Is there more? Are there more children that we don't know about? What about Alexandria? Now that she has been found, will she admit to what happened with my father some forty-seven years ago, as well as to what happened with Jack Winterbottom? Only the Good Lord would know for sure. I just did not want to get my hopes up. After thinking about this, I thought I should call Leonard and explain everything to him.

I got back on the phone, and I called the number for Leonard that Michael had given me. I was thinking that maybe I should wait until later on in the day to call him, but taking Michael's advice, I went ahead and made the call. Leonard answered the phone and said, "Hello?" I explained who I was and why I was calling. I had explained to Leonard that I had been looking for Alexandria for over twenty-five years, and she left me in a hospital in Las Vegas. I told Leonard the whole story about me and how I never knew who Alexandria was until now. Leonard replied by saying, "I think I speak for our family, Michael, when I say welcome to the family."

Leonard had this deep, raspy voice like mine. If he had not been a truck driver, I would have thought he would have been a radio disk jockey. He thought I may have worked in radio, as well. Leonard got a kick out of it when I told him that I had worked in radio a long time ago but no longer did that kind of work. I spoke to Leonard on the phone for about an hour about different things. He mentioned that he was a water truck driver for all of this work in the mountains where they have been drilling for natural gas. He explained to me how the system worked and what his role was by delivering the water to the drill. It was fun talking to my brother, Leonard, about the trucking business.

I also told him that he had the kind of career that I always wanted. I had told him that Kenworth was my favorite brand name of truck and that was because of two television shows that featured Kenworth trucks. Those two shows were: *Movin' On*, a show on NBC that ran back in the 1970s, and during the 1980s, there was a show called *BJ and the Bear*. That show ran on NBC, as well. Leonard had told me that he had watched those shows, as well, and that it was those television shows and some other people he knew that inspired him to become a truck driver. It was sometime later when I was talking to my brother, Michael, and he would tell me that when Leonard was a teenager, he got to ride along with a friend of his who owned his own semi-truck and took him across the country. I thought to myself, I would never get the chance to do something like that. I know people who are truck drivers, as well, and when I was thinking about this, I would have never been allowed to ride along in a semi-truck. First, I would have never stopped talking about it, and I know that being able to do that would just be a wish. I guess that would have to go on the bucket list, as well, and that would be to learn how to drive a semi-truck…Preferably a Kenworth, W-900 conventional, kind of like what Sonny Pruitt drove in the television show, *Movin' On*.

Anyway, while talking to Leonard, I kind of got the feeling that Leonard and Alexandria did not see eye to eye on a number of things. My brother told me that it was very tough growing up around her when he and Michael and Jackie were younger. Leonard did not go into specifics, but he mentioned that he just did not trust her and did not believe anything she ever said.

Leonard said, "Mike, I kind of have to tell you, I have not seen her in a long time. I can't get too specific, but I will tell you that it has been rough, even as an adult, to have Alexandria as a mother. Alexandria and I are not on speaking terms right now. Our relationship has gone right down the toilet, for a number of reasons."

Leonard then continued, "To tell you the honest truth, Mike, not really anybody in our family is really on speaking terms with Alexandria right now. I guess our brother Michael still sees her from time to time, and so does our dad, Leonard Sr., but from our family, that is pretty much it."

Somehow I saw a wild and nasty pattern of behavior here. According to my brother, Leonard, Alexandria has got so bad to deal with that not a lot of our family will speak to her. Michael kind of told me that same thing when I spoke to him during that three-hour marathon phone call. Michael really did not say anything bad, but Leonard really told it like it was. Anyway, I figured that I would have to deal with that when the time came.

I was still on the phone with Leonard when I asked him if he was on Facebook. Leonard said no he was not, at the time, because he is so busy with his job, as well as his wife and family. It was great talking to Leonard, just like it was great talking to my brother, Michael. I looked forward to talking to my sisters at some point. I just did not know how I was going to present myself. I didn't know how this whole thing was going to play out, but now at least two of my five siblings I now know.

I knew where Alexandria was and that she was alive. She is alive, and now I had the chance to meet her. I now know that I am part of a six-child family. I am the oldest brother in the family. Now, I feel like I have more responsibility. Maybe now I can live at peace with myself. Again, I just have to be careful as what I wish for because what I wish for just may come true.

Before I hung up the phone with my brother, Leonard, I was able to get his phone number, and we exchanged e-mail addresses. Since Leonard was not on Facebook, the only way at the time I would be able to talk to Leonard him was either by phone, e-mail, or in-person. Leonard asked me when I was going to make it up to Pennsylvania for a visit. I said I did not know at the time, but maybe after the first of the year. Leonard said, "That's cool; I'll be looking forward to it."

After our conversation, I hung up the phone, and I had this feeling like I had never had before. I was tired, but I was not ready to go to sleep. I had one more day of work, and then I would be off for Christmas vacation. What a Christmas this would be. What a way to ring in the New Year. I went to bed about four in the morning. It would only be a few hours later that I would wake up.

I guess it was 8:00 or 9:00 A.M. when I woke up that Friday. I just could not fall back to sleep. I was just too excited. That Friday was going to be a very busy day, and I still had to go to work. I had one more work day before it was vacation time and for me to pack, go to Orlando International Airport, and get on a plane and go home to Valparaiso.

I could not wait. Then I thought about calling Mom and Dad again. Then I found myself talking myself out of calling them. I just could not tell them something like this over the phone. I was going to be home in two days, and I would tell them when I got home. I thought it would just make pure sense to do that. I opened my computer again and looked again at Michael's family picture. I could not believe it when I found out he is my brother. Now I have two brothers. What a feeling, and to think I now have three sisters, too! The next morning, when I looked on my Facebook page, I then realized that I had two friend requests. One was from my sister, Natalie, in Arkansas, and the other was from my sister, Jackie, in Michigan. I accepted their friendship requests and then started looking at their pictures. My older sister, Natalie, kind of did the same kind of work I did. We started to chat on Facebook, then Natalie gave me her phone number to call, so we could talk in person.

This feeling I had was kind of like when I spoke to my sister, Katy, for the first time. I was nervous but intent on explaining my situation. Natalie and I started the conversation by saying, "It's nice to meet you, Mike." She went on to say, "You know, when our brother, Michael, told me that we had another sibling in the family, I was kind of hoping you would be a girl."

I replied, "Well, I am sorry to disappoint you, but I think I just leveled the playing field in this family."

We both got a laugh out of that line of mine, but the conversation got serious really quickly. I had told Natalie my story how I found Alexandria. Since Natalie's dad was married to Alexandria, she and our sister, Nancy, grew up in Chicago. Natalie talked about all of the Bears, White Sox, Bulls, and Blackhawk games that they had gone to. I had mentioned that I had my first heart surgery at Children's Memorial Hospital in Chicago. I mentioned about all of the Chicago auto shows I had been to, as well as museums and sporting events.

I know Chicago is a huge city, but what would have been the chances of bumping into my sisters in Chicago? But then I thought about the possibility, and they were pretty much less than zero. It was a long time ago, I remember my mom, as well as my grandfather, telling me that I had two sisters die in a house fire or a car accident and, to their knowledge, they no longer existed. I then thought that if my Granny Fran was told this, along with my grandfather, there would have been no reason for a search. Alexandria had told people this, so that if and when she had other children, nobody would ever think to look. There would be no names to look for, and unless I would have known what was Alexandria's first husband's name was, there would be no foundation for a search. Natalie had told me that her parents had moved from the Chicago area to Arkansas after Natalie went to college at the University of Arkansas. Natalie told me that Alexandria may have told people that story because after Natalie's father and Alexandria had split up and were divorcing, Natalie's father had told Alexandria that he was going to get custody of his daughters instead of Alexandria. Natalie's father had found out that Alexandria had been cheating on him, possibly with my father (Tom Dowd), and because of that, he was going to see to it that he would not let Alexandria raise his daughters by herself. Natalie said that Alexandria must have agreed to it, so I am guessing that when Alexandria and my father started their fling, she told everybody about the loss of her daughters. The truth was, Alexandria's daughters were alive and well and living in the city of Chicago. Not even my Grandparents knew that. Not even my father knew that. Not even my mom and dad knew that. No one in my Valparaiso family knew anything about this. Because of what everybody was told, there was no reason for any kind of a search. Who would have known? I guess if somebody had hired a private investigator, maybe we would have known what the truth was. I guess that was not an option, either. I had asked Natalie if she was like me and wanted to confront Alexandria.

Natalie explained to me how she found Alexandria. After I had explained how I had been looking for Alexandria for all of these years and how I found her, it suddenly occurred to me that she would have been looking for Alexandria a lot longer than I had. Natalie had said that after her father remarried, her father and Alexandria were married in a Catholic church. This was the second time I had heard that Alexandria was Catholic. Michael had mentioned it on the phone the night before. But Natalie went on to explain that since the rules of the church have changed dramatically over the years, Natalie's father and stepmother had tried to get their marriage blessed, so that they could take communion.

In order for you to get your marriage blessed, you have to have your former or previous marriage annulled. Years ago, back in the 1960s and 1970s, and well into the 1980s, the rules of the Catholic Church have been changed over the years, and so Natalie's parent's put the plan in motion to go through with the annulment. In order for the annulment to happen, the Church had to find Alexandria and have her sign the papers. The Church found Alexandria, and Natalie eventually found Alexandria, too. So, now, Natalie knew where Alexandria was and, like me, she had questions. I mentioned to Natalie that we may never ever know the real truth.

According to our brothers, Leonard and Michael, Alexandria was not talking, and she was so good at covering things up that she may never believe that we were her children. I had a feeling that Alexandria was in denial about all of us. Natalie and I talked for about forty-five minutes or so.

The more and more I talked to Natalie about our family situation, the more and more we realized that Alexandria lied to us in hopes that we would never find each other. It is kind of amazing when you think about it because I found Alexandria's third husband's name on an envelope. Natalie had (along with her older sister, Nancy) found Alexandria during a search for her father's signature on annulment papers.

Like I said before: Who would have known? I asked Natalie again if she wanted to see Alexandria and confront her like I did. Natalie told me she wanted answers, but at the time, did not want to upset other family members doing it. Natalie thought at some point, like later this summer, she and her husband, Charles, and our sister, Nancy, and possibly would drive up from Arkansas and be able to visit and meet our family. Natalie had spoken with Leonard, Michael, and Jackie, and now with me. But, like me, she had never met any of the family.

I wrapped up the phone call with Natalie because she had to go to a sales meeting. Natalie sold ad time for the local cable television system. I had told Natalie what I did and worked in the same business. I told her that I was the one that played those commercials on the air at the television station I worked at in Master Control. Natalie and I exchanged phone numbers and e-mail, and then we hung up the phone. I was getting kind of tired now, so I needed to go back to sleep for a couple of hours. I must have been tired, so I set my alarm on my clock radio and went to sleep. I woke up a couple of hours later when my alarm clock alarm went off and got ready for work. This was my last day of work before Christmas vacation, so I was ready to get this day started and finished. I made it through work and finished and got home around my usual time at 9:30 P.M. I would have all day on Saturday to get ready, and then I would leave early Sunday morning.

That Saturday morning, I had slept a little longer than the previous two nights. I had another message on my voicemail, and this time, it was from my newly found sister, Jackie. She had called for me sometime Saturday morning, and I needed to return her call. I had her phone number from my brother, Michael, and picked up the phone and called the number. The phone rang a couple of times, and then a girl's voice answered. I asked the voice on the phone if it was Jackie I was talking to. She said yes it was. I told Jackie that I was Michael Dowd from Florida. I told her that we were possibly brother and sister.

As it turned out, Michael and Jackie had an extensive conversation on the phone before she called me. I kind of expected her call because we had already found each other on Facebook. Jackie was excited to speak to me because she was so surprised she had another brother. Jackie, like me, had no idea about any of this and had no clue until recently that there were more family members. Alexandria had lied to Jackie, as well. Jackie grew up like I did, never knowing anything of this because Alexandria had kept it all a secret.

It was just like sweeping it under a rug, or something, and never revealing anything to anybody. Alexandria only said things that were not true. I believe Alexandria did that because she did not want people to figure it all out, like I did. Like Natalie did, too. It all kind of blew up like a giant volcano, with the ashes and damage that landed right back on Alexandria's lap and shoulders.

Like Jack Winterbottom had told me, it was easier for Alexandria to lie than tell the truth. Alexandria did this, so she would never thought she would get caught. I talked about me being a liar for many years. It started as a bad habit, and then, like Alexandria, it was just easier to lie than to tell the truth. It is no wonder my parents hardly ever believed me when I was a teenager. I was so full of shit that it did not matter if it was the truth. Whether it was the truth or not, my parents and former wife had no reason to believe me.

I am sure there are others, too. I mentioned when you run your mouth and keep adding to the cause, it just makes you look stupid. Now that I realize that I had been lied to my whole life, I wonder how much of anything that Alexandria says is the truth. As I got the chance to meet my family members, I would find out more things that would be questionable. I suppose I could go by the theory that Alexandria deserves the opportunity to tell her side of the story. I would welcome that chance any time of the day or night. I would love to take my television interviewing skills and just grill the crap out of her just like the late Mike Wallace used to do on the show *60 Minutes*. It is too bad he is not still alive because if I knew the man, I would have asked the best interviewer I know to talk to Alexandria and grill the shit out her. Put Alexandria on the hot seat. Turn those hot television lights on and see her sweat. Then you know if she is telling the truth or not.

The more and more I spoke with my sister, Jackie, the more she told me about our family. Jackie told me about her son, James. I got to speak to him on the phone and found him to be a really cool nephew. He was into a lot of things: karate, video games, and girls. That is all normal, and I was looking forward to the chance to meet both Jackie and James. Jackie asked me what part of Indiana I was from. After explaining that I was from Valparaiso and that I was going home to Indiana for Christmas, Jackie asked me if I had ever been to the Four Winds Casino in New Buffalo, Michigan. Jackie mentioned that she knew the place well and had been there before. I had mentioned I had been to that casino before, as well. Jackie said that she was living in the suburbs of Detroit and that she could meet me there during the week of Christmas when I was home with my parents in Valparaiso. I mentioned that it was just a few minutes to New Buffalo from my parent's house in Valparaiso.

Jackie said, "You know, Mike, with us only being a short drive apart, we could meet at the casino, maybe for an afternoon, and finally meet each other."

I replied and said, "That sounds like a good idea, Jackie. Maybe you could bring pictures of Alexandria and other family members, so that I can see what everybody looks like in our family."

Jackie agreed and said that I was to call her when I got to my parents' house in Valparaiso, then we could make plans. I told Jackie that I would have to explain to my parents about this whole ordeal, and I would have to explain the situation right when I got home. Jackie and I said our goodbyes, and then we hung up the phone. I was excited. I was thrilled. I was gradually solving this mystery of mine. All of the theories, some of the questions, and maybe just some of the answers I had been looking for a lifetime, were now being answered.

Now, the thought suddenly occurred to me. How was I going to tell Mom and Dad? I had so many things to do, so I thought I would think it out while I am packing and getting ready. Then I thought of something else. How do I tell Sharon? Susan? Katy? My friends like Bill, Norman, and George? How about my friend, Tim King? I had known Tim for over twenty-five years, going all the way back to one of my first jobs in radio. I had to find a way to tell him. Tim and his father had taken me to my first Indianapolis 500 back in 1986, and that was how I fell into that sport. I think I have been to the Indianapolis 500 many times now. I would have gone to more, but that was when I moved to Central Florida.

I had laundry to do before I packed my bags for my trip. After I did my laundry, I packed my bags and I was then ready for my trip. It was Saturday afternoon, and I was going to be leaving in the early morning, so that I could get to Mom and Dad's house by the noon hour. I was getting nervous because I had no idea what I was going to tell them. So, I thought I would call Tim King and let him know what was going on. If anybody would understand this situation, it would be Tim. I looked up his phone number and got him on the phone at home. I told him about me leaving in the morning, but I had something else I had to tell him. I went on and said, "Tim, I think I have told you about some of my life's situations that have been going on for a long time. I just wanted you to know that my birth mother has been found."

I heard a long silence on the other end. Then Tim asked me, "Oh, my gosh, how did you do that?" I then told Tim the whole story.

Then I mentioned that not only I had found my birth mother, but it turns out that I have five siblings that I did not know of either. Then, Tim says, " You have to be joking?"

I told Tim I was not kidding around. This had been my discovery, and he was one of the first persons I had told. I asked him not to mention it yet, as I have not told my family members about it.

Tim said, "Mike, no problem. I'll keep it quiet until further notice."

I said thanks and that I would have to explain this story to my parents. Tim wished me the best of luck, and then we wished each other a good holiday season. I hung up the phone with Tim and then I thought right then and there I needed to call my sister Katy. I had to just tell her. Over the almost thirty years since I found her and saw her for the first time, Katy knew about my birth mother. Katy knew that Alexandria had left me at birth and that I was brought from Las Vegas to Valparaiso and grew up there. She knew I had been looking for Alexandria, as well. Katy knew my story, and she knew it well. I decided right then and there that it was only fair that I call my sister and tell her the news.

I had Katy's cell phone number and, since it Saturday night, I had no idea what she might be doing. I dialed the number and, after a ring or two, Katy picked up. Katy said, "Hello?"

I then said, "Katy, this is your brother, Mike, in Florida. How are you doing?"

After exchanging our hellos, I asked Katy what she was doing. Katy said she was at a mall in Virginia doing Christmas shopping for her family. Then, I dropped the big one on her. I said, "Katy, you remember all of the times you and I talked about finding my birth mother? Well, she has now been found."

Again, like with the conversation with my friend, Tim King, there was a brief silence and then a reply.

Katy, surprised by my news, said, "Oh, my gosh, how did you find out?"

I then proceeded to tell her the whole story, how I found Jack Winterbottom, and how Jack led me to my brother, Michael. I told her about Nancy, Natalie, Michael, Leonard, and Jackie and how I now had five additional siblings I never knew I had. I told Katy about all of the nieces and nephews I now had, as well as great-nieces and great-nephews. Plain and simple, I told Katy that I had just hit the jackpot with the whereabouts of my birth mother, Alexandria. Katy was surprised, and she had no idea of what I had found out. After I had explained to Katy about how this all happened, Katy said, "Michael, this has the story of a well-written book."

I said that it was either a book or an episode of *Oprah* or *Jerry Springer*. Katy got a good laugh out of that line, and we talked for more than forty-five minutes or so. Katy had to get going, though, because she had to finish her shopping. My sister's work schedule did not allow her to have a lot of time for shopping, so she had to make the best out of it. She said she wanted me to keep her informed as to what I was going to do, as far as going to Pennsylvania or whatever I wanted to do. Katy was interested in my findings, and she only wished me the best. She wanted me to stay in touch and keep her informed on what was next with me. I told her I would, and I would call her when I found out more information. I had thought about it and then I realized that I had not seen Katy or her husband in about fourteen years or so. Since then she and her husband had two boys and was raising them. I guess I had just lost track of time. The last time I had seen my sister was way back in 1996 when we had Tom's memorial service.

They had come out for the weekend, and we did it right up with a special dinner, service at the Indiana Dunes State Park, and another after service dinner at Strongbow's. I'll never forget that weekend and being how I did not get to see Katy or her family very often, I could remember those times vividly. I hung up the phone with Katy, and now I was tired. I had to set my alarm early because I had to be at the airport to be on a flight to Chicago's Midway Airport. I was flying home for Christmas, and after I got home, what a Christmas this was going to be. Before I went to bed, I remembered something that I had posted on Facebook earlier in the week. I had mentioned that I was in the "process of solving a forty-seven-year-old mystery."

Just before I went to bed that night, my sister, Susan, was wanting to chat on-line. Susan wrote, "What is this post you mentioned on Facebook. Did you find family or something?"

I had told Susan that I had found family, but I could not explain it until I told Mom and Dad first. I told her that I was going home early Sunday afternoon and that I would explain it to them and to everyone. I then went on to chat: "I know you like to talk to Mom and Dad on Sunday nights. That is fine, but could you call about two hours later than you usually do, so I can have the time to explain everything?" I asked Susan to call after 9:00 P.M., then I should have everything explained to them by then.

Susan said, "Okay, but 9:00 P.M. is the cutoff because I have to get up and go to school the next morning." I said that should work, and I told Susan that I would explain things in about twenty-four hours or so. For once I am glad I spoke to her and told Susan that. I signed my computer off and then put everything away. I now had everything ready to go on my Christmas vacation, and all I had to do was wake up early and get showered, dressed, and get my things in the car and take off to the airport. I had to catch a plane early.

CHAPTER 10: THE TALK

I woke up about four-thirty in the morning on that Sunday, and when my alarm went off, I woke up and stayed up because I did not want to take the chance of falling back to sleep. I could not miss my flight because I had to get home. I had to get to my parents' house and do some serious explaining before my sister Susan chimed in.

I got showered, shaved, and dressed and then packed my few, remaining things. I had to make sure I had my printed boarding pass, my luggage, my keys, and some other stuff that I was taking with me. I really did not have any Christmas gifts for anybody yet, as I figured I would have the time to do my shopping when I got home. I was slated to be in Valparaiso for about ten days, and that should give me the break I needed. These last nine days have been interesting, to say the least, and I was just really nervous about the whole thing. I grabbed both of my pieces of luggage and locked the door behind me. My roommate was going to be staying in the apartment while I was gone, so I knew the place was going to be not completely vacant. I was just really in a hurry to get home.

I put my bags in the trunk and then started my car and headed toward Orlando International Airport. From where my apartment was, I lived about a forty-five-minute drive with lights and traffic from it. I got to the airport and parked my car in the long-term parking lot. I locked up my car, then I got my bags out, closed the trunk, and headed over to the bus stop and the terminal. Even as routine as air travel is for me, I am always edgy about traveling. I got on the shuttle bus, and I was on my way to the terminal to get on my Southwest Airline flight to Chicago. I got dropped off by the sky-cap service and took my bags and went into the terminal for check-in. There was a long line to get checked in, but I did not have to stay in line very long because I had already had a boarding pass printed. I got up to the counter, checked my one bag, and now I was ready to go through the security area. After a brief wait to get cleared, I got into the secured area and got everything checked and made it through. I got on the people mover and I was now on my way to my gate. A few minutes later, I arrived at my gate with my flight showing that it was on-time, so I thought then there would be no delays. My flight was at 8:30 A.M., and I was at my gate about forty-five minutes early. I would normally get something to eat before I board my flight, but I was just too nervous to eat. I thought again about how I was going to tell Mom and Dad about these last nine days. I drew a blank. Before long they called my boarding zone, and I got in line, gave the gate attendant my boarding pass, and walked down the jetport to my airplane that would take me to Midway Airport in Chicago.

I got on board and was welcomed by the flight crew then, since it was open seating, I went to the back of the plane and found an empty window seat. Before I gave it any more thought, the flight door closed, and we pushed back from the gate. The flight attendants gave their pre-flight instructions, and then we took off for Chicago. If there is one thing I like about flying, it gives me time to think. At that point on my way home, I needed time to think. I had to come up with a way to explain just what has happened these last nine days and then explain that we might go to New Buffalo, Michigan, to the Four Winds Casino and meet my newly found sister, Jackie. I think that Mom and Dad were in for a bit of a surprise when I get home, and now I was on my way there.

Again, during my two-hour flight, I thought about what I was going to say. Then, for some unknown reason, it finally hit me: I finally figured out what I would tell my parents. They knew that I had been looking for my birth mother for a long time. That was no secret. They both knew I wanted answers to my questions, so I could be at peace with myself. I somehow knew that Mom and Dad would understand what I had done and why I went to the extreme detail to find Alexandria. It just made sense. I had a feeling they would understand me and support me, no matter what the cause, and they would understand that it was my cause that was the benefit.

My flight landed a little early in Chicago, and now I had to get off the plane, walk down and get my luggage, and hit the rent-a-car-counter and leave for Valparaiso. I got off the plane, and I remember walking past the statues of Jake and Elwood Blues in the concourse that had a store for the House of Blues. That is kind of a welcome home thing when I get to that airport.

I passed the statues and walked down past the secured entrance and then down the escalator to the first floor to get to the luggage carousels. I found the carousel that had my flight number on it, and then, a few minutes later, my bag came out and I picked it up. The Hertz-rent-a-car counter was nearby, so I went over to the counter and got my car. I wound up getting a Toyota Yaris, so it was good on gas. That Toyota Yaris turned out to be a fun little car. Not only was it good on gas but it was a great handling car around the Chicago area. I put my bags in the rental car from the garage and then took off. I was now on the last link of traveling to Valparaiso. On my way home, I thought about it some more. I knew I would have to tell my parents everything, and tell them from start to finish. I had to just explain it all. I took the Indiana toll road home from Chicago, and it took me about an hour to get to my parents' house. I pulled in the driveway and parked my car. I took my bags out and made my way into the house. I arrived home on time, during the noon hour, like I had planned, but I had no idea what Mom and Dad's plans were. When I had arrived, I must have awakened Mom anyway because she had been taking her daily afternoon nap. I thought I could tell them right away about the whole thing, but now was not going to be the time. Later, I thought…it would just have to be later.

I was hungry when I got home, and Dad said go ahead a fix a sandwich or something that was in the refrigerator. So, I opened up the door, pulled out some lunchmeat and fixings, and made myself lunch. They had cottage cheese and potato salad in there, too, so I grabbed that and some milk to drink. I was kind of hungry, so I think I ate two sandwiches. After a filling lunch, I was getting kind of tired from the trip. I was not ready for a nap, either, so I watched some professional football on television. My Chicago Bears were not playing until Monday night, so there were other teams on television. So, because it was the NFL, I watched whatever game was on. About 3:00 P.M. or so, Mom and Dad woke from their nap and said that they had to go to Chesterton and pick up a poinsettia plant that had been given to them from my cousins, Judy and Harvey Blomburg from Minnesota. I suggested that we take my rental car up to Chesterton and leave the driving up to me. Mom and Dad had no objection, so off we went. Before we left the house, Dad suggested that we go see Mary Ellen up in the nursing home in Chesterton since we would be right there. Then I thought I just might be cutting this thing kind of close. The time was now 3:30 P.M., and I had about five hours or so to tell Mom and Dad.

I kept thinking to myself, *I have to tell them.* Then, I would think, and then say to myself, *Not now, just wait for the right time.* I got on the bypass and drove up to Chesterton. We had to go to some floral and gift shop to pick up the poinsettia plant. It turned out that this store was quite the place. It was right on Calumet Avenue in Chesterton, which is the main street through town. The store had two levels with a candy shop, and since it was the Christmas season, they had all kinds of Christmas stuff, too. Downstairs was the flower pick-up counter, and since we were in no hurry, I decided to do a little shopping. I found something to buy, and while Mom and Dad were in line to get their plant, I made my purchase. Then, just about the time I was done with my purchase, I met Mom and Dad with their new poinsettia. It was all wrapped up, so we took our things and left. I got everybody in the car and then we left for the nursing home to see Mary Ellen. Since the nursing home was just a mile or two away, it did not take very long to get to the place. I had been to the nursing home once before with Mom and Dad when I was home for the Thanksgiving holiday. I dropped Mom and Dad off at the front of the building and then parked the car. I then made my way to the front door and rang the buzzer, so that I could be let in. I walked in and walked down to Mary Ellen's room. It was always good to see my cousin, Mary Ellen. Mary Ellen had been married and used to live in the area in nearby Porter. Her husband, Larry

Miller, died just a few years before, and some of Mary Ellen's family still lived in the area. Larry and Mary Ellen had four kids: two daughters and two sons. The oldest son, Tom Miller, was in the National Guard and had been sent to Iraq on three tours of duty. The youngest son, Jim, was just a little younger than me, and he and I had been buddies for a long time. Mary Ellen's oldest daughter was about the same age as my sister, Sharon, and Mary Ellen's youngest daughter was about the age of my sister, Susan. It was always good to talk to Mary Ellen. She mentioned that she was going to her oldest daughter's house for Christmas and then be back at the nursing home later that night. Mom had told Mary Ellen that we were going over to Sharon's house for dinner and gift exchange on Christmas Day, like we usually did. We had a nice visit and left the nursing home about an hour later, after Dad had tried to talk May Ellen into going with us to dinner.

Mary Ellen had said she really was not hungry and did not care to go. So, we said our goodbyes and left. On the way back home, we stopped, and Dad bought dinner at the Dairy Queen in Chesterton. That place is a favorite of my family's, so it only made sense to go there. We went in, ordered our food, ate it, and went home. The time was now close to 6:00 P.M., and I had to tell Mom and Dad now, before Susan called and spoiled the whole thing. I drove us home and helped Mom out of the car. Then, the three of us went in and got comfortable. We all took our coats off and put them in the closet. I had kept a winter coat and Mom and Dad's house because I really did not need it in Florida. It was nice to leave my coat at their house, so I did not have to take it back and forth, and it would always be there when I got home. I hung up my coat, went into the bedroom, and took out the paper. That morning, on my flight home, I thought I should make a chart and put everything on paper to help explain things.

While Mom and Dad were napping that afternoon, I took a piece of paper and charted everything out, so I could explain where all of my sibling came from. I came back out from my bedroom with the paper and went to sit down at the table in the kitchen. When Mom and Dad and I played cards, we all kind of had our seats. I took mine where I usually sit. Then I saw Mom and Dad in the kitchen and said, "If you don't mind, I need to see you both here at the kitchen table." Mom and Dad looked at each other with a puzzled look on their face, and I thought what they might be thinking: *Oh, God, what happened now?*

Mom had already gone into the living room and turned on the light and television to watch *Wheel of Fortune*. Dad said he had to check his medicine, so he would be a few minutes. I suggested to Mom that she might want to shut off the television and lamp in the living room and come into the kitchen. I said, "We might be in here for a while."

Mom had shut everything off in the living room and sat down at the kitchen table like I had asked. We were waiting on Dad to finish, and a few minutes later, he came into the kitchen and pulled up his chair. I had the paper in front me turned over because I did not want them to see it just yet. After Dad took his seat, I just kind of sat there, and it was almost like a moment of silence. It was kind of like one of those awkward pauses they have in television sitcoms. Mom was the first one to speak, and she said, "What is on your mind, Michael?"

I said, "I really don't know how to explain this, and I really don't know how to begin to tell you this either, so I guess the best way to explain this whole thing is to tell you everything from the start and to tell you what I know. Over the last nine days or so, there have been a series of events that have taken place, and it has really changed my life in a very big way."

Mom quickly asked if I was in trouble or anything. I reassured her that I was in no trouble. "This conversation is not about anything like that. What this conversation is about, well, is something completely different."

Mom and Dad looked at each other again with another puzzled look. I then went on to explain: "I think it is fair to say and is really no secret that the two of you know that I have been looking for my birth mother for a very long time. I think I have been looking for her for about twenty-five, maybe twenty-six years or longer, I am not sure. But whatever the case is, I have reason to believe that my birth mother has now been found."

Dad was quick to ask, "How did you find her?"

"I quickly replied, "I will answer that and tell you everything I know." I had mentioned that it was kind of a long and short version answer to that question. Then I said, "The short version is this search for my birth mother all started with an e-mail and a phone call to Utah."

Mom and Dad again looked at each other and I went on and said, "But before I go on an tell you how I found my birth mother, Alexandria, there is something else you should know first. In my search for my birth mother, Alexandria, it has been brought to my attention that I now have five siblings that I did not know that I had."

Dad said, "Oh, my gosh!"

I said, "Yes, I know, somebody's Christmas list just got a heck of a lot bigger."

Dad or Mom really did not laugh at my response but found my findings very surprising. They both knew that I had been after the answers to my questions for a long time. I can't think of all of the conversations I had with my parents over the years about the subject of my birth mother. Since no one ever knew much about that part of my story, it was up to me to finish the story. I knew that it was up to me to finish and answer my own questions. It was up to me to find Alexandria, it was up to me to find my siblings, and it was up to me to find some, if not all, the answers as to why it had to be this way and just what were the circumstances that led to my life as I know it. It would only be another month or so that I would get some of those answers, but it was the series of events that took place over the last nine days that led me to finding the location of Alexandria, as well as my sisters and brothers. I found out that I now had five other siblings, and there was a huge story there. Where did we all come from? What were the circumstances? More importantly, why have I been lied to my whole life about this? I would find out about the answer to some of those questions later, but for now, I had to finish telling my parents the story.

I sure did have their undivided attention at this point. Just as bad as I knew I had to tell them, they wanted to hear how all of how this happened. I then continued to explain what I had found out: "I suppose this story goes back all the way to when my grandparents and when Tom was still alive. My grandfather and Tom really did not give me a lot of information about my birth mother, Alexandria, but it seems that it was enough to go on. I can remember when I was the age of fifteen or so, and my grandfather and I had a talk before he passed away about Alexandria. I never really took what he told me very seriously because, at the time, I was not really looking for Alexandria at that point in my life either. However, it seems that the information that Tom gave me was much more valuable. You both remember all of those trips I made to New Orleans back in the 1980s and 1990s? It seemed that just about every time I would go to New Orleans, Tom and I would have at least one conversation about Alexandria. Tom had no pictures of her. But, one time after several other past discussions, I remember being at his apartment in the French Quarter, and I remember Tom telling me about how the two of them had split up for whatever reason. Tom did not even know Alexandria was pregnant with me when they broke up. Tom said he never knew he had a son until his mother happened to be in Las Vegas when the hospital called and said that he needed to come and pick up his son from the hospital. Tom had told me my arrival into the world was a complete surprise. Tom, for the longest time, had thought my birthday was November 19, instead of November 17 because it was two days later after I was born when he and my Granny Fran came to get me. Then, I guess it was sometime after that when I was brought to Valparaiso, Indiana, and everything happened after that. Tom had even mentioned that during that time that after I was born and before I came to Valparaiso, I was looked after by a very nice Mormon family that lived out by Lake Mead. Tom had mentioned that this family lived in Boulder City, Nevada, which is a mostly Mormon community. I was told this area of Nevada was the only place in the state will you not find any places that serve alcohol, nor are there any casinos or gambling of any kind. Tom had told me that this family had wanted to adopt me, as well, but he put an end to that. Then, I came to Valparaiso, had my first heart surgery, and grew up and went to school. But it was that one visit to visit Tom that kind of changed things. Tom had mentioned that he thought that by the time I was born, my birth mother had already remarried. I had asked Tom if he knew the name of the man who was married to Alexandria, and he said he could not remember. But, Tom did say that this man had a funky-sounding name. Tom had said that this man did not have a common name like Smith, Jones, Johnson or Williams. Tom had remembered that this man had a very different last name. Then, you know, Tom passed away, and it was then about 2008 when I got a little more savvy with the internet, I was searching a free and public website from the State of Nevada. This site had a section on it that had marriage records. These marriage records were for all of Las Vegas, which included all of Clark County. All you had to do is put in a name, and if there was a match, the match would come up with both names on the marriage record, the day, month and the year it took place. So I typed in Alexandria's name. The website came up with a match, dated July 23, 1963, to my birth mother and a man named John P. Winterbottom.

"Then, after I found this man's name on this marriage record, I thought maybe if I could find this man, maybe I could find the whereabouts of my birth mother, Alexandria. I guess it was about sometime in 2010 when I heard about this website called mylife.com. I saw a television commercial about it and I then checked it out. I had to pay a small fee to get to use all of its features, but I thought, if I could find this man named John Winterbottom, maybe, just maybe, I could find my birth mother.

"So, I joined the website, paid the small membership fee, and started looking. I typed in the name John P. Winterbottom. As I recall, I really did not get very much in return to look at, but then I realized that when you type in a name into a search on this website, the search function will continue to look at the name, and the website will send you an e-mail when it finds the name you are looking for.

"One week ago last Saturday, I was at work and was checking my e-mails toward the end of my shift. It was then I had received an email from Mylife.com, and it said something like is this the John P. Winterbottom I was looking for. Since it caught my attention, I thought to myself, out of all of the years I had been looking for my birth mother, is this just another route down the road to nowhere. So, I thought, what the hell? Nothing else worked, so I might as well as check it out. So, I clicked on the e-mail, and it gave me a Utah address and phone number. Then I thought, what the hell? I might as well call the number because if I did not try, I would never know if it was the right path or not. So, I called the number, and a woman answered the phone. I asked if this was the Winterbottom residence I was calling and the voice said that it was. I then told the woman's voice who I was and that I was not a telemarketer and was not selling anything over the phone. I had also told her that I was calling from Orlando, Florida, and I then asked if John P. Winterbottom was there. The woman's voice then asked me if I was looking for Jack Winterbottom. I mentioned that I had his name as John P. Winterbottom, and the woman's voice said that John P. Winterbottom was his legal name and that he went by the name of Jack. I guess it was back in the 1960s or so that some men who went by the name of John also took the name of Jack. I did not really knew that then, but then I remembered that President John F. Kennedy also went by the name of Jack Kennedy."

"So, the woman went on and told me that she was Jack's present wife and asked why I was calling. I told this woman who was Jack's wife that I had information that Jack might have been married to a woman named Alexandria L. Jones. The phone went quiet, and I thought she was going to hang up on me. But then this woman said that Alexandria was Jack's first wife, some forty-plus years ago. Then it hit me that I had hit the right path. I now had something to go on."

"My conversation with Jack's wife then continued. I asked Jack's wife if she was ever told that Alexandria was pregnant with another man's child when the two of them got married in Las Vegas in July 1963. The woman said she could not remember, but then I said that I was the child that she gave birth to in Las Vegas after she and Jack had been married. I told this woman that I had been looking for Alexandria since she gave birth to me, and I thought that I was now on the right path. I went on to speak to this woman for about twenty minutes or so, and she told me that I needed to speak to Jack, and he might be able to tell me more about Alexandria since he was married to her. This nice woman had told me more information in a twenty-minute phone call that what I ever knew about my birth mother. This woman was very nice, open, and honest about what she had told me and that she wished me well in finding what it was I was looking for. She gave me Jack's phone number and had mentioned that Jack had moved on to Bakersfield, California, and that the two of them were no doubt getting divorced at some point. I had mentioned that I had been divorced earlier that year, so I knew what she was going through. Again, she wished me well, and I hung up the phone. Before we hung up the phone, she had given me Jack's phone number. About that time, it was the end of my shift, and when my relief came into work, I then went to the news conference room to call Jack Winterbottom."

"So, I got to the news conference room and made the phone call I needed to make to Jack Winterbottom. I remember the phone ringing, and a man's voice answered the phone. I asked him if this was Jack Winterbottom I was on the phone with. He said that yes, it was. I then told him my name was Michael Dowd and that I was calling from Orlando, Florida, and that I was not a telemarketer, and that I was not selling any products, goods, or services. I then said that I was given some information that you might have been once married to a woman about forty-seven years ago named Alexandria L. Jones. I had asked Jack if I had the right person, and he admitted to me that, yes, he was once married to a woman of that name. I asked him if he remembered the fact that she gave birth to a son in Las Vegas. He mentioned that he remembered he witnessed a birth that she gave to a son, not long after they got married. Then, I said that I had reason to believe that I was the son that she gave birth to. I told him that I had a birth certificate that stated Alexandria was the birth mother and that my birth took place at Southern Nevada Memorial Hospital. I told my parents about how I thought that there were several times during that life-changing phone call to Jack Winterbottom that I thought he was going to hang up the phone on me. I know Jack must have been floored by my phone call. It was a huge surprise to him, as well as me. I mean, here it was, just about twenty minutes or so after I spoke to his wife in Utah, that I have the man on the phone who was married to my mother when I was born. He told me he witnessed my birth and nobody had ever told me this before in my lifetime. It is no wonder he was floored by my phone call. Those long pauses in between conversations must have been shocking to him, and the reason he was shocked by all of this was because he never saw this phone call coming. I guess nobody thought that on one Saturday afternoon that he would get a phone call, be asked about his first wife, and then be told that the son she gave birth to forty-seven years ago was on the phone to speak to him."

I went on and told my parents that I had asked Jack if he knew where Alexandria was. "Jack had then told me that he and Alexandria had been divorced about three and a half years later after they were married in July 1963. Jack had no idea where Alexandria was or even if she was still alive. But then Jack started to talk about this conversation he had with a man who had been married to Alexandria several years later after Jack and Alexandria had been divorced. Jack went on to tell me about this phone call he got out one day from this man who was in the United States Air Force and had told Jack that the two of them had two sons together. Jack said to me that he thought now I had two brothers I did not know about. I had mentioned to Jack about how I had found him. I mentioned that I had found him from that website that had his name on the marriage record with Alexandria's name, and that I had found him through social media, mainly mylife.com. Then Jack mentioned something about two daughters Alexandria had but had been told that they had either died in a house fire or were killed in a car accident. I told Jack that I had heard that but was unclear what the situation was. Jack said that these were two sisters you had, and that you now have two brothers you did not know you had either. Jack knew something did not add up. Jack knew that I was in the middle of all of this and he was sorry he could not be of more help. Jack knew I wanted answers to some of my questions, but he knew he did not know all of the answers. Jack had told me everything he could, and he was open, honest, and helpful. Jack was extremely nice about the whole situation, and that if there was anything else he could do, I was told to just ask."

"Jack and I said our goodbyes, and we had each other's phone numbers, so we could call if we wanted to. Jack said I could call him anytime I wanted. I told Jack the same thing in return. I went on and told my parents that on that Thursday night, after I had spoken to them and told them what my travel plans were, that I had a phone call to make to Bakersfield, California, that Jack had called me back, and I had to find out what information he had for me."

I mentioned to my parents that I wanted to tell them about finding Jack Winterbottom, but I could not tell them because I was coming home in a few days, and I decided that I would tell them everything then. I'm kind of glad I did, because it was that phone call I found out who that name on the envelope was and who my two brothers are. My parents seemed to understand, but my story went on.

I then told my parents about the phone call I made that Thursday night. I told my parents, "I made the phone call and that Jack had told me that the man's name on that envelope was named Leonard Mitchell. I then said goodbye to Jack on the phone and went back to my computer and mylife.com and put in the name of my birth mother's third husband's name."

I told my parents about the two matches I had found on the website, and then how I looked at the name of the person in Pennsylvania and that match looked more promising. I then mentioned that on the column, I found what appeared to be my brothers' names, and I researched those names and figured out that those names in that list of relatives of Leonard Mitchell might just be my two brothers that Jack Winterbottom had mentioned.

My parents listened intently as I told them the entire story of how I had arrived at this moment, where I now had the name and location of my birth mother, as well as names and locations of my five, new half-siblings. It was such a relief to tell them. All my built-up anxiety about how best to have this conversation was over.

Then I had the task of telling my parents about the phone call I made to my brother, Michael. I had told them the whole story about how I called at ten-thirty at night and did not realize that I was calling that late. I then explained the story from there. "I called the number that I got from the website, and a woman had answered the phone. The woman who answered was very nice, and I had asked her if this was the Mitchell residence, and she replied and said that it was the residence I was calling. Then I asked if Michael Mitchell was there, and she said the he was there and if I could wait just a moment. Then a young man's voice came on to the phone and after exchanging greetings and telling him who I was and I was sorry for calling so late, he said that it was no problem, and that he gets phone calls at all time of the day or night. I then went on and asked if his father's name was Leonard Mitchell. Michael said that it was his father. I then asked if his father had been in the United States Air Force back in the 1960s or so during the Vietnam conflict. Michael said that yes, it was his father who had been in the Air Force for about thirteen years. Michael then asked me if I was looking for his father, and I replied and well no, not really, but sort of.

"I went on to tell Michael that I was looking for a woman named Alexandria L. Jones. Michael said in a very soft voice that the name Alexandria L. Jones was his Mother's name. I said to Michael that I had a birth certificate that had Alexandria's name listed as my birth mother on it. I explained that I was born Las Vegas, Nevada, and that my father's name was Thomas Dowd. I told Michael that my father was from Northwest Indiana and had met Alexandria at a bar in either Hammond, Indiana, or Lansing, Illinois, back in the early part of 1963. Then the two of them created me and left for Las Vegas because my father was going to work at a casino there as an accountant."

"After Alexandria and my father broke up, Alexandria was introduced to a man named Jack Winterbottom, and the two of them got married in Las Vegas on July 23, 1963, I was then born later that year in Las Vegas at Southern Nevada Memorial Hospital. Alexandria tried to give me up for adoption, but in the State of Nevada, you have to have both signatures on a document to allow that to happen. Alexandria told Jack Winterbottom that she was not going to take me with her. Alexandria left me in that hospital in Las Vegas and, about two days later, my grandmother and my father were tracked down, and they came to get me at the hospital and took me home. I guess it was about a year later that because of my health issues, and my father could not take care of me anymore, so Grandmother came back to Las Vegas and picked me up and took me to be raised with her and my grandfather in Valparaiso, Indiana. I am now forty-seven years old, and I have been looking for Alexandria for a very long time; maybe twenty-five or twenty-six years."

I then went on and told my parents more about this conversation with my brother. "My brother had told me that Alexandria was still living and was taking up residence in Brookvale, Pennsylvania, and that there were other family members to tell me about. Michael had told me that there was him and our brother, Leonard Mitchell, Jr., and our youngest sister, Jackie. Then Michael told me something else I had no idea about: He told me that just a few months before I called him and told him who I was, he got a phone call from one of Alexandria's oldest daughters. It was a phone call from our sister, Natalie, from Arkansas, telling Michael that Alexandria was her birth mother, as well. She told Michael that she has an older sister, Nancy, and that she was

Alexandria's oldest daughter. I told Michael that these must be the sisters that Jack Winterbottom and my parents had told me about, but I was told that these two sisters had died in a car accident or a house fire. Michael thought about it for a moment and told me that he was not surprised that Alexandria might have told people that, and Michael said that she has a track record of not telling the truth. Michael said that she might have said those things about our sisters because the fact was, she lost custody of her daughters in her divorce from her first husband. So, in Alexandria's eyes, they were both dead, and having said that, nobody would have looked for them until recently. Michael went on to explain that Alexandria and her first husband were married in a Catholic church, and when they were divorced, sometime later, Alexandria's first husband, or Nancy and Natalie's father remarried but their marraige was never recognized by the Church because the first marriage was never annulled. It was not until recently that the marriage was finally annulled and because of this situation, that is how we found our sisters, Nancy and Natalie."

"Michael had told me that Alexandria's late mother and late stepfather had told him years ago that Michael and his brother Leonard and sister Jackie that Alexandria may have more children, but like my family, had no idea who they were or where they might be. Since I was the one who found the rest of the family, these questions had been answered."

I told my parents that I was on the phone with my brother for about three and a half hours that Thursday night. I told my parents that my brother and I found each other on Facebook and friended each other, so that we could see each other's picture of each other. I also said to my parents that because of social media like mylife.com and Facebook, that by the next morning, I had friend requests from my sisters, Natalie and Jackie. I then told my parents that by Friday and Saturday, I had spoken with both of my sisters and they told me how I might be able to meet my sister Jackie at the Four Winds Casino in New Buffalo, Michigan, later on in the week. I told them that I wanted them to go with me and meet Jackie, as well, because I might need their support.

I finished and told my parents about the rest of the conversation I had with my brother, Michael, and how I spoke to my brother, Leonard, for the first time. I told Mom and Dad that Leonard had the job I always wanted and that he had driven a semi-truck for a living and was truck crazy like I was. My parents smiled, and my conversation went on about my newfound family.

I then turned the paper over to the side that showed them the paper I had written on, so they could see, and then I showed them how I charted out everybody from my family and who they were and how they were related to me. I had told them then about how I made up the chart while they were napping after I got home that afternoon. The chart had all six kids on it, our ages, and that all of had the same birth mother. After showing my parents the chart that I had drawn up, I then said something else that they did not know. I told them that this is our family as I know it now, but there could be one more, we are not sure.

"Michael had told me on the phone that Thursday night that he was told that there was another daughter, Jennifer. We had a sister named Jackie, who was the youngest in our family, but between the time after I was born and before the time that Alexandria had met her third husband, there was time to have another daughter. This was something both Michael and I figured out, and that it was a distinct possibility. We still do not know if this is real or if it is not real, but we would have to look into the matter further."

I had spent about two hours with Mom and Dad, telling them and explaining how I had found all of this out. I had asked Dad if he had a road atlas close by, and he went into a spare bedroom and got one. I then opened the atlas to Pennsylvania and showed them where everybody was. I then told Mom and Dad that I had kind of mentioned the story to Susan by way of Facebook and that she had asked me if I had found family or something. I told her that I had found some things out, but I said that I had not told the both of you anything yet and that I would explain everything tonight before she called. Well, it was about 9:30 P.M. on that Sunday night before Christmas, and just about five minutes later, the phone rang.

It was Susan on the phone. I had just told my parents everything I knew, just in the nick of time. I got to talk to Susan that night, and I told her everything, as well. Susan had told me that she had to write everything down on paper, so that she could remember how it all happened. I told Susan that we would be meeting my sister Jackie later on in the week, just as soon as we could get everything arranged. Susan was amazed by my story, and wished me well. Susan and my parents asked me when I would be going to see my brothers in up in Pennsylvania and maybe see my birth mother. Then I told Susan I did not know for sure, but I would try to get up to Brookvale, Pennsylvania, possibly in January.

I told Susan that I would talk to her on Christmas since she and her family were not coming to Indiana for the holiday. Susan, her husband Bill, and teenage daughter, Jessica, were staying at home in Swainsboro, Georgia, for the Christmas holiday. Susan wished me the best and asked me to make sure I told her about meeting my sister, Jackie, and to have fun with our family for Christmas. I said goodbye to Susan on the phone, and I would not talk to her again for another few days until Christmas arrived.

After my parents hung up the phone with Susan, it was then I had mentioned about how I felt about finding my family. I told Mom and Dad that I had no idea until now just how powerful the internet is; in particular, social media, and I also stated that if I had died as a result of that aneurism that I had about nine years before, I would have never found this out. I could have gone to my grave, never knowing who my family was and knowing where my birth mother was. God had spared my life for a reason; not just once, but twice, and I believe that.

Mom and Dad agreed with me on that, and the big conversation I was to have with my parents was now over. Then my mom had asked me if I knew about Jack Winterbottom before I called them on Thursday. I said yes, I did, and then Mom said something like she knew I had something to tell them; she could just tell by the tone of my voice. It was then I thought to myself that my parents know me better than I think.

CHAPTER 11: SAFE TRAVELS

The next day I was up in the morning, just a little while before my parents went to exercise class. I decided to have a bowl of cereal before I showered, and I figured that I would have to do some Christmas shopping and make some phone calls. I was talking to my parents again when the phone rang, and it was my sister, Sharon, on the phone. Sharon and Mom were talking about the menu for our Christmas family dinner. Then I heard Mother drop the bomb on Sharon. I heard Mom tell Sharon that I had found my birth mother. I'm not sure what Sharon's response was, but I think she was surprised and wanted to hear how I had accomplished my twenty-five-year goal.

Then I heard Mom tell Sharon that I found out that I had five other siblings, as well. Mom had explained how I had investigated and researched and used a computer to find my family that I did not know I had. It was after that phone call that I was overhearing that I realized that I had my parents' support in all of this. They were not mad at me, and by telling them this story as to how I accomplished my task and telling my parent's the truth, I now realized that they truly supported me in all of this.

They knew I had been looking for many years. They knew I had no answers to my questions. They knew I was frustrated. There was only so much they knew that they were able to tell me and that some of the information was helpful, but it was not until I found Jack Winterbottom, who was married to my birth mother when I was born in Las Vegas, that I really started to know the truth to the story. Then, after finding my brothers and sisters and having the three-and-a-half-hour conversation with my brother, Michael, it was then that the whole truth came out. After talking to my brother Michael, he was the one who told me who my family was and, more importantly, where my birth mother was and that she was alive and living not too far from where Michael's house is located. My story was out of the bag, and it was no longer a secret. My parents knew the whole story, and now I had a story to tell to others. My sisters, Sharon and Susan, both knew the story, as well, as did my sister, Katy. Christmas 2010 was really special, but being able to tell my family my story about everything that had taken place was just really special. But it was about to get even better. I had to get on the phone and call my youngest sister, Jackie, and make the arrangements to meet her and her son at the Four Winds Casino in New Buffalo, Michigan. Jackie, at the time, lived up in the suburbs north of Detroit, Michigan, and she had told me that she and her son James had been to the casino before, about the time when it opened. It also turned out that Jackie knew some people who ran the resort, and we both agreed that the Four Winds Casino would be the right place to meet.

We decided to meet the following Thursday and, weather permitting, we would get to see each other for the first time. We decided that we would go to the casino and have their buffet for lunch and that we would have the whole afternoon to talk and get introduced. So, we decided to meet at 1:00 P.M., Michigan time, and Jackie was going to be bringing her son, James, as well as pictures of Alexandria. It was when I had hung up the phone with Jackie that I realized I had no idea what my birth mother looked like. I had only heard what she looked like from Tom; that she was kind of tall, slim build, and had jet black, thick, long hair. Jackie also had pictures of our brother, Leonard, and said that she was really excited to be meeting her big brother.

I decided that when I went out to go Christmas shopping, I would pick up a couple of things because I did not want to go and meet Jackie, especially at Christmas, empty-handed. So, while I was out shopping, I picked up a container of multi-flavored popcorn for Jackie, and a NASCAR calendar for my nephew, James.

The day I spoke to Jackie on the phone to make our arrangements at the casino in New Buffalo, I asked my parents if they wanted to come with me. I was too nervous to go by myself. I asked Jackie if it was okay to bring my parents, and she said it would be great to meet them, so Mom and Dad came along.

I had my rental car so, for them, it was a free trip to the casino. The drive itself is only about a half hour or so from their house, so I thought it would be nice to bring them along. It would also be a great idea to have them there for my nervous support. I am glad I did.

I may had mentioned how very nervous I was when I met my sister, Katy, for the first time. I was in a nervous sweat when her brother, Tom, answered the door and let me in their house to see Katy for the first time. My heart rate jumped, and I know that my blood pressure must have been elevated at that point. Then, there was the day my former wife and I got married, and it was that same kind of nervousness and high heart rate that made me thirsty and almost caused me to pass out during communion of the wedding mass. Since I was not Catholic, I was not allowed to take and drink of the wine or indulge in the bread, but I had asked our priest, Father Dave, for a small container of water. Then one of the two altar boys delivered a small Dixie-cup container of water. I was just that nervous. My former wife told me during our honeymoon in the Bahamas that she thought I was going to pass out. The truth was, I thought I *was* going to pass out. The only other thing up until now that I got nervous about was the time I used to get up really early for the one day trip to the Indianapolis 500. I used to get really nervous before the start of that race, too. But now this was meeting a sibling that I had never met before and it was more like the nervousness I felt when I met Katy for the first time. I got up that morning, as usual, showered, shaved, and dressed for our visit. I was too nervous to eat anything for breakfast, and since I was going to be eating a buffet later in the day, I skipped out of having a bowl of cereal, but I did have some orange juice, so I could take my early medicine. After I got ready, and realizing that Michigan time was one hour ahead, the three of us set out in my rented Toyota Yaris and set the course for New Buffalo, Michigan. The weather was decent that day, meaning there was no snow storms to drive through to get to our destination. That was good for us, and even better for my sister and her son to drive to. We only had a forty-minute drive to where we were going, but Jackie had a three-and-a-half-hour drive to get there. Jackie said it was no problem to accomplish, and she was up for a road trip. Mom, Dad, and I arrived at the casino about a half-hour early that day.

That was fine because I had no idea what the roads were going to be. I did not want to be the last one there, and I did not want to be late. I had told Jackie on the phone a couple of days before what I was going to be wearing, so she could find me. I had also stated that we would be waiting inside the lobby in the rotunda where there are two fireplaces. The fireplace on the left was not being used, and there was a table in front it. The Four Winds marketing people were using that table to set up customers for some sort of club to join as most casinos do, so I knew Jackie would see us by the other fireplace.

Mom, Dad, and I waited by the right-hand fireplace in the lobby at the Four Winds Casino in New Buffalo, Michigan. I was really nervous at this point, and each time someone came through the door, I wondered if it was going to be Jackie. There was not much talking between the three of us at that point in time, and every minute seemed like it was on very slow time.

Then, finally, without fanfare or media of any kind, the door opened, and it was my little sister, Jackie, and her son, James. As I was looking straight at the revolving doorway as they came in, Jackie was looking right at me for the first time. She and I were all smiles as we met halfway in the casino rotunda. I think the both of us were in tears when we hugged for the first time right there.

After we hugged, she introduced me to her teenage son, James. Then, I got the chance to introduce Mom and Dad to my sister, Jackie. We got to take pictures, too, in front of the fireplace at the casino rotunda, and then we decided to make our way to the buffet restaurant. At his point, I was rather hungry, even though I was still nervous, but now I could calm down, take my heart and blood pressure medication, and chill out.

The five of us went into the restaurant, and then Jackie paid the lunch tab for all us, and then we were seated. Dad was ready to pay the bill, but Jackie had beat him to it. I had the money to pay the tab, as well, but again, my little sister beat me to the punch. We all thanked my sister for paying for our meals. We sat down at the table and ordered soft drinks. Then, at my parents' suggestion, Jackie, James, and I made our way to fill our plates. Then, after everybody got back with a full plate, we started to eat. As in any buffet, there was more than enough to eat, and there was more than enough to choose from. We all went through the buffet and, while we were eating, Jackie and I started to exchange conversation. I had asked her how the trip over here to New Buffalo was, and she said they there was only one patch of snow, but it was not a big storm, so they drove right through it. Jackie had told me that she was nervous to meet me in person and found it exciting that she now had a new member of the family. Jackie had explained how much fun it had been as a kid growing up with Michael and Leonard as brothers, and now that she had told me about the recent findings of our oldest sisters, Nancy and Natalie, like our brother, Michael, had already told me, and now the discovery of me.

I had mentioned that our brother, Michael, had said it was like finding the "missing link" of our family, so to speak. It was not as he was describing me as a Neanderthal, or something (and I know I have been called much worse), but I was the missing link to the puzzle that seemed so mysterious to everybody. Jackie went on to say said that she, like me, had been lied to for many years and, many years and like me, had no idea that there were other family members out there, until she was in her late teenage years. As it turned out, our brother, Michael, had found out from his dad as a teenager that he had reason to believe that there were more brothers and sisters to his family that might be out there, but he just had no idea where they might be.

Michael's dad knew this from that one phone call that he had with Jack Winterbottom, when Jack wrote that certain name on the envelope. That name on the envelope turned out to be an extremely valuable piece of real estate. Not just for me, but for my entire family. My parents enjoyed talking to Jackie, as well. They had asked Jackie what she did for a living, and she told them as she had told me that she had worked in a factory near Detroit and then became a bar tender. Jackie then cautioned me again about confronting Alexandria. Before I had met Jackie and had only talked to her on the phone, Jackie has cautioned me about how Alexandria may not accept me as one of her own. Michael and Leonard had made the same remarks when I talked to them for the first time. Jackie had mentioned that she had not spoken to Alexandria in about ten years, face to face. Leonard was the same way. He did not speak to Alexandria, either, and that left Michael as the only one who made any attempt to talk to her. Alexandria did not go out of her way to be accommodating, in particular with her own family members. I did not really know how to accept this news, but I thought that the only thing I could do is remain positive. I mean, I did not really know how she would react to me, but that was not for another month or so, when I would make travel plans and go up to Pennsylvania and see my family myself.

After we finished our lunch at the casino buffet, James went down a hallway to an arcade that was there at the casino for kids of parents who were playing the adult games in the main casino. Mom, Dad, and I agreed to meet in about two hours or so, near the front of the casino, so that this would give Jackie and I a chance to talk. I had told Jackie about my heart surgery back in 2002, and I mentioned that if that aneurism had imploded and killed me, I would have gone to my grave never knowing who my newly discovered family was.

I was lucky and fortunate to have this chance now with Jackie, as well as with my other family members. I mean, it suddenly occurred to me that I was so lucky to be alive after having this kind of surgery, that I now thought that this was another reason to thank God for my survival. First, I thought that I had survived that surgery to find my friend, Debbie, and tell her how sorry I was for all of the wrongdoing that I had done. Now, I was thanking God for the answers to some of the life-long questions that I had, in particular the ones that had to do with finding Alexandria and the rest of my family. I realized that God had answered my prayers, as well as prayers from others who prayed for me during that whole ordeal over the summer of 2002.

Here it was, a little more than eight years after surviving life-saving surgery, and here I am, talking to one of my sisters from a family I just discovered. Not only I had found my birth mother at this point, but there were others. Many others. Brothers, sisters, nieces, nephews, great nieces, and great nephews. Then when you think about it, there are two former stepfathers in all of this, as well: Jack Winterbottom and Leonard Mitchell Sr. What a family

I was coming into. I am fortunate to have my parents and family anyway, as well as their support, but this situation, this is kind of epic. This kind of story is the kind thing you see on a television show, or even a Lifetime movie, or even a soap opera like *Days of our Lives*. Then, I got to think about it, and I thought that my story was something you can't make up on television or in the movies. This was real. This was my life. This is what happened to me. It is kind of an amazing story, if you think about it, but nonetheless, this really happened. Now things were starting to unfold. It took time to meet my sister, Jackie, just as it would take time to make arrangements to go to Pennsylvania for the first time. Jackie and I talked and walked around the casino until our two hours were up. We both played some slots, never winning anything, but having fun while it lasted.

Then, we met my parents at the front of the casino, and we all walked back to the arcade, where James was playing some really cool video games. Then we all went up front and waited for the valet parking people to bring up the car that Jackie had driven to see us with. Since I did not want Mom and Dad to walk far and go to the car, I went out to the other parking lot and brought my rental car over to the drive up area and waited while they brought out Jackie's vehicle. A little while later, I had two Christmas presents to give to James and Jackie, and when Jackie's vehicle showed up, she then gave us a bag of freshly made brownies, and something else I had never seen before.

What I had forgot about was the fact that Jackie had brought pictures of Alexandria. She had brought a picture of our brother, Leonard, too, but the ones with Alexandria were the most intriguing. I mean, let's face it, I had been waiting my whole life for this moment, and I was not even meeting my birth mother yet. So, after Jackie gave me the bag of brownies, and I gave her the two Christmas presents that I got them, Jackie then handed me the pictures and explained that these were some of the pictures from the past. About that time, Mom and Dad were seen getting into the rental car, but Dad was waiting outside the car, for some reason. I did not know it at the time, but Dad was watching me, and he was watching my reaction to viewing the pictures of my birth mother for the first time. It was almost like he knew what was going to happen. He knew it, and he was right. I saw the picture of Alexandria with our brother, Michael, for the first time. I had seen pictures of Michael before, but this one was different. This was with Alexandria, and after going all of these forty-seven years, I finally had seen what she looked like.

Jackie was standing right there with me. I did not see him at the time, but Dad was watching me. Like any good parent, he knew what kind of a reaction that I was about to have. He just knew me that well. I saw the picture of my birth mother for the first time. I then started to cry. I don't usually get this emotional about things, and I usually don't cry, either, but this was different. This was seeing a picture of Alexandria for the first time. She was alive, and I knew it. She was living among us, and I knew it. She was out there in this world of ours, and I knew it. Jackie said she had to get going, since she had a three-and-a-half-hour-long drive back to her home. She and James thanked me for the Christmas gifts. I returned the same gesture, and we wished each other a Merry Christmas. I mentioned to Jackie that she sure did know how to make a big brother cry. She asked me if I was going to be all right, and by that time, I was done with the tears.

Before Jackie got into her vehicle, she went over and thanked my parents for coming with me to the casino to meet her and James, and then we said good bye one more time. Jackie got into her vehicle and drove off. While she was still in sight, she blew the horn at us, and she and James both waved at us. By this time, I was back at the car and Dad, along with Mom, who was safe and sound in the warm car. I had the pictures that Jackie had just given me and sat them on the middle console, near the shifter. I got into the car and buckled up, and then we pulled away from the Four Winds Casino. Before we got out of the long driveway out of the casino, I then showed Mom and Dad the pictures that Jackie had given me. I said to the both of them, "Here are the pictures of Alexandria that Jackie just gave me. I about lost it when she showed them to me, when I saw them for the first time."

Dad then said, "You did lose it, I was there. I saw your reaction to them."

Dad was right, and I was busted, I guess. I got caught in the act. Dad was standing outside the car and watching me for a reaction. He was there the whole time, just watching. He was also there to make sure that I was okay because he knew that this was all so new to me. He knew that I wanted this day to come for a long time, and he did not even have to mention it. Dad just knew me that well.

After we got home, I drove the three of us back to Chesterton to the Dairy Queen, where Mom and Dad were ready to eat again. It was after 5:00 P.M. and this was the normal time that they ate dinner. I was still full from lunch, but since Dad was buying, I guess I could make room for just a few more things. Needless to say, when we got home from the casino, I was stuffed. No need to raid my parents' refrigerator tonight. Just no room for anything. I was tired, too. Considering I was up early that morning, and the fact that we spent nearly all afternoon at the casino, I was rather tired from all of the excitement. That night I stayed home with Mom and Dad and chilled out. I even fell asleep in one of their recliners that night and was told I was snoring, as well. I guess I was that tired. I thanked Mom and Dad for going with me that day, and I really appreciated their support in all of this. They enjoyed it, too, and really thought my story was really something to share. I mean, let's face it, being raised since I was one and a half years old, and then growing up and when I am forty-seven years old, not only do I find the whereabouts of my birth mother, but find out I have five siblings to boot. That is a story to share. Over the next day or so, I was able to finish my Christmas shopping, and we celebrated Christmas the following Saturday at Sharon and Bob's house. My two nieces were there, as well as my great niece and great nephew. When I was playing with my great nephew with one of his new toys, it was then I realized that is how I was related to my parents. I was their raised son, but I was also their great-nephew. Now here I was, having fun with my great nephew. It just does not get any better than that. That is what family is about. Generations. Christmas was really fun that year. Just like it is fun every year. I get to come home to Valparaiso for Christmas and celebrate it with my family. This year I got to see my family and then some more of my family. Yes, it DOES NOT get any better than that.

The following Tuesday, I had to pack and go back to the airport. I had a late afternoon flight back to Orlando, but I had to get back and get ready for work the next day. The sooner I got back to Orlando, I could start making plans to go to Pennsylvania for my visit.

But first I had a couple of things to do. Since the holiday now was going to be for New Year's Day, I had won tickets to the Capital One Bowl that takes place in Orlando every January 1. Then, after that, it was time for my annual company holiday party, which was held about a week later. Now, most companies have their holiday parties before Christmas, but we have ours after the first of the year because of all of the people on vacation during the month of December. This way it gives more people I work with the chance to go to the party.

I had met a woman who like me, was from Valparaiso, and was now living here in Central Florida. Her name is Tammy. I had met her on Facebook, and it turns out she graduated a year behind me at Valparaiso High School. Tammy had graduated in 1982, and it turns out she and I had an accounting class in high school together. She had a better memory than me, but nonetheless, it was neat to know someone from Valparaiso. She not only knew who I was, but she knew a lot of people that I know, as well.

Then, again, I knew a lot of people she knew, as well. Then, what was even more surprising was that Tammy had told me that she used to go to the First United Methodist Church in Valparaiso, like I did. She had told me that she and her family had a house next to Dr. Steele, who was the lead minister at the church when we were both in high school. After Tammy and I had met online, we agreed to meet in downtown Orlando at a restaurant called the Wall Street Cantina, which is right across the street from where I work at. They have good food there, and I thought it would be a nice place to talk and have lunch and talk about old times in Valparaiso. Tammy and I kind of hit it off that Saturday afternoon, and I had the urge to ask her out for the Capital One Bowl Game on New Year's Day. Tammy said she would go, so the two of us met, and I drove us to the Citrus Bowl stadium in Orlando for the game and pre-game hospitality.

The football game was between Michigan State from the Big Ten conference and Alabama from the South Eastern Conference. The game turned out to be a blow-out, as Alabama won easily, and then after the game, I asked Tammy if she wanted to go to the company party the following Saturday night. Tammy had to get back to me later on in the week, but then she said she would go with me to the party. I had told Tammy about my story at the pre-game tent before the football game on New Year's Day. Tammy, like others I had told the same story to, was amazed how I found out everything. After I told my story to Tammy, she mentioned to me that I need to write a book about all of this. I told her that it might be a good possibility, but first I had to go to Pennsylvania and possibly meet my family first.

Now, after the discussion I had had with Tammy and others about my discovery, so many people have encouraged me to write a book on my experience. So, now I have. I guess when you have friends and family say that my story would make a great book, I guess maybe they are correct.

About two weeks passed after the holidays, and I talked again with my brother, Michael. I had enough funds put together for a trip from Central Florida to Pennsylvania. I was going to leave the last Saturday of that January 2011 and stay through the first part of February. Since my brother is a minister, I wanted to get up to his house on Saturday and be there to hear him preach on that following Sunday.

Then, my brother's birthday was on Groundhog's Day, February 2, so I wanted to be there for his forty-second birthday. I had talked to my sister Katy, as well, and she had invited me to her house in Virginia to visit. This worked out great because I could then give her more details about my trip to Pennsylvania and spend some time together for a while. I had never been to Washington, D.C., and I had always wanted to see the sights of our nation's capital. Katy had said that she could pick me up at the airport, and then she would take that Friday off from work. Then, we could spend the day in Washington, seeing the sights.

Now, my trip was set, and I was going to be gone for about ten days or so. This was really going to be some vacation, I had thought. I would get to see my two brothers, as well as my birth mother, and then spend the rest of the week with my sister, Katy, and her family. This was going to be awesome, I thought.

After I got home from work on that Friday, I had to do laundry and get my stuff packed for my trip. Since I was leaving early in the morning on that Saturday, I had to get everything together and packed. I finished my packing around 11:00 P.M. and then set my alarm and went to bed. I had to get up around 4:00 A.M. or so because I had to shower and shave and put on a suit and tie. I was going to be dressed up for this trip, just like when my grandfather took me to Colorado to visit Aunt Bonnie and family in Denver back in the 1960s. Back then everybody dressed up when you flew on an airplane. Back then it is just what you did. I woke up when my alarm went off, and I went to the bathroom to get showered and ready. After I got dressed, I packed my few, remaining things, shut off the lights, and locked my apartment up. Then I rolled my two bags of luggage out to my car and put the luggage in the trunk. I pulled away and started my journey to Orlando International Airport. I got to the long-term parking lot and found a place to park, not far from the shuttle bus stop. I got my luggage out of the trunk, made sure my car was locked up, and then made my way to the shuttle bus stop. I did not have to wait long, and then the shuttle bus came by and picked us up. There always seems to be somebody traveling all the time at Orlando International Airport, so I had to wait my turn to get on the bus. I got on the bus and took a seat, and before we left for the terminals, the bus driver had to ask what airline everybody was taking. But first the driver came around and asked everybody on the bus what row they were in, and he then wrote down on a small piece of paper, so that you knew and remembered where you parked your car. He then took everybody's airline request, so that he knew where to drop all of the passengers. I got dropped off in front of the Air Tran airline counter, then I got off the bus and gave the guy a small tip for getting my large bag off of the bus. I said thank you to him and then went inside to check in. I got my boarding pass, then checked my one bag. I was then on my way toward the secured section. The line was not very long, but it still took about twenty minutes to get through security. Once I got through security, I had to put my stuff back together and put my shoes back on. Then I had to walk over to the people mover to get on the small rail system that would take me to my gate to catch my plane. I got off the people mover and then headed toward my gate. It always figures, my plane would be at the gate at the very end and in the corner of the terminal. I found the gate that I was looking for, and through the giant glass window I could see the airplane that was going to take me to Harrisburg,

Pennsylvania. I had given my flight information before I had left Orlando to my brother, Michael, so he knew when to pick me up at the airport. The flight was on time for departure, so I then took a seat by the Jetport and, by the looks of things, this was going to be a crowded flight. I had an assigned seat by the window about halfway in the plane. Before the plane was loaded with passengers, I took up a conversation with a nice man who was going on the same flight. This man had asked me if I was going home or visiting. I told him that I was going to see family for the first time. I had explained the whole story to this man, a complete stranger, like Forrest Gump did in that movie while sitting on that park bench while waiting for the bus to see his girlfriend, Jenny. There were other folks who were listening, too, as I could tell there were some people intrigued with my story. After I was done explaining my story, this man was kind of blown away, and he wished me his very best. He wished me good luck, and then our boarding zones were called, and we got on the plane. The flight was almost sold out, so it was going to be a crowded flight. There were some young kids on the flight, but they, for the most part, were well-behaved. It was a long, two-and-a-half-hour flight from Orlando to Harrisburg. Even though the flight was crowded, I was sitting next to a guy who had come to Orlando for vacation. He was traveling in a group of people, as I think it was some of his extended family. He and I got to talking, and he had told me he was working for the State of Pennsylvania Child Protective and Family Services. I guess he was a case manager or something like that, and then our discussion came back to me. He asked me what I was going to be doing in Pennsylvania on my trip. I told him I was seeing family for the first time and how I had found my birthmother and some of my siblings. Again, here I go with the Forrest Gump thing but, you know, even to a number of complete strangers, people were interested in my story. The guy sitting in front of me was traveling with the guy sitting next to me, and he heard my story and offered to buy me a drink. He said something like, "I'll gladly buy you one; you might need it."

He was right. I had not noticed how nervous I was, but I told him no thanks because I was on an empty stomach. Although a bloody Mary did sound good at the time. It would be my luck that I would spill it on my suit and then stain it up and not be able to wear it on Sunday for church. Then I had thought about the smell. That was not going to be a good impression on my newly discovered brother and his family picking me up at the airport, and then taking me, a complete stranger, into their house and feed me for the next several days. I mean, how nice was that? I was so worried about making that first impression with my brother, Michael, that I knew we both had a lot of catching up to do over the next several days. I was not only going to get to meet Michael and his family, like his wife, son, and two daughters but also his father, Leonard Sr., and our brother, Leonard Jr. Then, at some point, he was going to be the one who would introduce me to Alexandria. I got nervous just thinking about that. I had no idea what was going to happen over the next several days, and I guess that is the surprise in life. Like Mr. Gump used to say, "Life is like a box of chocolates, you just never know what you are going to get inside."

Like Mr. Gump, in my case, I had no idea just what was in store for me.

My flight was on time, and it was very scenic to fly into Pennsylvania during January. As we made final approach, we flew right over the Three Mile Island power plant, located just a short distance from the airport runways. The pilot of the airplane got on the horn and told us we were flying over it. It was kind of cool to fly over this historic power plant. If memory serves me correct, the Three Mile Island power plant meltdown happened about the week that I was with my family in Macon, Georgia, at Susan's house over spring break back in March 1979, just after my grandfather had passed away. Not only did this power plant have the worst meltdown in history, but that was the week that I had that conversation with my father that caused the meltdown in our father/son relationship. Here is was, almost thirty-two years later, and just like my life, this whole thing had come to full circle. I mean, who would have thought? I saw all of the news that week because of the severity of the story, and here I was, some thirty-two years later, flying into Harrisburg, Pennsylvania, and going to meet my brother, Michael, his wife, and son for the first time. Who would have thought that then? I sure would not have. I did not get a good view of the power plant because by the time we got below the clouds, there it was snowing outside. It was not snowing hard, but there was some accumulation on the ground. Just enough to make it scenic, I guess.

We landed with no problems and pulled up to the gate. There was still a small amount of snow in the air, and I was getting nervous at this point. So nervous, in fact, that my palms began to sweat.

After we pulled up to the gate, most all of the passengers got up to get their bags out of the overhead compartments. After deplaning and collecting my luggage, three or four nice people who had been sitting around me and heard me tell my story wished me the best of luck. I had mentioned that my brother and I had kind of looked a little alike, so I wondered if people on my flight would notice the resemblance. I got to my carry-on bag and then made my way off the flight. It was finally time to meet Michael and his family. I came out to the main area, wiped off my hands that were sweating, and then made my way up the Jetport to the gate, where the plane had pulled up. I got to the gate and looked for a sign to follow, so I knew where to get my other bag of luggage. I started walking toward the secured area, knowing Michael would be there to greet me. The Harrisburg Airport was a nice airport to fly into. It looked rather new and modern and was very clean. I walked up to the secured area and came out to the main area, headed toward the luggage area. There, looking right back at me just like when my sister, Jackie, was looking right at me when she walked into the door at the Four Winds Casino, in New Buffalo, Michigan, there was Michael, his wife, and their son, looking right at me. Michael smiled and waved at me, and I waved back and smiled right at him, as well. There was no need for me to be nervous anymore. This was family, and like meeting our sister, Jackie, it was a lot like that same feeling. I guess it was like meeting Katy for the first time, too.

It was just that emotional. The three of them were standing next to a large, floor-to-ceiling beam, off to my left. I walked over, dropped my bags, and Michael and I hugged like brothers for the first time. It was like no other emotion I had felt. I heard laughter from him and laughter from Michael's wife and I felt tears running down my face. It was just that emotional. After so many years of frustration, and after so many years of sort of knowing that I may have had other family members out in this world, including my birthmother, this was it. Like the great football commentator John Madden used to say after the Super Bowl was over and the celebrations that starts, "It just does not get any better than this."

At this moment of time, meeting Michael and his family for the first time just did not get any better than this either. We collected all my things and were ready to go.

Unlike other reunions that you see on television and so forth, here at the Harrisburg Airport, there were no television crews or reporters. Even though it would have made a great news story, I was glad there was no television news crews there. It was kind of neat, though, because when we all walked over to get my luggage, you could tell that the folks on my flight that knew my story were talking about us and how we very much looked alike. In fact, the nice gentleman that I was sitting next to at the gate in Orlando saw the two of us together and pointed at us, and without even saying anything, you could just tell that he was happy for us and he could tell we did look somewhat alike, too. The four of us waited for my luggage, and then it popped up on the carousel. Michael grabbed it, and since I already had my carry on, we were ready to go. The weather was cold and snowy, but I was just glad to be there. We all walked to their car and got in while Michael loaded the luggage. We had one stop to make on the way to Michael and his wife's house, a grocery store just south of Brookvale. Michael, his son and I stayed in the car and talked about this whole story of ours. I had asked Michael what was going through his mind when I had called that Thursday night that he and I were on the phone for the first time for three and a half hours. I had to apologize again for calling so late.

Michael said, "I honestly thought it was a call from my daughter's boyfriend. I know sometimes he calls late, and I thought I was going to have to tell him not to call so late. But as it turned out, it was not him; it was you. There really is no reason to apologize for your call, brother, because like I said, because I am a minister of the church; we get phone calls just about any time of the day or night. I just had no idea that it was going to be a long lost brother of mine who I really never knew existed. The way our conversation first started out, you were asking me questions about my dad, and I thought you might have been in the Air Force with him or something and you were looking for my dad for a reunion.

"Then, when you mentioned you were looking for Alexandria for all of these years, I knew you were not looking for my dad. You were looking for Alexandria. I am sorry it took you so long to find us, but if we had known you were out there, we would have looked for you. But the fact of the matter is, we had reason to believe that there were other family members out there; we just had no idea who they were until you called and explained everything. What you said makes perfect sense about our whole family situation."

"You have to remember, too, that it was just a few months ago that we found our sisters, Nancy and Natalie, and found out they were long lost sisters of ours, too. Then, here it is, a few months later, and on one Thursday night in December, I get a phone call that tells me that you are the long lost brother we never knew about. I knew and my dad knew that there were other children out there that Alexandria had; we just never knew who or where they were, but now we do. Again, you are like the missing link to all of this. My brother, Leonard, and I, along with our sister, Jackie, kind of knew that there were others out there, but again, we just had no names or anything. Then, like I said, all out of nowhere, we get a call, and we find out about our oldest sisters, then, out of some amazing thing or something, you call me out of the blue and tell me your story, and that story fits the missing link to our family. There are six of us now, and this is a God-given gift to all of us."

I thought about what Michael had said, and he was correct. This whole story was sort of a shock to him and our other family members, just like it was shocking to me. I can't imagine now what it would have been like to find my family at an earlier age. I mean, would I have been mature enough to handle it then? I knew I was not good in relationships, so would I have been able to handle all of this? First, I find my sister Katy; then, almost thirty years later, I find Michael, Leonard, and sister Jackie, and then I am told I have two more sisters on top of that.

And with all of this, just how would I have handled meeting my birth mother back then? Would I have been mature enough to handle that? Definitely not, I think. Whoever was writing my book upstairs, either God or my guardian angel, knew that I would not be able to handle it back then. It just made perfect sense to find all of this out now.

We left the store and made it to Michael's house just in time for the lunch hour. Michael's wife was making a big meal for lunch, and I was hungry from the trip. Like I had mentioned, I did not eat before had left Orlando, so I was famished. When we got to the house, we all got out of the car and went in. Michael grabbed my big bag of luggage, took it into the house, and then took it upstairs to my room where I was going to be staying. I had been wearing my suit for a while, and now it was time to get out of it and get into some comfortable clothes. I changed into some jeans and a sweater and then came back downstairs. When I got downstairs, I was introduced to Michael's daughters, Mary and Marcy. Before we went to eat, Michael asked me if we could take some family pictures together. Of course, I told him yes, we could. This was going to turn out well because I had promised people that I would post some pictures with my family members on Facebook. Facebook is an amazing social network. You take a picture with a digital camera, and then you put it on your Facebook page. It was that simple. After we took some pictures with the family, I had asked Mary to tag the picture, so that I could post it on my wall later on that afternoon. Mary, Marcy, Michael, and I were friends on Facebook, so this all worked out well. After a prayer and a big meal, I could not stay awake any longer. I had to take a nap, or I was going to fall asleep. I was gone.

CHAPTER 12: THE MOMENT IN MY LIFE THAT I HAVE BEEN WAITING FOR

After a short nap of about an hour or so, I woke up about the time Michael's wife and daughters were helping get dinner on the table. It was good to sleep after waking up early and traveling more than 1,100 miles that day. My mind was still in a little fog as I had just woken up; nonetheless, it was good to sleep. Michael had taken a nap, as well, but he got up to help his wife in the kitchen. After a prayer and dinner, Michael and I sat and talked about more of our families. As we sat down to dinner, Michael and I talked about our early childhoods and about different things that had happened in our younger lives. Michael is a minister, too, and he had to finish and polish his sermon that he would be giving the next morning at the Christian Church in Brookvale. Being able to see Michael preach that Sunday was one of the reasons why I wanted to leave and go to Brookvale on Saturday. I had not been to church since the day after Christmas with my parents at the United Methodist Church in Valparaiso, so it was good to get back to church.

My brother, his family, and I got to discuss a lot of things that night, but most of the talk was about Alexandria. Michael told me that he and our brother, Leonard, and our sister, Jackie, used to all live together when his father was married to her. Then when they divorced, Leonard Jr. and Michael lived with Alexandria for a while, but then when that did not work out, the boys went to Pennsylvania to live with their father. The boys grew up with their father until they were adults, and then the boys ventured out on their own. Michael and his wife were high school sweethearts, and they got married about two years after they both graduated from high school in July 1989.

Leonard Jr. got married before that, and Jackie was married sometime in the 1980s, as well. I had told Michael that Pam and I got married in June 1990 and was divorced just a month before what would have been our twentieth wedding anniversary. Michael never asked me what happened between Pam and me, because he knew as a minister, he knows how things can happen to couples.

Now, I wish I could have known Michael long before Pam and I got divorced. Maybe, just maybe, the influence of one of my brothers could have helped me help save my marriage. For me counseling did not do much good. I felt like I was dragged to an office and had to spill my guts to a complete stranger about my issues. I still take the blame for our breakup and divorce, but I just think perhaps if I had one other voice to listen to, maybe things could have been different. Then again, I just do not know if would have done any good anyway. Michael told me that what he had done for a living, including owning a car repair garage outside of Brookvale and a Goodyear tire dealership at the same place. Michael had then told me that he'd then moved he and his family to Virginia to go to Bible college. This would be the school that Michael would attend to become a minister. After four years of school, Michael then came back to Brookvale and was offered a job as the lead minister at the Community Church of Brookvale.

Brookvale is a smaller community, but the church is very well attended by locals from the area. I told Michael about my own professional journey to where I currently was in Florida and about working in the field of local radio and then making the switch to television. I also told him about my first job in television, going all the way back to my days at US Cable of Northern Indiana in Merrillville, Indiana, then going to TCI of Gary, Indiana, and then my short stint at WYIN-TV-56 in Merrillville, Indiana, and then my move to Florida when I went to work at Toyota of Orlando. Then I told Michael about my current job at Central Florida News 13 in Orlando, Florida. It was kind of ironic that I had been in the television business all of these years, as well as a brief career in radio, because at one time, Michael had thought about going to college and taking up the career of either radio or television. Like me he is also a musician. I told Michael that I had played piano for almost ten years but gave it up my senior year of high school. Michael told me that he loved playing guitar and enjoyed playing in a band when he was younger. I told him that I never played in a band, but I had performed in front of small crowds. I never got paid for any of my performances, but I also knew I was never good enough to play in a band or anything like that. But the one thing that Michael and I had in common was the fact that he got to buy audio and visual equipment for the church. We talked microphones, audio consoles, and speakers, as well as computer systems that allowed the congregation to see visual displays while the church service was going on. I was really looking forward to that Sunday to spend with my newly discovered family. Again, I just had no idea what was going to happen.

About 11:00 P.M. or so, it was time for bed, and I was still tired. I took my nighttime medicine and went up to my room and crashed.

Sunday was going to be another big day.

I had slept well that night, and Sunday morning came, and I was awoken with a knock on the door by Michael about 7:30 A.M. I had time to shower, shave, get dressed, and get ready for church, and well as go downstairs and eat a big breakfast before church. I had to get used to this three-meal-a-day thing. Michael's wife had cooked a big breakfast with eggs and bacon and other things, and I had to eat it kind of quickly, so that we could get to the church before 10:00 A.M. Michael had gotten up early that morning, so that he could get to the church and get everything opened up for when people got to the church, things were ready. Lights had to be turned on, coffee had to be brewed, and since there was fresh snow on the ground from the night before, the steps and sidewalks had to be cleaned off. The parking lot had already been plowed, but the steps and sidewalks had to be shoveled off. Then when this was done, Michael came back in the church van to pick us up.

Michael's wife, Mary, Marcy, Mark, and I had to get to the church on time. We arrived at the church a little before 10:00 A.M., and people were still arriving because of the snow on the ground. Michael expected a small crowd today because of the weather. It was kind of a late-arriving crowd, but there was still a good turnout. My brother introduced me to many members of the congregation, and I found that I was very welcomed to the church. There were some people who did not know that Michael and I were brothers, but then again, we just had found out about a month or so ourselves. There were folks who said that we kind of looked alike, as well.

I remembered at the Harrisburg airport, when I was waiting for my bag of luggage and some of the people who knew my story realized the same thing. Before the church service started, I had taken a seat next to my niece, Mary, and she and I struck up a conversation. I had asked Mary when the last time she had spoken to her grandmother, Alexandria. Mary told me it had been about five years. When Mary told me this, I realized that I might be in for a tough day if I got to meet Alexandria. Michael had made a visit to see Alexandria two days after I first spoke with him on that Thursday, and two days after I had that three-and-a-half-hour conversation with him. I had spoken with Michael on the phone that Saturday after, and he had told me then that Alexandria had denied everything, including being married to Jack Winterbottom and giving birth to me in Las Vegas. She also denied that she knew my father, Thomas Dowd. It would be later that day that it would be known. I was to find out soon just how bad the relationship was between Alexandria, Leonard Jr., Michael, and Jackie. Now there was me to contend with, and seeing that Alexandria had signed those Catholic annulment papers, she had to have realized that those two daughters she gave birth to before me were still around. I could then tell by that conversation with Mary that I had a bad feeling about where this was going. But I had to remain positive and pray for the best. Let's face it, I was in the house of God, and I was here to worship. I was also here to hear Michael preach and deliver the sermon. I then did just that.

Michael introduced me to the congregation at the start of the morning church service, and while I was given an applause, I then gave a wave to the congregation of thanks for the nice welcome and they applauded. That Sunday at church, I got to take communion, as well as pray. I listened to a very moving sermon from Michael, and he kept the congregation well informed of other people who were missing from church from sickness and other issues. The Old and New Testaments of the Bible were read, and of course we sang hymns. After the service was over, he introduced me to more people from the congregation, and again, it was more of a thanks from coming all the way from Orlando, Florida, to visit the church. I met a lot of wonderful people that day at the Community Church in Brookvale, and it was even sweeter to see Michael up there delivering the sermon, and it was even more gratifying to know how much the congregation responded to his word.

I had found out something else about my brother Michael that I did not know. As it turns out, Michael had a religious dictionary that was co-written by my Great Uncle Ron Youngblood. Uncle Ron was my dad's brother-in-law and was married to one of my dad's sisters. It was kind of cool to tell Michael that I was related to Uncle Ron, and it was cool to see that my brother had one of his books in his office. I was hoping one day that I could introduce the two of them. I'm sure they would hit it off and have plenty of things to discuss. I guess it was about a half hour after the church service was over that we all got into the church van and went back to Michael's house. On the way out of the church parking lot, I asked Michael if it would be okay to drive past Alexandria's house. Her house was not that far off the beaten path home to the house, so Michael said he would drive us by, but not stop. The snow had stopped, but there was about four to six inches of stuff on the ground at this point. The temps were above freezing, so the ground was wet with puddles in the streets. Alexandria lived in a mobile home out in the country, on a heavy, wooded lot. She had a rather long, gravel driveway to her house, but she had no garage for her car. As we drove closer to Alexandria's house, I started to look. Then, for some unknown reason, something caught my attention to the other side of the road, and I missed it. I looked back quickly, but all I could see was a person with a long, dark coat, and it was a quick flash before we were gone.

Michael said to me, "Did you see her out shoveling snow?"

I said, "No, not really. For some reason, I was looking the other way and only saw a flash of somebody up on the porch."

Michael just kind of smiled and then I said something like, "I have been waiting my whole life to meet her, and then when I get the opportunity to finally see her, I'm not looking at the right time. Just my rotten luck, I guess."

With that said, Michael drove us home because we had to get ready for Sunday dinner, and we were going to be visited by our brother Leonard, Jr. and his wife, JoAnne, as well as Leonard Sr., my brother's father. I was looking forward to meeting them both and talking to them about things, as well talking about Alexandria.

Sunday dinner was served in the noon hour and, once again, there was all this wonderful, home cooked food on the island in the kitchen. I mean, there was so much food it was like being at a buffet, or something. I guess it was sometime after 1:00 P.M. or so, when Leonard Sr. came over, and I was introduced to him. Here is the man I know as Husband Number Three, as Jack Winterbottom put it. Here is the man, because of that phone call made to Jack Winterbottom, that led to Jack writing Leonard's name on the envelope of Jack's divorce papers with Alexandria. It was that envelope with that name on it that Jack Winterbottom had stored away in a box of old stuff after he had moved from Utah to Bakersfield, California. Then, for no explanation, when I called him to tell him who I was and who I was looking for, this kind man tells me he has this name on this envelope with Leonard Mitchell's name on it as Husband Number Three.

If it was not for the communication of these two gentlemen, done more than forty years ago, I would not have found what I was looking for. Even more, here it was more than forty years later when I made the discovery. Who would have thought it? Just what were the chances of this? I mean, I don't like to sound dramatic or anything, but really, only God must have known this or my guardian angel must have known this, too, just like a treasure in a shipwreck and it being discovered many years later. This envelope, with this man's name on it, had become my sunken treasure. Like me SCUBA diving in my favorite place in the Cayman Islands, then finding the most valued treasure one could ever find in the ocean depths. This envelope was like finding gold bars under the sand in the ocean. This discovery of mine was the biggest discovery of my search, and now one of the men who was responsible for this discovery was about to be introduced to me.

Leonard came to the door after we had already started to eat. He came in the kitchen door from outside where he had parked his van. Leonard was a farmer and a business owner, too. He had two businesses in town, as well as his farm. I would find this out later, but Leonard was a very popular man in town. Most everybody knew him through some connection or did business with him. My brother Michael was like that, too, mainly because he had that automotive repair shop on the outskirts of town. It seemed that most everywhere we went around Brookvale, everybody knew Michael and everybody knew our brother Leonard Jr., and their father Leonard Sr.

Leonard Sr. walked in the kitchen door and Michael was there to greet him. I got up from the table from where I was eating and walked around the island to go and meet him. I had to meet this man because he was like three other men who had been married to my birth mother, Alexandria. Michael introduced us, and we both took out our hands and shook them. Leonard had this big smile on his face when we met, just as I did. Leonard took his coat off, and Michael took it. Then Leonard and I walked over to the table. Leonard sat down but did not go up to the island and get any food. I went back to my seat, and our conversation started.

Leonard Sr. had taken a seat next to my sister-in-law, Joanne. Joanne is Leonard's wife, and she had arrived for dinner when we started eating. Leonard had a job at the time that he worked overnights, and had slept in a little later and joined us after Leonard Sr. had already arrived. Leonard Sr. and I started to talk. Leonard had asked me what airline and airport I had flown. I responded and told him that I had flown into Harrisburg Airport and flew in on AirTran and got here in Brookvale on Saturday. I had mentioned to him that I had wanted to get in a day early, so that I could see Michael preach that Sunday morning. Leonard asked me about the flight, and I told him it was on time but crowded. I had mentioned that I got to fly right over the Three Mile Island power plant. He asked me how I was enjoying the weather here in Pennsylvania, and I told him it was nice to get out of Florida for a while. The snow really did not bother me. Then, after a few minutes of small talk, I decided to get right to the punch. I needed to speak to him about why I was here.

I said to Leonard Sr., "I hope you don't mind me asking you, but I was told by a man named Jack Winterbottom that the two of you had a conversation on the phone over forty years ago. This phone call that the both of you had has led me to find Alexandria, as well as my brothers and sisters. Do you remember that phone call, and if you do, what were the circumstances behind that call?"

I felt like Mike Wallace of *60 Minutes* fame asking him that question. If there was one person who could grill anybody in front of a television camera, it was the late Mike Wallace. I had to ask. I had to find out the whole story.

Leonard then said in a friendly voice, "As it turned out, I was in the Air Force, and we were on this plane flying all over the world to different air bases back then. That is what I did; I was a flight engineer when I was in the service back during the Vietnam era. Alexandria and I had just divorced not long before I made that phone call, and I was in Utah at an air base and had Jack's name and phone number. He was surprised to hear from me, as he and I had never met. When I had told Jack about being married to Alexandria, he seemed to take interest because he was once married to her, as well. I am not sure how long we talked, but I told Jack that Alexandria and I had been married and divorced, and the two of us had two boys together."

"I had asked Jack if he knew about Alexandria's family. Jack said he really never met any of Alexandria's side of the family, like her mother and stepfather, who were still living at the time, or Alexandria's two brothers, who were both alive at the time, too."

"Jack told me about the fact that there were two daughters of Alexandria's that had either died in a house fire or were killed in an automobile accident. Then, I think, I remember Jack stated something about you being born in Las Vegas. It was a long, long, time ago, and I really don't remember just what we said word for word, if you know what I mean. Then, all of a sudden, a few months ago, I get a call from your sister, Natalie, and she tells me that she is one of Alexandria's daughters that your mother had when she was married to her first husband. This is how we found out that the story of your sisters was not true. They did *not* die, either in a house fire or in a car accident. That was the story that was told by Alexandria so that nobody could find them and trace them back to her. She told people the story of her daughters' deaths when we were married, and she lied about the whole thing because, well, she did not want anybody to find out that she had lost them in the divorce from her first husband."

"Now, you find Jack Winterbottom, kind of like I did all that time ago, and then find us. I must say, this is a very interesting story, and I also have to say, I am glad you found your family. I am happy for you. I hope all six of you can eventually get together and talk about this sometime in the future."

After what Leonard said, I then told him the story as to how I found him. I told him how after Jack Winterbottom had given me his name from that envelope, how I found him through mylife.com. I explained that after I found out that he was in Pennsylvania, and I thought I had the right person, and that Jack and I figured out that the two brothers of mine would be in their forties. "When I found Leonard's name, and then there was a Leonard Jr., and a Michael listed as possible relatives, I kind of knew I had the right family. For some unknown reason, I was the one who called my brother, Michael, first and woke him up with a three-and-a-half-hour phone call."

Leonard responded, "I guess I really don't understand social media, as it is called, but I guess in your case, you were able to find us. That is really an amazing thing."

For the next half hour or so, Leonard and the rest of us talked about our family situation. We were all fortunate that this kind of all came together because Alexandria would have never told anybody. Alexandria would have kept this whole story like dirt swept under a rug. Nobody would have known. Jack Winterbottom had no idea what my name was until I explained to him how I was named. That was long after he and Alexandria left Las Vegas and went to Utah. Leonard Mitchell had no idea who I was, either. But he did know one thing: Leonard had told Michael and Leonard, Jr., when they were younger that there was a possibility that there were other kids that Alexandria had.

Other people in my family had told me the same thing—that there might be more children in the family. I was just fortunate that I found this out when I did. I just wish I had found my family sooner. I guess my one regret is in all of this is that Alexandria's mother, our maternal grandmother, and her second husband had passed away some years earlier and were not around to be a part of this newly discovered family of ours. I have seen pictures of them, and from what everybody had told me about them, they were awesome folks. It's just too bad, as I said, I did not find them sooner.

I guess it was around 2:00 P.M. or so when Leonard Jr. made it over to Michael's house. Like Michael and myself, he was about our height and was all smiles when he walked into the kitchen from the back door. Michael and I got up from the table again, Michael took Leonard's coat and hat, and I came over to introduce myself and shake hands and hug. We were all smiles when we met, and I noticed that Leonard had a really hard grip when we shook hands. Hands of a truck driver, I guess. When you log over three million miles driving a semi-truck, I guess you had better have hands with a hard grip. Leonard was hungry, and he came over to the island, grabbed a plateful of food that was still there, and came over to the dining room and grabbed a chair. Leonard asked for a glass of iced tea to drink and somebody got that for him in a plastic glass and delivered it to him. Leonard then asked me how I was doing and how I enjoyed the weather in Brookvale, Pennsylvania. I told him it was fine with me, as I really don't spend time in the snow much anymore, so it was welcomed by me. Leonard apologized to me because his snowmobile was not running at the time, as he is a really big snowmobiler. He was not sure what was wrong with it, but he just knew it was not running properly. It was a shame, too, because there was several inches of fresh snow on the ground, and it would have been fun to be out messing around on one. Oh, well, I guess we would just have to do some other activity. After we all finished our dinner and had some dessert, Michael, Leonard, and I left the dining room and made our way into the family room. It was really cool that the three brothers would be together for the first time. Leonard Sr. walked in, and I suggested that we all get a picture taken of the four of us. We took several pictures, and there were a couple of pictures that got taken of just us three brothers. Michael and Leonard were standing on each side of me and were messing around with me in the middle. I swear, it was like a mild bit from *The Three Stooges* or something.

After a few pictures, Leonard Sr. decided he had to leave because he had some farming duties to attend to, so we all said our good byes, Leonard put on his coat, and left the three of us brothers to chat in the family room. While the three of us brothers were talking about stuff, I asked Leonard how he felt about the three of us going out to Alexandria's place and introducing me to her. Leonard was not crazy about the idea, but I had to give him some encouragement. I talked Leonard into going out to Alexandria's house that Sunday afternoon, and then a few minutes later, the three of us had put on our coats and left the house and were now on are our way. Again, I had no idea what was about to happen.

In a previous chapter of my book, you remember when I told you when I heard the song from the group U2. I was in my car, had just left my therapist's office, and was at a stoplight in Winter Park, Florida, when I heard the song, "I Still Haven't Found What I'm Looking For" on the radio. To a certain extent, that song rang a bell with me because it was so true at the time. As I recall, I had just found Jack Winterbottom, and he was in the process of finding that envelope with a name on it that I needed to find my family. Just think about it for a minute, at that moment in time, that was a song about me and my journey through all of this. I still think to this day, it was a message from God. I still had not found what it was I was looking for.

It was only a matter of time before I would actually *find* what it was I was looking for. And it was that night, after I got home from work around 9:30 P.M., that I would get the voice mail from Jack Winterbottom and call him back with the information he had for me. He had the name on that envelope. Jack had that name on that envelope just for me. After I had spoken with him the previous Saturday, he had written that name down, even though he had no idea why. But it would be some forty years later or so that Jack would get a phone call from me, and I would tell Jack who I was, and so forth. Then, on the phone that night in December, Jack would give me the name of husband number three. That was what I was looking for; the key and major piece I needed to solve the biggest mystery of my life of forty-seven years. To this day, I just find that amazing. Now, at this moment of my life, on that Sunday in January, I was now going with my two brothers to see Alexandria. It never really occurred to me that another song fit that scene of my life. If you remember the song by Phil Collins back in the 1980s, "In the Air Tonight," a song that I have heard maybe hundreds, if not thousands, of times on the radio and other mediums. It was that song that I realized that fit the scene when the three of us brothers went for that faithful visit. Little did I know, just what this scene of my life would turn out to be. Like the song I just mentioned, "In the Air Tonight," there are two verses that come to mind. In the first verse, "I have seen your face before my friend, but I don't know if you know who I am." How this verse relates to me is having seen a few pictures of Alexandria I now had seen her face before, and like the back half of the verse says, I wondered if Alexandria would know who I was. I mean, she had not seen me since she had given birth to me, would she really know who I was, even if I tell her. Then, on another verse, "I saw what you did, I saw it with my own two eyes, so you can wipe off that grin, I know where you've been, it's all been a pack of lies."

It would be no grin she would have on her face when we meet, but I had an idea of where she had been. Alexandria had been married four times and divorced from all four of her husbands. Alexandria had met Jack Winterbottom when she was living with my father, Tom Dowd, and for whatever reason left my father, as well as Jack Winterbottom to go on to something else. And, to make things even worse, the way that Alexandria had lied about so many things, including telling people that my two older sisters had died in a car accident or had died in a house fire, that was nothing but lies. As Jack Winterbottom had once told me by phone, it was easier for Alexandria to lie than tell the truth. It's all a pack of lies. Just all of it. I knew that, and so did my brothers and sister, Jackie.

The three of us, Michael, Leonard, and I, pulled up to Alexandria's house in the country and off the beaten path. Her gravel driveway had been plowed out by somebody, but at the moment, I did not care who had done the job. The three of us got out and walked up to the front porch of the mobile home. The sun was still out at this point, and there was no wind. It was as quiet as a Hollywood movie set at that moment, and that was fine with me. We then walked up the stairs, walked down the porch, and headed to the front door. There was a snow shovel next to the front door; that must have been when she was out shoveling snow when we drove by after church. The time I could have seen Alexandria for the first time, but because I was not paying attention, and got distracted for whatever reason, I had missed the chance to see her. The air was cool, but not cold. The sun was out, and Leonard and I had our sunglasses on. I was nervous, at this point, and I mean *nervous*. I know I was shaking, but I paid no attention to myself. This was the moment I had been waiting for my whole life; forty-seven years, waiting.

And, like the song, I could feel it coming in the air tonight, even though it was actually late afternoon. Michael knocked on the door, as I stood in the middle of him and Leonard. Again, I had to be just freaking nervous, as we were just waiting for Alexandria to answer the door. We kind of figured she was there, because her dark blue Honda Civic was parked right in front of her home. Finally, the door opened, and I heard Leonard say something like, "It's about time you opened the door. It is cold as hell out here."

There she was. My God, it was her. It was Alexandria. She looked at me briefly, as well as Michael and Leonard. Here is the woman who had given birth to me more than forty-seven years ago, and here she was just a couple of feet from me. She was almost in touching distance. I could have reached out to her, but I did not.

I was frozen, and not because of the winter weather. I was stunned, I was nervous, and even more, I just could not think of anything to say. As Alexandria opened the screen door, I could hear her say something to Michael about something that had to do with their last visit. Alexandria was mad at Michael for whatever had been discussed in their last visit together. Then, Leonard started with the obscenities. I won't repeat what Leonard was saying at that point, but Leonard was really upset, to say the least.

Then when the moment came, Alexandria looked at me and asked, "Who are you?"

Leonard then blurted out, "He is one of us, Alexandria!" Then Leonard started in with the obscenities again. Again, not printable. I could hear Michael trying to talk to Alexandria and trying to explain who I was and what we were all doing at her house. But with Leonard's deep, scratchy voice, and with his obscenities screaming in the background, and Alexandria yelling back at him,

Michael could just not reason with her.

This swearing festival, of sorts, between Leonard and Alexandria went deep. I mean, there had to be something more to it. I knew from conversations with Leonard on the phone that he was not pleased with the way things had gone with Alexandria in the last, few years. Leonard and Alexandria had been toe-to-toe about several things for several years, and the situation between them was just not getting any better. Again, Michael was trying to talk to her and reason with her, but Alexandria would have nothing to do with it. Alexandria was fuming mad at both of my brothers, for whatever reason or reasons. Leonard was just as fuming mad at Alexandria.

Alexandria seemed to be fuming mad at most everybody in her family. Now, she was getting introduced to me, and she was going to be fuming mad at me before the afternoon was over. I looked at Alexandria again. I had no idea if I would ever get to see her again. Here it was, I had spent all of this time looking for this woman, and here she was right in front of me, and here she was going at it screaming abusively at both of my brothers. It would only be a few, short minutes later that she and I would start going at it, too, just not like she and Leonard were doing. I now look back at this scene of my life and now realize just how ugly this whole visit turned out to be, when I was glad that there was no media present. What was going on here was like a typical episode of *The Jerry Springer Show*. It was just horrible.

I remember seeing Alexandria and Leonard argue and Michael trying to calm Leonard down, and then I remember saying something to Michael like, "I knew she was a tough customer, but this is unreal."

By this time, I had my urge to speak to Alexandria, and when she asked me again who I was, I told her what my name is. I said, "You gave birth to me in a hospital in Las Vegas in November 1963. You were married to a man named Jack Winterbottom when I was born. You and Jack got married in Las Vegas on July 23, 1963, after you split up with my father, Thomas Dowd. You gave birth to me and left me there in that hospital until my father and grandmother showed up two days later to claim me. I have been looking for you for a long time, over twenty-five years, and I came here to introduce myself to you."

To my shock, Alexandria responded, "I know none of those people you just spoke about. Hell, I've never been to Las Vegas, either. You are wrong, you are *not* my son, and you have no idea what you are talking about."

I then responded, "I have proof, Alexandria. I have a birth certificate right here in this envelope. All the proof is right here, and you know it."

Alexandria just shook her head no and closed the screen door. Then, she said to us all, "Now, get lost." She slammed the door in front of all three of us and left us on the front porch.

Then, Leonard started again with the obscenities. After swearing up a storm again, he started to knock on a window. After the knock on the window, you could hear Alexandria get on her phone and speak to somebody. Then, we realized Alexandria was calling the police on us, and then we decided to leave. About the time we were getting off of Alexandria's porch, we could see somebody walking over from next door and heading up the driveway.

Michael, Leonard, and I got into the car, and then it turned out that this guy walking up the driveway was the cop Alexandria had called. Michael was the last one to get into the car, and when the cop showed up, Michael rolled down his window and said hello. As it turned out, Michael knew this guy, as he had gone to Brookvale High School with him. After exchanging pleasantries, the county police officer asked Michael what the problem was. Michael told the county police officer, "The three of us went to pay our mother a visit, and she was not to responsive to us being there. It got kind of ugly, and when she called you, we decided to leave."

The police officer then said to us, "Why don't you guys go ahead and leave, and I will go in and talk to her and try to calm her down. She seemed really upset when she called me."

Michael said, "Okay, we will get on out of here and take off; sorry for your troubles."

Michael then put the car in reverse, and we backed up far enough, so that we could turn around in the driveway. After we got out to the main road, we turned left and made our way back to Michael's house. On our way out of the driveway, I could see Alexandria letting the cop into her house. That figured, here it was, she called the police on us for no reason and denies us into her house, but she allows a cop into her house to lie to him about why the three of us were there. That just made me sick! I mean, really, would any normal person do that? Would any normal person just stand there and lie about this whole thing? Alexandria would. Again, for her, it would be easier than telling the truth. It made me think: What if she ever had to testify in a court of law? She certainly has a major problem telling the truth. Alexandria gets up there on the stand, and the bailiff has her put her hand on the Bible and swear to tell the truth, the whole truth, and nothing but the truth, so help you God? Yeah, right, this woman would not know the truth if it jumped up and bit her in the arm…or any other body part for that matter.

The three of us went back to Michael's house and discussed the whole episode in the family room, so we would not be bothered. Leonard felt very badly and must have apologized to Michael and me about a dozen times or so for all of the foul and greasy language his dished out at Alexandria's mobile home.

Michael and I told Leonard not to worry about it. I had no idea just how bad it was between him and Alexandria. After seeing all of the outbursts of obscenities during our visit, I was just now getting to understand the situation. Alexandria had really pissed off just about everybody in our family, including former husbands, her own children, and others. It was only a matter of time before I would find out that she was not talking to her grandchildren and great-grandchildren. It was bad enough I had to witness what I saw out there at Alexandria's house that Sunday afternoon. But now, it kind of all made sense. Alexandria was not a sociable person, at least with her own family. Alexandria wanted nothing to do with any of us. I would only assume that because it took me so long to find Alexandria as an adult, as well as my six siblings (Katy included), that there had to be more to this story.

Over the next, several days, until I left Brookvale, Pennsylvania, Michael and I would talk about Alexandria and some of things that led to her being that type of person. Michael was really sorry for what had happened out at the trailer that afternoon, but as I told him and Leonard, that was not anybody's fault but Alexandria's. She just would not accept the truth to the matter concerning me, which is why she was in denial about the whole thing. Plus, as I told Michael when she said she did not know me, she actually was telling the truth. She and Jack Winterbottom had left me in the hospital in Las Vegas, and at the time, all they knew was that my birth certificate at that time stated my name was "Baby Winterbottom." That's it.

She had no idea that the hospital called Tom Dowd and his mother and told them they were to come to that hospital and pick me up. So, since there was a law in the State of Nevada that stated that if I was to be adopted, both parents would have to sign the papers to make it legal and, since Tom would not sign the document, Alexandria left me in that hospital and some sort of Social Services took custody of me until Tom was found. My grandmother just happened to be in Las Vegas visiting her son at the time, so it was perfect timing, I guess.

So, getting back to my explanation, I do think Alexandria was telling the truth regarding my name. She had no idea what my name was, and that made it easier for her to deny knowing who I was. But the proof was in the pudding, so to speak, and the next day or so, Michael dug up some pictures that he found in some boxes that were stored in the basement of Michael's house.

Michael had a picture of Alexandria in a red party dress that looked like she was at a wedding or some special event. That picture that Michael had given me showed a profile side of Alexandria sitting at a table at this social function of some type. Michael told me that when he saw this picture again, it was really then that he knew I was his sibling.

Michael said, "You know, brother Michael, I always believed your story, and I always believed that you were our brother; not just from your story, but with all of the factors involved in your story. But when I saw you in our house, sitting in one of our chairs, and I got to see your profile, that reminded me of this picture of Alexandria. After comparing this picture of Alexandria's profile with your profile, this was the proof that was in the pudding, so to speak.

There was another picture of Alexandria that intrigued me, as well. The picture was dated sometime in 1966, and it was a picture of Alexandria in a dark green dress and pregnant with our brother, Leonard. She and Leonard

Sr. were already married at this time, but what intrigued me about this Polaroid picture was taken about three years or so after I was born. I could now see what Tom saw in her. Alexandria was a very attractive lady, who had this incredibly thick, jet-black hair. I remember when Tom would talk about Alexandria from those visits in New Orleans that Alexandria's thick hair was one of the things he always spoke about.

I remember that visit back when I was a teenager when Tom had come to Valpo and visited with my grandfather and me, and I remember Tom speaking of that same thing. At that time, as a fourteen-year-old, I had this thick, dark, brown hair, which kind of matched Tom's hair color, but the thickness of my hair at that time was like Alexandria's thick hair at the time. You heard me talk about Alexandria, when I saw her for that first time that Sunday afternoon, she still had this thick, black hair with some grey in it.

After seeing Alexandria's pictures from when Jackie gave me those pictures going back to when she and I met for the first time at the casino in New Buffalo, Michigan, I could tell Alexandria had this jet-black hair, too. However, this picture of Alexandria in this green dress and pregnant with our brother, Leonard, was most intriguing. Alexandria was one, big mystery to me, and finding her and my siblings were just the tip of the iceberg. Since my brothers and sisters were all fine with meeting me, that was the opportunity to get to know them. Alexandria was a problem because she was so secretive about everything with regards to our family, and trying to keep things hidden from three of my siblings about me, as well as our two older sisters. Who would have known?

That Monday, after the famous Sunday visit with Alexandria, I woke up to breakfast once again, this time from Michael. Michael was up early and, because of the inclement weather that was going on outside, Michael's three kids were off from school. After the snowfall on Saturday night, the weather had turned into a rain/sleet event, and the schools in Brookvale and the rest of the County were closed. So, while eating a delicious breakfast of bacon and eggs that Michael had made, Michael stated that he wanted to take me up to Williamsport, Pennsylvania, to see the Bill Elliot McDonald's. Then, after lunch, we would go up to find the Little League baseball complex. When I had arrived in Brookvale the previous Saturday, Michael and I had talked about the complex in Williamsport, and how I used to watch the Little League World Series when I was younger.

After I finished breakfast and got showered and dressed, Michael, his son, and I got into the car and took off to Williamsport. The drive took us a little longer to get to the restaurant than usual, because of the weather. The sleet had turned to rain and, despite the weather, the roads were wet and not snow-covered. About an hour later, we arrived at the restaurant with all of this cool Bill Elliot racing items that were in the inside of the place. If you are not familiar with the sport of NASCAR racing and were wondering who Bill Elliot is, Awesome Bill from Dawsonville was, and still is, a NASCAR legend. Bill won two Daytona 500 races in 1985 and 1987 and then won the driver's championship in 1988. I had actually met Bill Elliot at the Indianapolis Motor Speedway, during qualifying for one of the Brickyard 400 races back in the 1990s. My meeting with Bill Elliot was very brief, so it was more like a quick hello, and off he went. But, still, I got to speak to him. The Bill Elliot McDonald's is actually a museum, of sorts, with the restaurant as an added bonus. Even though Michael and I had only met just a little more than a month before, he and I had discussed racing a great deal. I had spoken about all of the Indianapolis 500 races I had been to, as well as being a former ticket holder for that race, and I had mentioned that I had seen the Brickyard 400 at the Indianapolis Motor Speedway, as well. I had mentioned that my friend Bill Frank and I had gone to several Daytona 500 races, as well. Michael had told me that he was in the auto repair and tire business, and he used to get tickets to the races at the Pocono International Raceway, which was just about an hour's drive from Brookvale. Michael, like me, had also met Team owner Roger Penske. I had met Mr. Penske at an IndyCar function back in 2003 at EPCOT theme park at Walt Disney World. Michael told me that he had met Mr. Penske at one of the Pocono NASCAR races in the Goodyear hospitality tent before the race started. The more time Michael and Leonard and I spent together, the more things I found out how much we had in common. Leonard had told me that he is a big James Bond fan of the books and films. Leonard told me if he still had the books, written by one of my favorite novelists, Ian Fleming, he would have given them to me. Unfortunately, those books perished in a fire several years before that and were never recovered. I guess finding all of these things out were like making up for lost ground or lost years with my siblings. That was a good thing.

Michael, his son, and I went up to Williamsport and found the Little League complex. The weather in Williamsport had turned to snow, and there was about four or six inches of new white stuff on the ground, and it was coming down that Monday afternoon. The three of us had parked in the front by the museum, but the museum was not open. We then walked down the hill and saw the complex that was behind the museum and mall type offices. The baseball complex was kind of like a small college campus with the way it was laid out. There was another hill that was at the bottom of the hill that led to the main baseball stadium. The grounds and stands were all covered in snow, and you could see the stand out over the fence in centerfield. That was the television camera stand for all of the games that were broadcasted from that complex. There was nobody playing on any of the eight or so diamonds, but there were some kids going down the hill on a toboggan, which looked like fun. Michael took a few pictures of his son Mark and me at the complex and at the Bill Elliot McDonald's. Those pictures were all taken with a digital camera, so that I could put them all on my Facebook page that I was documenting. That worked out really nice. On the way back from Williamsport, and in the coming days, Michael and I talked more about Sunday's visit with Alexandria. Michael had come to the conclusion that Alexandria may have acted the way she did because she was embarrassed. That was still no excuse, but maybe the truth. Later that day, I was speaking to Leonard Sr., and he kind of told the same thing. Then, Michael and I talked about doing one more thing, so that maybe Alexandria would just understand all of this. Michael and I agreed to co-write a letter and include a copy of my birth certificate that I had brought with me. I had talked to Michael about one other idea ,too, and, during this discussion, Michael and I were going to get Alexandria a bouquet of flowers and put the envelope with the two things in it and give Alexandria the envelope with the flowers. We had no idea how she would react, but we both thought that this might be the best way to soften her up, so to speak.

That next day, Michael and I went to Berwick, Pennsylvania, as the weather had gotten a lot better. The sun was out, and Michael had wanted to get the car cleaned, since it was covered in salt from the roads and all of the bad weather. Then, afterwards, we would go to a grocery store, Giant, and get Alexandria a nice bouquet of flowers.

The store had a nice floral department, so we picked one out and had some red roses put in the bouquet, too. The florist added the roses for us, and Michael and I split the tab for the flower bill. Then we went back to Michael's house and made a copy of my birth certificate and wrote the letter of explanation. About an hour later, after lunch, Michael had some errands to run, and then we took the flowers out to Alexandria's house. Again, we went up the long, gravel driveway that led to the house. Michael would not get out of the car, so it was going to be up to me to make the delivery. Before I got out of the car, I made sure that we had the letter, as well as the copy of the birth certificate secured in the envelope. I asked Michael if I should write Alexandria's name on it. Michael replied yes, so before I made my flower delivery, I wrote Alexandria's name on the outside of that envelope. Ironically, I mentioned to Michael, "You know, Michael, one day I just may write a book about all of this. This is a huge chapter of my life and how my life has come in one full circle, there is only one name I could call this book on my life. I would have to call it *The Name on the Envelope*.

"I think that this story has been a very interesting journey for me and, after finding all of this out, and with all of the things and situations that we have discovered, I honestly think that this would be a very good story to write about."

Michael concurred, saying, "Yes, brother, this *has* been interesting, to say the least, and I suppose if there is any consolation out of this whole ordeal, it would be that we now know who our family members are."

Michael was right about this ordeal. He was spot on. Our story was really like no other could imagine. Our story was as interesting for him and his side of the family, as well as for me. It just seemed like every time either he or I spoke about it, we would always learn about something new, just by discussing our story.

After putting Alexandria's name on the envelope and talking about an auto-biography about our story, I said to Michael, " I'll go make this delivery, and I will be right back." Alexandria's car was where she usually parked it—

right in front of her house, not far from the porch on the trailer. I was not sure if Alexandria was home, but I knocked on the door anyway. There was a small, two-seat bench on the porch, and when I did not think she was going to answer, I started to put the flowers on the bench.

Then, all of a sudden, the big door opened, and Alexandria was there. She never said hello to me, and she never opened the screen door. I looked at Alexandria, and she looked right back at me. I said to Alexandria after she opened the door, "These flowers are for you with this envelope."

Alexandria was immediately agitated, and then she replied in a feisty manner, "Take those flowers back; I don't want them!"

Again, I said, "These are for you, Alexandria; enjoy them!"

Once again she slammed the door on me, just like she did on that previous Sunday afternoon. I did not care, though, as I now had seen her twice, and I now know who she is. For what it was worth, despite all of the issues, Alexandria can believe the story or not. At that moment in time, she can deny everything if she wants to, but all of us kids from her family know the truth. Alexandria was just too stubborn to admit and too dishonest to accept the truth.

I would not see Alexandria for another six months or so, when I would return to Brookvale for the Fourth of July and meet our sister, Natalie, and her husband. Once again, during that trip, I went to Alexandria's house in the country. Michael drove us out to the house, and our sister, Natalie, went with us. Natalie and Michael stayed in the car, and I walked up the gravel driveway and again knocked on the door.

This time Alexandria had been out mowing the yard, and she had bought a new car. Her Honda Civic and been demolished in a car accident, and she had got what looked to be a brand new car. The car was silver in color, and it reminded me of my silver Ford Taurus that I used to own before somebody ran a red light in downtown Orlando and demolished that car. Anyway, Alexandria was home, I thought, and I knocked on the door. This time on this visit, I brought not only my birth certificate but I also brought pictures of me when I was younger. I just thought Alexandria wanted to see them. I was wrong, dead wrong. My birth mother answered the door, and I heard her scream through the screen door. "Who are you, and what do you want?"

I said, "Alexandria, this is Michael. We met last January when Michael introduced us and you flew into a rage and screamed at us."

Alexandria then came back and yelled, "I told you then, I don't know you, and we are *not* related. Are you the one who plowed my driveway shut so I could not get my car out of the snow?"

I replied, "No, Alexandria, I live in the State of Florida, and I don't own a snow plow." Alexandria, who was still screaming, said, "Well, somebody did, and I want you to know I did not appreciate that when it happened. Who are you, what is your name, and why are you here? Just what do you want?"

I then repeated the story: "Alexandria, you know my name, and you knew my father, Thomas Dowd. You were married to a man named Jack Winterbottom in July 1963 and gave birth to me later that year in Las Vegas. You mean you don't remember?"

"I have *never* been to Las Vegas, and I *never* gave birth to you!" She then slammed the door slammed on me for the third time. That would be the last time I would see Alexandria. I would make one more trip to Brookvale in the spring of 2012, over the Easter holiday weekend, but I made it clear that I had no desire to go back to Alexandria's front door and get the door slammed in my face. I just did not care to have that happen again and be so humiliated. That was not going to happen to me again.

The next day, February 2, was Michael's forty-second birthday, and Leonard had told us he was going to come over and we would go to Brookvale Pizza restaurant for lunch. The three of us had a fun time that day for lunch, and it was cool, just hanging out with both of my brothers once again.

Leonard was again very sorry for the scene he had caused when we were out at Alexandria's house. Leonard said that he was sorry that the situation was just that bad and that he knew it was not the best way to introduce me to Alexandria. I told Leonard not to worry about the issue and that it was all water under the bridge. I also told Leonard that I just had no idea that it was so tough between the two of them. I was going to be leaving Brookvale the next day and travel to see my sister, Katy, and see her husband and family. So, I said my good byes to Leonard and, after lunch, I told Leonard that I would try to get back to Brookvale for the Fourth of July later that year because we thought that Natalie and her husband might be here then, too. So, again, Leonard and I said our goodbyes, and Michael and I went back home. I was going to call my therapist, Natalie Bogart, and call my parents, as well as my sister, Katy. I wanted to update everybody on the situation here in Brookvale and let Katy know when to expect me in Washington, D.C. at the Ronald Reagan Airport. I was really looking forward to seeing Katy and her family on this trip since we had not seen each other in about fourteen years or so. To add to that, I had never really spent any time in our nation's capital, so it was going to be a sightseeing trip, as well. So, after speaking to my parents and updating them on my trip so far, I then spoke to my therapist and updated her, as well. Then, after those two phone calls, I called Katy and let her know when to expect me at the airport. Then, a really cool thing happened. I was on the phone with Katy, and then I got to introduce her to my brother, Michael. I was not sure what was said exactly, but it was just cool to hear the two of them talk for the first time. Michael had heard all about Katy from our conversations, and Katy had heard about Michael through me after I made my discovery. Michael then handed the phone back to me, and I once again said that I would see Katy on Thursday afternoon, as long as my flight was on time. I then hung up the phone, and now it was time to celebrate my brother's forty-second birthday. After another filling meal, we all gave him gifts when we had birthday cake. It was a fun celebration to be a part of, and I was just glad that I was there to help celebrate Michael's birthday. As I said in past chapters, it is times like these you just don't forget. And, on top of that, times like these just do not get any better!

CHAPTER 13: MY FULL CIRCLE OF LIFE

The day was Thursday, and on this day, I was going to be traveling to leave Brookvale, Pennsylvania. I was traveling to Alexandria, Virginia, to go see Katy and her family. It was time to leave to the airport in Harrisburg and catch a connecting flight to Philadelphia, then from Philadelphia to Washington-Reagan Airport. My flight was leaving around 2:30 P.M. or so, but with the drive time to the Harrisburg Airport, I was up early again so that we had plenty of time to get there. Michael and I talked about my trip to Brookvale and asked me when I was coming back. I had mentioned that I would like to get back around the Fourth of July, if we could talk Natalie and her husband to come up then, as well. I was counting on coming back to Brookvale, as I now had family there. It was relaxing to go there and very scenic. More importantly, it was time to catch up with my family members who lived there, with the exception of our birth mother.

Alexandria would not admit to the truth in all of this, and that issue had become frustrating. The story for me and my family members with regards to our mother was very frustrating. Alexandria would not talk to any of her children, grandchildren, and great-grandchildren. It was just that frustrating. Michael and I talked a lot about that issue on our way to the airport in Harrisburg. Michael knew it, Leonard knew it, Jackie knew it, and so did I. I think it was frustrating for at least two of Alexandria's former husbands, as well. I think it had to be frustrating for Jack Winterbottom, as well as Leonard Mitchell Sr. Like I had said before, Alexandria had been married four times and divorced all four times. I knew three of her former husbands. I had spoken to one on the phone several times, and I had met one other one, as well. Both former husbands I spoke with both told me that Alexandria had a really bad habit of not telling the truth. My sister, Jackie, and my two brothers had told me the same thing. At least for the time being, Alexandria had tried and tried to keep her past a secret: the marriage to Jack Winterbottom and her marriage to her first husband, William Gardison. Alexandria had lied to people about those marriages. She also lied about her two, oldest daughters because she had lost custody of them to her first husband. Alexandria lied to me about everything, including knowing my father, Thomas Dowd, and then she lied to me again about not knowing or being married to Jack Winterbottom. Alexandria had covered it all up, just like former President Richard Nixon. I guess you could say that for me, anyway, finding my birth mother, Alexandria, was kind of like discovering my own kind of personal Watergate cover-up.

First, my brothers and youngest sister find out that they have two older sisters, thanks to the search that was done for the marriage annulment by Catholic Family Services. Then I find one of Alexandria's former husbands, and he has a name written on the envelope of his divorce papers with her. Then I find out I have family members....five more of them. At that point in my life, I just felt like my life had become a story line for the soap opera, *Days of Our Lives*, except I was not battling the evil Stefano DiMera; this time I was taking on my actual birth mother. Alexandria had hosed us all, and she did not care. The way I see it, she is and was only hurting herself. She wanted it that way. If Alexandria was embarrassed about the whole ordeal, I could understand it. But not admitting the truth to any of this story...that was just wrong.

Michael and I got to the airport in Harrisburg, and we parked in the airport parking garage. Michael got my luggage out of the car, and we ventured into the airport terminal. We got there early, so I took Michael to the MacDonald's restaurant they had in the terminal building. I got checked in, and I was told that my flight was on time. I took my boarding pass, and we went into the restaurant. It was kind of disappointing to leave Brookvale and the State of Pennsylvania, considering everything that had happened. Michael was just so understanding about everything, and he knew what I was going through. He and Leonard, along with my sister, Jackie, understood it all. I was happy I had found them. My brothers and sisters were happy I found them. I had brothers-in-law and sisters-in-law. I had a whole slew of nieces and nephews, as well as great-nieces and great-nephews. This was awesome! And I had my family that I grew up with, too. My parents in Valparaiso, my sister, Sharon, and her husband, Bob, and their two daughters, Melissa and Rebecca. I have a great niece and nephew in that family, too. I have my sister, Susan, and her husband, Bill, and their daughter, Jessica. On top of all of these family members, I have cousins from the Dowd, DeHaven, and Johnson families. In addition to all of the family members, then I have my friends, too. One of the things I realized in all of my story of discovery, If was that if I had died at any point of my life before I had found any of this out, I would have gone to my grave never knowing the truth to the matter. My newly found brothers and sisters would have never known either. I broke the code. I solved the mystery. I found the sunken treasure. I won the lottery jackpot. This kind of feeling was like no other. I guess it goes way back to when I got to see my sister, Katy, for the first time. Now I was on my way to see Katy again almost thirty years after we saw each other back in Naples, Florida.

Michael and I finished our lunch at the airport, and then it was time to get through security and get to the gate. Michael and I said our goodbyes, hugged, and I stood in line at the entrance to the secured area. I made it through the line, and I waved one more time at Michael through the security opening. I knew I was going to be back for the Fourth of July, so I knew we would see each other again. There will always be times again to go to Brookvale, and as long as Alexandria will not speak to us, or admit the truth, there will always be unfinished business in Brookvale, too.

I walked down to my gate, and the gate attendant said that the flight that was going to Philadelphia was late getting to Harrisburg and was delayed about fifteen or twenty minutes. Once the plane finally arrived, the passengers got off the plane, and then I saw some airplane mechanics go out to the plane and work on one of the propeller engines. The plane I was taking to Philadelphia was a puddle jumper, as it was called. The aircraft had two propeller engines on the wings and held about fifty passengers or so. The mechanics worked on the plane for about an hour, and then we were cleared to get on the plane and leave. I called Katy's house in Virginia to let them know. We boarded the plane, and after all of this delay, we were on our way to Philadelphia. The weather was nice and sunny, so I was hoping that weather should not be a factor in getting to the Philadelphia airport. After flying at a low-level altitude to the airport, we were soon on the ground in Philadelphia and pulled up to the terminal where we got off the plane. Because we were in the commuter section of the airport terminal, I had to get off the plane, get my carry-on, and walk into the terminal building. Then I had to take a bus to the area of where my connecting flight was to Washington. After a short bus ride in the secured area, I got off the bus and went back into the terminal. I had to go up an escalator and find my gate. Now, if any of you have ever been through the airport in Philadelphia, it is not very new or clean. In fact, I would have to say, that out of all the airports I have been in, Philadelphia has to be the oldest, most outdated, and dirtiest airports of them all. I thought I would have time to get one of those famous Philly cheese steak sandwiches while I was there, but the place was so dirty, it just left me feeling like I needed to take a shower after I had left. I had to wait until the airplane I was taking to Washington arrived, and then my flight was called, and I boarded the plane. The flight was going to take about an hour, and I could not wait to see Katy. My sister was going to pick me up at the airport, and we would have the chance to catch up after all of these years. My flight got to Washington, and when we landed, I could see the Washington Monument all lit up, like it was glowing. There was a full moon out, too, which kind of made sense on this trip anyway, so everything kind of had a glow to it.

My plane arrived at the gate, and since I was in an aisle seat, I was able to get my carry-on and get off the plane quickly. I made it off the plane and onto the jetport, and then I was inside the airport terminal in Washington. The first thing I noticed when I got off the plane was a Five Guys burger place off to my right of where I walked into the gate. I also noticed that my airplane was parked at the very last gate in that part of the terminal. So, I followed the signs, and I was hoping that Katy was going to be there when I got out of the secured area. I am sure she got my message. So, I walked down to the exit of the secured area and make a left turn to the luggage carousels to get my one bag of luggage. I make that left turn out of the secured area and, lo and behold, just around the corner was my sister, Katy! She was waiting for me with this big, wide smile on her face. We hugged, greeted each other, and exchanged pleasantries. We had not seen each other since Katy and her husband, Mike, had come to Valparaiso, for Tom's memorial service. Now, so many years had passed, and she and her husband had two young boys, and I had two more nephews. I could not wait to meet my two nephews, either. I could not wait to see Katy's husband, Mike, again, either. More importantly, I could not wait to see Katy again. She and I had so much to talk about. It was almost thirty years since I first got to see Katy as an adult at her house in Naples, Florida. Katy knew what my new family situation was, and she knew that I had been looking for my birth mother for all of these years. She had been a supporter of mine all of these years, and I could not wait to tell her what my experience was in Brookvale. It was like I was sitting on a time bomb or something. This story of mine was just that explosive. But little did I know what was in store for me. I just had no idea what my sister had planned.

There is nothing like a little surprise in your life, particularly when you are with a sibling who you have not seen in a long time.

As I got closer to my sister, I had a big wide grin on my face, as well. It was almost like getting rid of fourteen years of frustration or something. Katy always had a very busy schedule, and I was just glad she had invited me to her house for a few days. I had actually never been to see Washington, D.C., before and played tourist. I had always wanted to see the historic buildings of our nation's capital, but I just never made time for it. The feeling was kind of like going to Disney World.

I thought I was the only one in the world who had never been to the Walt Disney World. So, to eliminate that problem, when I moved to Central Florida back in 1999, one of the first things I did was get an annual pass so that I could go on my days off to any park at Disney World. Now, I have been to all of those parks so many times, I actually have lost count. But Washington, D.C. was a different story. I can remember hearing about some kids when they go through school, they sometimes got to get on a bus and go to Washington for spring break. Me, I never got to do that. My grandfather never had the need or want to go there, and even though my parents had been there on vacation many years before, I never was invited to go with them. Now, I think I know why they never took me. I did not realize it until some many years later, but about the time my parents went to Washington, D.C. for a vacation, they had gone to see one of my cousins, Paul DeHaven. Paul was a cop on the streets of Washington during some of the most violent times in our nation's history. During those violent times of the 1960s and 1970s, there were a lot of sit-ins, stand-offs, as well as demonstrations and even riots. All because of the conflict that had been going on while our American troops were over in Vietnam. Ironically, Paul had been in the service during some of those years and had been a military policeman during his tour of duty. When Paul got honorably discharged from the service, he was quickly recruited by the Washington, D.C. Police force. It was during those violent times in Washington that Paul and his fellow police officers had to control the crowds of demonstrators, including using tear gas and arrest large groups of people. I can remember after my parents got back from Washington, about some of the stories that Paul had told his aunt and uncle about some of things that he had been a part of while he was a policeman there. I can remember my dad talking about it when I was really young and we lived on Oak Street. Friends and relatives would come over and visit. Dad would talk about the tear gas they used in those riots and demonstrations and talk about how the jails would be so overcrowded that the police force would have to put all of the overcrowded inmates on the floor in handcuffs on a high school gymnasium floor until they could be processed. Many years ago, I can remember my mom saved a *Life* magazine, and the reason she had saved it was because there was an article on some of the things like the riots and demonstrations going on in Washington. The other reason why my mom had saved the magazine was because there were pictures of Paul in full color in it. In that *Life* magazine, there were at least two pictures of Paul on duty during those riots and demonstrations.

As it turned out, there was another reason why Paul was an important person in my life. It was Paul's untimely death in May 1999 that I had made the decision to leave Valpo. From about May 1998 until May 1999, there were four, major events that happened in my life that made me want to leave Valpo and leave for good and never come back. First, in the spring of 1998, my former wife, Pam, and I filed for divorce, with Pam eventually moving to Orlando, Florida, to take her new job. Second, about a month after Pam left me and left for Orlando, Florida, the company I was working for was sold, and the new owners decided that they would cut management jobs, which included mine. I was lucky because I got a different job about three weeks later, but I was angry when they cut me loose. Third, I went on a scuba diving vacation with about thirty-five other friends to Cozumel, Mexico, during March 1999 and, on that trip, we lost a friend and fellow diver, who somehow fell off the dive boat that we were on and died when he got caught under the boat in the propellers. Then, the fourth and final straw in all of it was when Paul died suddenly at a private function in Merrillville, Indiana. Paul worked for the Merrillville, Indiana, police force and had passed away in May 1999. There was this huge wake and funeral procession and, no doubt, I know that had to be the biggest procession that I had ever been a part of. They had streets blocked off in Merrillville, including parts of Broadway, which is no doubt one of the busiest streets in Northwest Indiana. There was the wake, the funeral the next day, and then the procession from the church to the cemetery. I can remember going past the Merrillville Police Department building on Broadway, and we stopped right out in front of the building on Broadway. They had Paul's unmarked police car on display, with black flags draped on the dashboard on the inside of the car. There was a multi-gun salute that took place there. Then, we went to the cemetery for the interment, and afterwards, there was a dinner that was hosted for by the Fraternal Order of Police. Like any funeral for any police officer who dies while they are employed by the police department or dies in the line of duty, there were police cars from many other areas in Northwest Indiana, as well as from different parts of the State of Indiana. This included the Indiana State Police, the local county police from Lake County, Indiana, as well as other surrounding counties. Paul had been employed by Merrillville for over twenty years and knew many, many people. It showed because of the turnout at the funeral and wake. We lost a great man that year, and not just a Merrillville cop. We lost a cousin, nephew, father, husband, brother, friend, and cop. Paul was all of that and more...a lot more. So, I guess that it was only fitting that there was such a huge celebration of life for him.

I talked about 1979 as the absolute worse year I ever had. I would guess that from May 1998 until May 1999 would no doubt be the second worst year of my life. How I made it through all of that I'll never really know. I guess in that year of time, it was yet another full circle of time. First, Pam and I had split up and had filed for divorce. Pam would never sign the divorce papers, so we stayed married, but she moved to Orlando, Florida, to take her new job. That took place in July 1998. Then, just about a month later in August1998, after TCI was sold, and AT&T took over, they decided to eliminate a lot of the management jobs. My job was in management and I, along with many others from the Hammond/Gary/South Chicago Suburbs Division, were let go. Now, I was out of a job, had to pay the mortgage, and try to find a new job. About three weeks later, I got a job at WYIN TV Channel 56 in nearby Merrillville. The job was only part-time, but it helped pay the bills. Then, about March 1999, I went on a scuba diving trip with a group of friends from the local scuba club to Cozumel, Mexico. While in Cozumel, my roommate and diving partner, Bill, got caught under a dive boat after we got back from a dive. The accident happened when my diving partner lost his balance when the dive boat was put in gear, and he lost his balance and fell off the boat. Then the boat turned, and he went right under the boat and got caught into the propeller of the boat. My friend Bill died instantly. There was nothing anybody could have done to prevent it. The accident was tragic. Our friend was brought back to the boat with a fatal head injury that exposed his brain. That next morning, in Cozumel, another friend and myself had to go to the local police station and give a statement. Because of the accident, the boat captain and the two deck hands were put in jail until the accident was investigated. They were released about twenty-four hours later. The rest of the trip was tainted, and I never went back to Cozumel again after that trip. The fourth and final thing that caused me to want to move from Valpo was when I heard about the sudden death of my cousin, Paul DeHaven. As I said before, it was his death that became the last bad thing that happened, and I wanted nothing but a clean start somewhere else. Not long before Paul's death, Pam had come back to Northwest Indiana and had said that she wanted to reconcile and get back together. I told her that I would think about it. Paul's sudden death took place a few weeks later, but for me, it was just the last straw that helped me make the decision to leave Valpo. As it turned out, Pam and I reconciled and got back together, and it was June 1999 when I quit my job at Channel 56 and sold the house that Pam and I had bought in Washington Township, just outside of Valpo. That decision to move to Central Florida turned out to be very beneficial for me. Not only did Pam and I get back together, but it would only be a couple of years later, in 2002 that I would be hospitalized and would wind up having life-saving heart surgery. That life-saving surgery that I had would really turn out to be a life saver for me. It would only be about eight years later when I was long recovered from that heart surgery that I would get re-acquainted with Debbie and apologize to her for all of my wrongdoings. Then, just a month after that, I find my siblings and birth mother, as well as two former step-fathers. I would discover what some of the answers were to many questions that I had that were a mystery for me and most of my life. That *is* the full circle of life. But there would be at least one more circle of life that I would discover at my sister's house in Virginia.

After Katy and I got re-acquainted again after fourteen years, I got my luggage off the carousel at Washington-Reagan Airport, Katy and I left the building and headed for her car. I put my luggage into her trunk, got in her car, and we took off. Katy said she wanted to take me out for dinner since her husband was at a basketball game for one of her sons. So, Katy and I went to a restaurant in the Old Town section of Alexandria and went to a wonderful seafood restaurant. It was so good to be with Katy again. Like I had said, it had been a very long fourteen years since she and I had seen each other, as well visited. During those fourteen years, we did talk to each other on the phone, but it is just not the same when you get to visit in person. In these fourteen years, She and her husband, Mike, had two boys. They were young boys growing up and going to school and doing things like I used to. The oldest, Brent, was really into sports. He played, baseball, lacrosse, ad basketball. Brent's younger brother, Eric, was only in first grade at the time, but he was very smart like his older brother, and very mature for his age. He like to play sports, too, like basketball, but he just had not developed his full athletic potential just yet. Because it was early February, both of my nephews were playing basketball at the time, and the really cool thing was I got the chance to see Brent play one night in Virginia. It was kind of funny to see my nephew play the game, and even though he was only in sixth grade at the time, I could not believe how well their team played. It was even more fun to see my brother-in-law, Mike, and see how animated he got at the games. If the referee made a bad call or missed a call, Mike stood up and let the ref know it. Katy had told me Mike had even been thrown out of one of Brent's games, due to his reactions of one of those blown calls. While Katy, Mike, and I were at one of Brent's games, I got to see Mike's temper come out. He never got a technical foul or anything, but Mike was a basketball player himself back in the day, kind of like me when I was in ninth grade at Thomas Jefferson Junior High School. Mike, like me, had played the game and, like me, was a student of the game.

Katy and I were having dinner at this wonderful restaurant, and after we ordered, I then got the chance to start talking about my trip to Pennsylvania. Before our dinner arrived, Katy and I had an interesting conversation about my trip. I told Katy about my visits with my two brothers and meeting them, as well as our meeting with our birth mother. I told Katy about the door being slammed in our faces…not once, but twice. I also told Katy about what it was like seeing Alexandria for the first time. I had mentioned about how nervous I was and how it reminded me of when Katy and I had met in Naples, Florida, for the first time as adults. I told Katy the whole story of my experience with Alexandria, and we both agreed that Alexandria must really be a sick person or something to deny and lie about it all. If I had all of this evidence that Alexandria was my birth mother, why would Alexandria just lie and deny it? Why would Alexandria deny being married to Jack Winterbottom, as well as knowing our father, Thomas Dowd? Then, even deny that Alexandria lived in Las Vegas, with my father Tom Dowd and then getting married to Jack Winterbottom. Then, after giving birth to me, in Las Vegas, Alexandria left me in the hospital until my father and grandmother could get there to claim me. But now I realize that my life had not come full circle just yet. Yes, I had related to Katy all about my trip to Brookvale, Pennsylvania, and how everything took place, but more was to come. I could tell Katy had something up her sleeve, and I had no idea what it was. I guess that is what surprises are about. This is what puts the grin on my face. When something is a total surprise and that you have no idea that it is coming at you. Something so surprising, you just never saw it coming.

About two nights after I had arrived at Katy's house in Virginia, Katy and I were talking about things about our father and families when, all of a sudden, Katy goes and gets a book or something and returns to the family room of their house. Katy took a seat right next to me and said, "I have something here I think you might want to take a look at."

She handed me what appeared to be a wedding album. It wasn't just any wedding album. As it turned out, it was the wedding album of our father Tom, and Katy's mother, Doreen, from November 1958. I had never seen these photos before, and I do not even remember Tom ever talking about it. Tom never really talked about his first marriage, unless I had asked him about certain things; in particular, when it came about talking about my birth mother, Alexandria.

However, this was different. This wedding album was the tangible proof that I needed to write this book. The proof of existence. The timeline from the beginning, for both Katy and myself. I guess it was the beginning for my brothers, Michael and Leonard, , as well as my youngest sister, Jackie. With my two older sisters found in Arkansas, Nancy and Natalie, I now had that tangible proof about my story. My life's story. Our life's story. The story about me, as well as the rest of my siblings. This is the start of the story and proof of why things happened the way they did. Not only was it the beginning of Katy's life, as well as mine but also the other people involved in our lives: Our father, Thomas Dowd, our grandparents, Katy's mother, Doreen, Jack Winterbottom and Leonard Mitchell, my great aunt and uncle, my parents, Harold and Aileen Johnson, and their daughters, Sharon and Susan, Aunt Bonnie and Uncle Chuck, and my cousin, Shawn Kenworthy. All these relatives had some decisions regarding the future of my life, as well as Katy's. The funny thing was, at that time, neither one of us was born yet. It was these decisions that were made, for whatever the reason, that somehow helped Katy and I get to this point in our lives. That thought suddenly hit me like a speeding race car at the Indianapolis Motor Speedway. As I was sitting next to Katy on the couch that night, I then mentioned my thought to my sister. I said, "You know something, Katy, this wedding album is the tangible proof of the beginning of our lives. This kind of all makes sense, now that I think about it, this is the beginning of our time, and this wedding album is the proof. This album is proof that we both exist because of the decisions that were made by people like our parents and other relatives.

"Our father married your mother and then, a couple of years later, you were born. Then, for some reason, our father met my birth mother, and that series of events led to the bitter divorce between your mother and our father. Then, while Tom and my birth mother, Alexandria, were living together, they produced me. Your mom re-married, and your family moved to Naples, Florida. I was born in Las Vegas, then brought to Valparaiso, Indiana, and grew up there. In 1981, we find each other and re-unite at your family's house in Naples, Florida. Then, over the next thirty years, we live our lives and stay in touch here and there, and now I find my birth mother after looking for her most of those thirty years, and then also finding out that I have five other siblings, as well as you. Now, here we are, looking at these photos from the past, and I am thinking that somehow, this scene out of our lives was meant to happen. I would almost bet that your mother, Doreen, as well as our father, Tom, and our grandparents, Charles McKinley Dowd and Francis Irene Dowd, wanted you to have this album for many reasons. But, even more so, I'll bet your mother and our father and grandparents somehow knew that someday like today, that you would eventually show me these photos from this album, and we would both realize that this was truly our beginning. Your life and timeline, as well as mine.

"I was wondering that when you invited me to come to your house after being in Pennsylvania for my trip, if seeing this wedding album was just the inspiration I needed to write a book about all of this. I do think that this will be some of the inspiration I needed anyway, to write a book, and I have you to thank for showing this album to me."

Katy was short on words and just did not know what to say or how she was going to react. I could then see her reach for a tissue and wipe her eyes after I spoke. My eyes watered up, too, and then I found myself reaching for a tissue. By this time, we were looking at the pictures, and then we came across some pictures that included Charles McKinley and our grandmother, Francis Irene. The more I looked at some of the photos, the more overwhelmed I got. The sad thing was, Katy did not even know who our grandparents were.

It kind of reminded me of when I was shown pictures of Alexandria's mother and stepfather from my brother, Michael. It was kind of sad for me because I never got to meet them. They both had passed away long before I had even found Alexandria or my siblings. If we only had social media back in the late 1990s and not 2010, maybe I could have found them. It was just too bad that Katy never got the chance to meet her grandfather, Charles McKinley Dowd. I told Katy that she would have loved him like I did. She, like me, would have found him to be special. I then told Katy that I was sorry for the fact that she never got to meet her grandfather and her grandmother. My sister said that it was not my fault, but it was just the situation we were both in. Again, it was those decisions that were made by other people in our lives and decisions that were made by those my sister and I never knew who they were until we got older. However, it was those decisions, or at least some of them, anyway, that helped my sister and I get to this point in our lives. As if it was meant to be. In other parts of this book, I use the example of the DeLorean Time Machine that was fictitiously used in *Back to the Future* films. In our case, at least with my sister Katy and me, I could have taken us back to Valparaiso, and I could have introduced her to our grandparents. That would have been nice for the both of us.

CHAPTER 14: FINAL ADDITION

In looking back on the time it took me to write this book about my life, I never really thought that I would ever write a book. The writing of this book has been another major accomplishment for me, and also writing this book has been like a giant English paper assignment that I had to write. Writing this book has also been fun, and the things I remembered along with the people who share or who have shared my life with me. I never thought I would be a writer. I never knew that my life was worth telling my story to anyone. But, the truth is, writing this book has been like therapy. I mentioned in my book that I saw at least two therapists before I wrote this book, and for that, I am grateful for their help. For me having to re-live some parts of my life that I thought I would never have to remember, like the year of 1979, and other years that were just as bad, the writing of this book has made me realize that I am fortunate to still be able to tell my story and move forward.

As I said in my introduction chapter, I have a lot of family and friends that I owe a lot of thanks to. I will mention them again, and I will say I could have not written this book without their inspirations, as well as what they did for me in my lifetime. I personally would like to thank all of you who helped me along this journey of my life. There are so many family members and friends who have inspired me to write this book and tell my story, that now I hope they, like you, have enjoyed reading it. As I said also, this book is about me, my life, my perils, pitfalls, failures, and yes, even some success and happiness. I am also grateful to God for giving me this life to celebrate this writing of this book and for giving me a story to tell people to inspire and, hopefully, go on and inspire others to do the same. I will say this, just like the old saying, "Be careful what you might wish for, because you just might get it." I encourage you to do the same. If you are looking for long lost family or friends, I urge you to do so. If you do, just remember there might just be a story to tell like mine. If you don't, you will never know what that story might just be. As I go back to Chapter One of my book and I talk about how I found my birth mother, as well as six siblings, I never had the urge to quit looking. I suppose I could have hired a private investigator and have them do the leg work, but for me, my story was more fulfilling now that I realize I did that task by myself. I strongly believe that God wanted me to find my birth mother and siblings, despite the outcome. God knew how frustrated I was about the situation, and God knew I needed to know the answers. I found my birth mother and siblings. I found some of the answers I was looking for. For that I wish to thank several people for their help.

First, I wish to thank my parents, Harold and Aileen Johnson, for their support my whole life, as well as for their inspiration for my writing of this book. As I said in previous chapters, I will, and will always, owe my whole life to both of them, and I have nothing but the biggest of thanks for all of their help. They took me in when I was about a year and half old. They raised me as one of their own. They have now seen me grow up and live my life and write this book and have helped me with just about everything you could ever ask for. I am extremely grateful that I had both in my life. You just don't know what that means to me now. At this time, I also wish to thank my sisters, Sharon and Susan, and their husbands, Bob McCasland and Bill Andrews, for all of their help and support, as well. I just could have never accomplished some of the things I did in my lifetime without the help and support and guidance of this family, and what this family means to me. I will always be indebted to them and their husbands and families for their love and support.

Second, I wish to thank Jack Winterbottom for all of his help. Out of deductive reasoning, I thought that if I could find him, the man who was married to my birth mother at the time I was born, I could find my birth mother, and I did. As I said, it was Jack's help and information he gave me over the phone about facts that happened back before I was born and after I was born. I named this book, *The Name on the Envelope* because it was Jack's handwritten name on an envelope he had put away for more than forty years that helped me find the long-lost family I was looking for. That name on that envelope story still blows me away even now after writing about it. Jack was also very honest and friendly and upfront with me going all the way back to when I had that first conversation on the phone with him. That conversation all started with an e-mail from mylife.com, giving me the phone number to Jack's former wife in Utah. It was that one phone call that let me to calling Jack in Bakersfield, California, later that night. Then, it was another phone call that informed me just who was that name on that envelope he found a few days later. That name was the name I needed to find and complete my search to find the people who I had been looking for all of those years. I cannot ever thank Jack enough for all of his help and how nice he was to answer all of my questions I had about everything I had gone through to find my birth mother and siblings. I will always be grateful for Jack's help.

Third, I wish to thank my brother, Michael Mitchell, for his friendliness and openness in helping me find the one person who I was just never able to find until now. As I wrote about it earlier in my book, I told you about the three-and-a-half-hour conversation we had with each other that night in December 2010, and I cannot begin to thank him and his wife and family for helping me solve the mystery I had been after to solve after looking for over twenty-five years. Because of that conversation I had with Michael, he told me about all of the other siblings I had along with the answer I wanted to know about the whereabouts of my birth mother, Alexandria. For all of this, I will always be grateful. Along with my brother, Michael, I wish to thank my Natalie, and Jackie, and their families, for all of their openness, honesty, generosity, and understanding in all of this story. It makes me feel wonderful to know that I have found a great family, and I am proud to be part of theirs, as well.

Fourth, I wish to thank my sister, Katy, for her help and kindness and help in my remarkable story. From the time I first got to meet my sister when I was eighteen, until the time I was forty-seven years old and had just found out how I had found my birth mother and siblings, I had mentioned about how Katy had supported me in my endeavors to write a book and tell my story. What I did not realize was that my story was about Katy, as well as me. It was like one full circle of life going all the way back to the days of when our father had married her mother and then split up and divorced, and then our father's hooking up with my birth mother and producing me. I never realized that when I started writing this book that Katy's life had cross paths with mine and that the photo album she showed me of when our father married her mother was the proof of the beginning of the both of us. My story, along with part of Katy's life story, has been the foundation of my book. Our story as brother and sister has been sort of the outline for the writing of my book. I will always be grateful for the help and inspiration she gave me to write this book.

Fifth, I wish to thank the people of mylife.com for writing and publishing a short story of me on their website. This thirteen-paragraph story was the final inspiration I needed to write my book. My thanks to Joe, who wrote the story, and all of the other wonderful folks who decided that my story needed to be told on their website. This short story as to how I found my birth mother was the story that charged me up to start writing my own story from start to finish and to write my story into a book form. My thanks to all of the wonderful people at mylife.com who went out of their way and wrote and published my story on their website that inspired me to write this book.

Sixth, I wish to thank all of my close friends and co-workers who listened to my story and inspired me to write my book. I have to thank a former co-worker, Stephan Chavarie, who I used to work with at News 13 in Orlando, Florida, who suggested the name of my book, *The Name on the Envelope*. I also wish to thank my former boss and General Manager, Robin Smythe-Weisman, for her support and helping me find a marriage record when I was doing my search for information during that nine-day period when I found everything out. I also want to take this time to thank all of my friends on Facebook who read my story on mylife.com. It was the inspiration from the reaction I received when people read my story on this website and recommended that I write this book. So, for them, and all of the others who read my story on mylife.com, I will always be thankful for your support and friendship. I hope that you will enjoy my story and will know what it took for me to write it.

Seventh, I wish to thank my book editors, Jean DeHaven and Katherine Adams, for helping me with the writing and editing of my book and story of my life. Jean is a cousin to me on the DeHaven side of my family. Jean took it up on her own to volunteer and edit my book, chapter by chapter, and word for word. I have trusted Jean to take the job as my editor because if there is anybody who knows my story of my life, it is Jean. Jean was there when I first came to Valparaiso, Indiana, and has been a mainstay cousin my whole life. Jean, like my family, has seen me from a baby, and has seen me grow up and write this book. If there is anybody I could have trusted with the task of editing my book, it is Jean. Jean has been fabulous to work with as my editor, and I will always be grateful for this and all of her wisdom she has given me all my life.

Eighth, I wish to thank all of the teachers I had during my lifetime of learning going all the way from the time I started kindergarten all the way through college at Vincennes University. This includes all of the teachers I had during the thirteen-year span in the Valparaiso Community School System in Valparaiso, Indiana, and again, all of the teachers and instructors I had in college at Vincennes University. Also, included in this select group of educators are two SCUBA instructors, Jay Phipps and Tom Moore, who taught me how to SCUBA dive and gave the valued experience of learning the skilled sport of SCUBA diving. I mentioned the sport of SCUBA diving in my book, and there is a very good reason for it. I love the sport of SCUBA diving for many reasons, and I am glad that I have had the opportunity to be able to enjoy the passion I have for the sport of SCUBA diving. There were some other teachers I mentioned during some of the chapters of my book, and I would like to thank again, my former ninth grade basketball coach, John Knauff, for teaching me and coaching me and letting me play on his team back in the 1970s at Thomas Jefferson Junior High School. That whole experience was a lot of fun, and I thank Coach Knauff and my teammates for the fun and experience I had when we played together. Again, I wish to thank all of my teachers from the schools of Banta, Central, Parkview, Ben Franklin Junior High School School, as well as Thomas Jefferson Junior High School and, of course, Valparaiso High School. My thanks to all of my teachers, as well as classmates; in particular, those who graduated with me on Wednesday, June 3, 1981. As I said in my book, that day on that football field will be a night that I will never forget. I hope for all of my classmates, both past and present, that you will never forget that night, as well. Also, there are a number of teachers from Vincennes University I wish to thank. I suppose it would be fitting that I thank my English Composition teacher, Nancy Pointer, as I know she would be proud of my writing of my own book. My thanks go out to former Vice-President of Student Services, Mr. Jerry Gegginheimer, as well as to the Broadcasting Department of Vincennes University, and to the Business Department and former teachers Jack Hanes, John Hitchcock, Jay D. Burks, John Windover, and Tony Cloyd. I learned a lot about different things in the radio and television business in the time I was a student at Vincennes University, and I have these and many other people to thank for it. With that said, I would like to thank George Varns, Alice Bond, and the whole organization of COPE special services of Vincennes University for their entire help while I was a student at Vincennes University, as well as their help after I finished. At this time, I would also like to thank President Emeritus Dr. Phillip Summers for his friendship and wisdom from the time I first came to Vincennes University as a pre-freshman and the friendship even after I graduated and came back to visit at Vincennes University. I was very proud to be a student at Vincennes University, while Dr. Summers was President at Vincennes University, and I am even more proud to be a fellow alum now that I have long graduated from Vincennes University.

Ninth, I wish to thank my grandparents, Charles and Francis Dowd, my father, Thomas Dowd, my father's sister, Aunt Bonnie Dowd-Wall, and my father's brother, Charles E. Dowd. I spoke a lot about these people who were a major influence in my lifetime at some point when I was younger when decisions had to be made about my life's future. I know I have made a lot of references to some of those decisions that were made in my lifetime from these family members, but I only suppose it was for my best interest and future that those decisions were made the way they were made. I wish to thank my cousins, Curt and Christy Dowd, as well as April Cafemeyer, Mark Kenworthy, Shawn Kenworthy, and Francis Kenworthy for their support in my writings and their support through all of the years of my life. For this support, as well as other things in my lifetime, I wish to thank you all.

Finally, I wish to thank some personal friends who have been with me over the years through the thick and thin of my life. I wish to thank my former wife, Pam, for all the fun we had while we were together and to tell her how sorry I am that our marriage did not work out like I had hoped. It took me two different therapists, the finding of my birth mother and siblings, and the writing of my book to figure out what caused me to do the things I did to cause our marriage to fail. I take full responsibility for all of the failures in our marriage, and I only hope that I could ever be forgiven for all of my mistakes. Also, at this time, I wish to thank all of my close, personal friends who I have known for a very long time, like Bill Frank, Norman Madrilejo, Jay Mathews, Tim P. King, and George Moncilovich. Just before I started writing my book in the early part of 2013, we lost George Moncilovich to a rare liver disease that he was not able to beat. He was my friend for over thirty-seven years, and he will never be forgotten. George, like my other friends listed, have been with me for a very long time, and we spent a very large amount of time together. Going through junior high school, as well as high school and through our college years and our adult years, I will never forget the laughs, the tears, the pain, and the friendship we shared and had. George will be missed by me, his family, and a lot of other friends and relatives. May God bless George Moncilovich, and I hope that he is in a much better place now. Along with my friends, I have to thank my friend, Debbie Watson, for her forgiveness, as well. I never knew this, but when you have an addiction problem that becomes a behavior problem like mine, you have to go through several steps of forgiveness. Debbie is one of those friends I got the chance to ask for forgiveness, and I thank her for that opportunity to do so. I still have a lot of other people to apologize to, but to forgive and move on takes a lot of courage.

The next chapter of my life I will be asking for a lot of forgiveness from a lot of people. There is one more person who I would like to thank for his advice in my writing of this book. That person is Dr. Ronald F. Youngblood, and the words of advice he gave me when I started my writing. Dr. Youngblood, who was an author of several, published books, gave me the advice to never quit writing until you are completely finished. I took Dr. Youngblood's advice and continued to write until I was finished. I thank him for those great words of advice. There are many, many more friends that I could list in this paragraph, but that would take a million years to do. I think that if you who know me personally, you will know who you are.

I suppose it would only be fitting that I thank the career that I chose a long time ago to work in. Over the twenty-five-plus years that I have worked in the radio and television business, I have met and worked with some really cool people. For that I am thankful and grateful. My work goes back to 1985 and continues on today with my work in the twenty-four-hour television local cable news channel, News 13 Of Orlando, Florida. I must say, my career has been a lot of blood, sweat, and tears, and just about every kind of emotion, as well. Over the years, I have worked with some really talented people who are no longer with us. Those include Dan Lynch and Butch Bennett from radio and Scott Harris and Troy Cutter from television. The first two names I listed were people I worked with in Valparaiso, Indiana, when I was a radio personality at WLJE-FM, and the last two names I listed were people I worked with at News 13 in Orlando. May God bless them, as well.

Last, but not least, I have to thank the one person who made my life a complete challenge: my birth mother, Alexandria. Throughout my whole book, I told you the story of how I wondered for thirty-three years who she was, where she was, what she looked like, was she living or not, and a number of other questions. I told you in my book about when I was a teenager about thirteen or fourteen years old or so, and in the hospital at Children's Memorial Hospital in Chicago, Illinois, when I saw my birth certificate for the first time with her name on it. The mystery of my life started then, back in July 1977, and it continued until I found what I was looking for, in December 2010. Through that time, I lived a lifetime. I had another heart surgery, graduated from high school and college, learned to SCUBA dive, and got married and divorced. For over thirty-three years, Alexandria was a mystery to me, and I have social media and others to thank for my help in my search. My search was challenging. My search was interesting and mysterious. My mission to see my birth mother took me to Indiana, Michigan, and Pennsylvania to find out different facts. Along the way, I found two stepfathers, three sisters, and two brothers. My mission had me call people in Utah, California, and Pennsylvania. Like Jake and Elwood from *The Blues Brothers*, I was on a mission. I was on a mission from God.

Now that my mission has been completed, may we now live in peace. I thank you all for reading my book.

Yours very truly,

Michael McKinley Dowd

Author of "The Name on the Envelope"

CPSIA information can be obtained
at www.ICGtesting.com
Printed in the USA
BVHW040704071119
562910BV00009B/12/P

9 781480 986756